Cross-Border Cooperation as Conflict Transformation

Has European integration helped to build peace in Europe and its neighbourhood? The book addresses this question through theoretically and empirically informed case studies that explore the successes of, and the challenges to EU cross-border cooperation as a tool for conflict transformation.

Conceptually, the contributors link the question of transforming conflict to changing understandings of borders and bordering. Empirically, the contributions represent case studies of practices and discourses of EU-sponsored cross-border cooperation, and challenges to it. The case studies encompass the multiple geographical perspectives of the EU internal boundaries, its (sometimes disputed) external borders, and borders involving third countries. From a thematic point of view, the collection focuses on the intersection of two levels at which bordering processes unfold and are enacted: the level of governance, devolution and international intervention and that of grass roots or civil society efforts, including cultural cooperation and artistic production. The collection thus offers a kaleidoscopic view of border politics and conflict that zooms in and out of the EU frontiers and their geopolitics of peacebuilding, security and cooperation.

The chapters in this book were originally published as a special issue of the journal *Geopolitics*.

Maria-Adriana Deiana is a lecturer in International Relations at Queen's University Belfast, UK. Her research deploys feminist and other critical IR perspectives to examine the interrelated issues of war, peace and security. Her publications include *Gender and Citizenship: Promises of Peace in Post-Dayton Bosnia & Herzegovina* (2018).

Milena Komarova is a sociologist and UK in a Changing Europe Initiative Research Fellow, based at the School of Social Sciences, Education and Social Work, Queen's University Belfast, UK. Her work intersects the fields of border, conflict and urban studies, including Brexit and the Irish border.

Cathal McCall is a professor of European Politics and Borders. He has published widely on the theme of European Union cross-border cooperation and conflict transformation, including *The European Union and Peacebuilding: The Cross-Border Dimension* (2014).

Cross-Border Cooperation as Conflict Transformation

Promises and Limitations in EU Peacebuilding

Edited by
Maria-Adriana Deiana, Milena Komarova, and Cathal McCall

LONDON AND NEW YORK

First published 2022
by Routledge
2 Park Square, Milton Park, Abingdon, Oxon OX14 4RN

and by Routledge
605 Third Avenue, New York, NY 10158

Routledge is an imprint of the Taylor & Francis Group, an informa business

Introduction, Chapters 1, 2 and 4–6 © 2022 Taylor & Francis
Chapter 3 © 2018 Rodrigo Bueno-Lact and Henk van Houtum. Originally published as Open Access.

With the exception of Chapter 3, no part of this book may be reprinted or reproduced or utilised in any form or by any electronic, mechanical, or other means, now known or hereafter invented, including photocopying and recording, or in any information storage or retrieval system, without permission in writing from the publishers. For details on the rights for Chapter 3, please see the chapter's Open Access footnote.

Trademark notice: Product or corporate names may be trademarks or registered trademarks, and are used only for identification and explanation without intent to infringe.

British Library Cataloguing in Publication Data
A catalogue record for this book is available from the British Library

ISBN: 978-0-367-75217-0 (hbk)
ISBN: 978-0-367-75218-7 (pbk)
ISBN: 978-1-003-16154-7 (ebk)

DOI: 10.4324/9781003161547

Typeset in Minion Pro
by Newgen Publishing UK

Publisher's Note
The publisher accepts responsibility for any inconsistencies that may have arisen during the conversion of this book from journal articles to book chapters, namely the inclusion of journal terminology.

Disclaimer
Every effort has been made to contact copyright holders for their permission to reprint material in this book. The publishers would be grateful to hear from any copyright holder who is not here acknowledged and will undertake to rectify any errors or omissions in future editions of this book.

Contents

Citation Information	vi
Notes on Contributors	viii

Introduction – Cross-Border Cooperation as Conflict
Transformation: Promises and Limitations in EU Peacebuilding   1
Maria-Adriana Deiana, Milena Komarova and Cathal McCall

1 The Irish Border as a European Union Frontier: The Implications
for Managing Mobility and Conflict   13
Milena Komarova and Katy Hayward

2 Small Diplomacy: Cultural Cooperation As a Factor Alleviating
Societal Tensions – The Case of Lviv and Its Polish Partner Cities   37
Klaudia Nowicka, Iwona Sagan and Dominika Studzińska

3 The Glocal Green Line: The Imperial Cartopolitical Puppeteering
of Cyprus   58
Rodrigo Bueno-Lacy and Henk van Houtum

4 EU's Cross-Border Cooperation and Conflict Transformation at
Contested Borders in the European Neighbourhood: Lessons from
the Turkish-Armenian Border   97
Gökten Doğangün and Yelda Karadağ

5 On (In)Definite Topography: National Identity and European and
Regional Imaginaries in the Post-1989 Croatian Literary Narratives   122
Ivana Trkulja

6 Re-Thinking Border Politics at the Sarajevo Film
Festival: Alternative Imaginaries of Conflict Transformation and
Cross-Border Encounters   142
Maria-Adriana Deiana

Index   163

Citation Information

The chapters in this book were originally published in the journal *Geopolitics*, volume 24, issue 3 (2019). When citing this material, please use the original page numbering for each article, as follows:

Introduction

Cross-Border Cooperation as Conflict Transformation: Promises and Limitations in EU Peacebuilding
Maria-Adriana Deiana, Milena Komarova and Cathal McCall
Geopolitics, volume 24, issue 3 (2019), pp. 529–540

Chapter 1

The Irish Border as a European Union Frontier: The Implications for Managing Mobility and Conflict
Milena Komarova and Katy Hayward
Geopolitics, volume 24, issue 3 (2019), pp. 541–564

Chapter 2

Small Diplomacy: Cultural Cooperation As a Factor Alleviating Societal Tensions. The Case of Lviv and Its Polish Partner Cities
Klaudia Nowicka, Iwona Sagan and Dominika Studzińska
Geopolitics, volume 24, issue 3 (2019), pp. 565–585

Chapter 3

The Glocal Green Line: The Imperial Cartopolitical Puppeteering of Cyprus
Rodrigo Bueno-Lacy and Henk van Houtum
Geopolitics, volume 24, issue 3 (2019), pp. 586–624

Chapter 4

EU's Cross-Border Cooperation and Conflict Transformation at Contested Borders in the European Neighbourhood: Lessons from the Turkish-Armenian Border
Gökten Doğangün and Yelda Karadağ
Geopolitics, volume 24, issue 3 (2019), pp. 625–649

Chapter 5

On (In)Definite Topography: National Identity and European and Regional Imaginaries in the Post-1989 Croatian Literary Narratives
Ivana Trkulja
Geopolitics, volume 24, issue 3 (2019), pp. 650–669

Chapter 6

Re-Thinking Border Politics at the Sarajevo Film Festival: Alternative Imaginaries of Conflict Transformation and Cross-Border Encounters
Maria-Adriana Deiana
Geopolitics, volume 24, issue 3 (2019), pp. 670–690

For any permission-related enquiries please visit:
www.tandfonline.com/page/help/permissions

Notes on Contributors

Rodrigo Bueno-Lacy, Karelian Institute, University of Eastern Finland, Finland.

Maria-Adriana Deiana, School of History, Anthropology, Politics and Philosophy, Queen's University, Belfast.

Gökten Doğangün, Centre for Black Sea and Central Asia (KORA), Middle East Technical University, Ankara, Turkey.

Katy Hayward, School of Social Sciences, Education and Social Work, Queen's University Belfast, Belfast, Northern Ireland.

Yelda Karadağ, Centre for Black Sea and Central Asia (KORA), Middle East Technical University, Ankara, Turkey.

Milena Komarova, Senator G. Mitchell Global Institute for Peace, Security and Justice, Queen's University, Belfast.

Cathal McCall, School of History, Anthropology, Politics and Philosophy, Queen's University, Belfast.

Klaudia Nowicka, Katedra Geografii Społeczno-Ekonomicznej, University of Gdańsk, Gdańsk, Poland.

Iwona Sagan, Katedra Geografii Społeczno-Ekonomicznej, University of Gdańsk, Gdańsk, Poland.

Dominika Studzińska, Katedra Geografii Społeczno-Ekonomicznej, University of Gdańsk, Gdańsk, Poland.

Ivana Trkulja, Centre for Advanced Study Sofia, Sofia, Bulgaria.

Henk van Houtum, Nijmegen Centre for Border Research (NCBR), Radboud University Nijmegen, Nijmegen, The Netherlands and University of Eastern Finland.

INTRODUCTION

Cross-Border Cooperation as Conflict Transformation: Promises and Limitations in EU Peacebuilding

Maria-Adriana Deiana ⓘ, Milena Komarova, and Cathal McCall

Can we continue to view European Integration as a project associated with conflict transformation and peacebuilding through the promotion of soft borders and cross-border cooperation? Or are we faced with yet another sign that the European Union (EU) has reached its limits? (Balibar 2015; Bhambra 2015)

As we developed this Special Section, we have witnessed the unfolding of inter-locking tensions around variously identified "Others" and security threats, a corresponding rising tide of ethnic nationalism and a reversal in the processes of debordering at the heart of the EU post-war project. From the state of emergency and enhanced security emerging in response to terrorist attacks (Burke 2015; Butler n.d.) to EU governments' calls for a revision of Schengen (Nielsen 2015), central elements of cross border movement and cooperation have been increasingly questioned (Hayward 2016). Since the heightened security alert of 2015, migrants and refugees fleeing instability, hardship and conflict have continued to attempt (and often tragically fail) to reach the shores of Italy and Greece, as well as access the EU on foot through the Balkan route. Frequently, those who make the journey are met with security forces, detention centres, tear gas and border fences. As a consequence of controversial deals with Turkey and Libya, migrants and refugees have faced deportations. They have become stranded at sea or in detention facilities where violations of human rights have been rampant. Within the EU Member States, populist and right-wing entrepreneurs have continued to fuel public anxiety around migration and fear of 'the Other' bringing borders to the centre of political debates, media and everyday life (Yuval-Davis, Wemyss, and Cassidy 2017).

Despite having faded from the media and political limelight, tensions relating to conflictual borders have been reignited or emerged anew across the EU external and internal borderlands, as well as in the EU's extended neighbourhood. The reverberations of the 2015 war in Gaza and violence in the West Bank serve as powerful reminders of the complex and ongoing conflict in the region. Despite the Minsk Agreement (2014), conflict also remains frozen in the border zone between Ukraine and Russia. Moreover, in the Post-Yugoslav space, two decades of peacebuilding efforts have often served to reinstate divisive ethno-nationalist politics. Questions of statehood and borders remain alive and contested as highlighted by recurring attempts to challenge the entirety of Post-Dayton Bosnia–Herzegovina in the name of the Bosnian-Serb entity Republika Srpska's self-determination, as well as by the renewed border contentions between Serbia and Kosovo. Despite numerous rounds of talks on the reunification of Cyprus, divided along the Green Line, intractable differences among the parties on territorial issues have failed to produce an agreement (Pelerin 2016). Even in a context such as Northern Ireland, where peacebuilding and cross-border cooperation had reached an advanced stage after decades of conflict, questions about the future of cross-border relations are at stake as *Brexit* brings about prospects of a return to a hard border in the island of Ireland (McCall 2018).

Contemporary pressures for increased securitisation and *rebordering* progressively undermine peacebuilding and *debordering* as key principles and articulating grammar in the project of European integration. In response to these multiple crises, the EU Global Strategy has seen a move towards more pragmatic and strategic approach to EU Foreign policy increasingly driven by stability and security concerns (Tocci 2016).

In the face of such developments, including the rise of right-wing populism and resurgent nationalism(s), we are compelled to ask critical and urgent questions about the commonplace of a borderless EU, its image as a political space produced through the logic of intergovernmental and cross-border cooperation, democracy and human rights, as well as its credentials as a peacebuilding global actor (Klatt 2018). In this Special section, we grapple with these questions by focusing specifically on the diffusion and limitations of EU sponsored cross-border cooperation as an instrument for conflict transformation in the current moment of global interdependence, renewed or unresolved conflicts, and increased securitization. This introduction first outlines the development of cross-border cooperation as a trademark of Europeanization and traces its ambivalences as an instrument of border politics at the EU external frontiers. It then contextualizes the collection within new trajectories in Border Studies that, gesturing to a more complex and situated conceptualisation of border landscapes, foreground a multiplicity of actors, issues and sites of border politics. As contributions in this collection illustrate, paying attention to multiplicity, locality and complexity is crucial if we are to understand practices of borderwork in the aftermath of conflict, as well as in peacetime.

Cross-Border Cooperation and Its Limits: trademark of Europeanization and Double-Edged Instrument of EU Border Politics

Since its very inception, the project of European integration has been regarded as a prime symbol/example of *debordering*, unification and cooperation. Both symbolically and materially, it has worked to reconfigure *hard* borders into *soft* borders underpinned by intergovernmental cooperation among states, the development of multilevel governance and the support for various programs of cross-border cooperation (McCall 2013; Anderson and O'Dowd 1999; Scott 2012; Hayward et al. 2011). Initially set against the backdrop of World War II, the suspension of borders as barriers and their divisive impact on international and inter-state relations has also essentially cast European integration as a project associated with conflict resolution and peacebuilding (McCall 2014). Within EU external policy and discourse, this long-standing tradition of conflict transformation is continuously mobilised to attest the EU's credential as a political project and peacebuilding actor.[1]

Established across different regions, cities and borderlands and involving actors as diverse as civil society, municipalities, local businesses and cultural institutions, cross-border cooperation has become a trademark of Europeanization. More than that, it has been a tool of strategic partnership deployed at and beyond the EU's ever-shifting external borders to extend its geopolitical influence and strengthen its image as a global actor (Bialasiewicz 2011). Born out of post-Cold War transformations, cross-border cooperation has increasingly assumed a paradigmatic status as an instrument for rapprochement and development. In this process, previously divided border regions can be brought together through various policies that aim to create a more cohesive European space (Scott 2015). By (even momentarily) lifting the territorial cage of the state that is pivotal to border conflict and by (re) constructing borders as resources for economic and cultural exchanges, intercommunal relationships and political dialogue, cross-border cooperation has a conflict transformational potential (McCall 2014).

However, the success of this strategy in some European contexts, for instance as in the case of the Irish border (Hayward et al. 2011), is also met with less encouraging examples of EU-sponsored cross-border cooperation, such as many of those launched in post-Yugoslav borderlands (Scott and Van Houtum 2009). In other words, while the promotion of cross-border cooperation has been intensive in EU rhetoric, in practice crossing borders is a much more complex and multi-layered socio-spatial process than envisioned in institutionalised EU practices and policies of cross-border cooperation. For instance, it has been found that less successful cases of cross-border projects have often merely served to enhance local budgets rather than stimulating cooperation (Scott 2015). The top-down and technocratic nature of cross-border cooperation often also presents a challenge for local participation and ownership (Popescu 2008). This is particularly true in the aftermath of protracted conflict where the eventuality of cross-border encounters might (re)produce insecurities and (re)ignite grievances. At the EU external frontiers, these ambivalences are amplified. As James Scott and Henk van Houtum observe: "rhetorical statements to the contrary, [cross-border cooperation] has become mundane, technocratic, underfunded and bereft of the historical symbolism of earlier cooperation at what, since 2004 and 2007, have become internal borderlands of the EU" (Scott and Van Houtum 2009, 273). As contributors in this collection illustrate, this analysis still rings true today. In the midst of pressures for securitization and multiple unresolved crises outlined above, the notion of cross-border cooperation as conflict transformation remains a seductive concept for those interested in peacebuilding. Yet, a key contribution of this collection is that the complexities of *really existing* conflicts and their historical legacy, actors with often opposite political agendas and identities, as well as the lack of transformative visions and adequate resources, complicate the realisation of cross-border cooperation's potential.

Cathal McCall (2014) has noted that in its current form, EU sponsored cross-border cooperation is driven principally by economic interests and thus often sidelines other sites, actors and resources that can mobilise initiatives for peacebuilding from below (Lederach 2005). Such a trend runs contrary to Lederach's notion of peacebuilding from below as a starting point in the critique of top-down and technocratic models of conflict transformation (Lederach 2005; McCall 2014). This understanding expands the range of actors and sites of politics that could contribute to transforming the legacy of conflict beyond elites, central governments and institutions to include grass roots activists, interpersonal relations and cultural practices. This approach can be fruitful given the fact that, despite borders often being central to (inter)national conflict as sites of cultural and political antagonisms, and of struggles over inclusion and exclusion, the experiences of borderland inhabitants frequently lie beyond the concerns of central governments (McCall 2014). Lederach's idea that addressing the legacy of conflict is a long-term and often tortuous process requiring change in the personal, structural, relational and cultural aspects of conflict, has been further examined and developed in critical peace and conflict scholarship (e.g. Mac Ginty and Richmond 2013; Väyrynen 2019). The so-called "everyday turn" is particularly poignant in the context of bordering processes and conflictual relations. It encompasses opportunities for local agency and transformation enacted through ordinary encounters and social practices which are often overlooked in mainstream peacebuilding approaches whereby local agency is often inscribed within a technocratic logic of NGOs, projects and funding cycles (Mac Ginty 2014). As Roger MacGinty writes:

> The unpacking of everyday peace reveals that interaction across sectarian, ethnic and nationalistic boundaries can be common despite a meta-context of societal division. Thus we can confront the often hegemonic narrative of homogenous, near-hermetically sealed groups that have no or only aggressive interaction with the outgroup. The everyday peace notion shows that a complex array of intergroup interactions can occur in many contexts and are sensitive to calibration according to gender, class, locality, and interpretations of decency and civility. (Mac Ginty 2014, 552)

While there can be no presumption that these interactions will have a conflict transformation outcome, studying everyday peace challenges deterministic understandings of the social groups, identities and socio-spatial imaginaries at stake in conflictual borderlands and shifts our attention from the formal political sphere to the vernacular as a site where these might be reproduced but also challenged. In a similar vein to Chris Rumford's 'borderwork' (Rumford 2013), the focus on the everyday spotlights the role of citizens as agents in the making and the unmaking of the social order and in the multidimensional negotiations of borders. In this sense, the notion of the 'borderscape' offers a sound conceptual framework to capture the multilevel complexity at stake in the bordering process as occurring at the level of geopolitics and governance, as well as in everyday negotiations and cultural encounters.

Borderscapes as Sites of Conflict Transformation

From an initial concern with the geographical, physical and tangible manifestations of borders, the interdisciplinary field of Border Studies has developed a processual understanding of borders as multilayered sites of inclusion and exclusion that are at the core of socio-political processes and everyday practices (Amilhat Szary et al. n.d.). This perspective allows us to see borders as serving vital economic functions; as instruments for the organisation of democratic practice; and as markers of identity and security. Yet, it also reveals them as the source of tensions over human rights abuses, stereotyping, conflict and violence (Kolossov and Scott 2013). As early as 1999, James Anderson and Liam O'Dowd outlined a new agenda for Border Studies that foregrounded the inherent complexity of borders as contradictory sites of politics:

> [C]loser critical scrutiny of borders challenges their reification and reveals them as far from simple. Instead, they appear inherently contradictory, problematical, and multifaceted. They are at once gateway, and barriers to the "outside world", protective and imprisoning, areas of opportunity and/or insecurity, zones of contact and/or conflict, of cooperation and/or competition, of ambivalent identities and/or aggressive assertion of difference. These apparent dichotomies may alternate with time and place, but – more interestingly – they can co-exist simultaneously in the same people, some of whom have to regularly deal not with one state but with two. (Anderson and O'Dowd 1999, 595–96)

Newly developed conceptual work since has shifted the attention from borders as an entity to bordering as a complex socio-spatial process. As the theorising of borders intensified in response to the complexity of contemporary societies, new conceptual tools have emerged to reflect the centrality of bordering in processes such transnationalism, migration, conflict and securitisation (Amilhat Johnson et al. 2011; Szary et al. n.d.). These new understandings illuminate the multi-level and multi-directional constitution of borders as "by no means ...

static line[s], but a mobile and relational space" (Brambilla 2015, 22). Drawing on the concept of the 'borderscape', which denotes "cultural and political complexities, contested discourses and meanings, struggle[s] over inclusion and exclusion, [and] involvement of multiple actors" (Rajaram and Grundy-Warr 2007), scholars have enabled a much more complex understanding of border politics as constructed, lived and experienced at the intersection between local, national and global dynamics (Rumford 2010; Amilhat Szary et al. n.d.; Wilson 2015). Essentially the 'borderscape' captures the complex relations and contentions between borders as sets of (legal, political and socio-cultural) rules, practices and spatial realities on the one hand, and identities, representations and imaginaries, on the other (Brambilla et al. 2015; Rajaram and Grundy-Warr 2007). As Chiara Brambilla writes, it enables an investigation of borders through a kaleidoscopic view encompassing "the 'variations' of borders in space and time, transversally to different social, cultural, economic, legal, and historical settings criss-crossed by negotiations between a variety of different actors, and not only the State" (Brambilla 2015, 25). The notion of 'Borderscapes' thus identifies zones of interactions and cultural production in which the contours of socio-spatial identities are continuously constructed and deconstructed (Wilson and Donnan 1999, 64). In this sense, borderscapes may be interpreted as potentially important zones for intercultural contact, communication and cooperation that might lead to conflict transformation (McCall 2014). Underscoring the agency of so-called "ordinary" citizens in making and re-making of borders in a 'bottom-up' fashion (Rumford 2010, 953), borders-capes are also important sites for exploring situated dynamics of "everyday peace" (Lederach 2005), as well as the practices and policies that might constrain them.

Informed by these conceptual developments, the contributions in this Special section explore the multilevel complexity of border conflicts, their reverberations beyond the line of the border and the intersections with questions such as ideology, power, culture, memory and emotions. In doing so the collection pays attention to the multi-situated, *pluritopical* and multilevel negotiations and contestations of borders. Contributors explore the practices through which borders are inhabited, crossed and traversed (Brambilla 2015), as well as the different border regimes, historical legacies and geopolitical dynamics that regulate and govern these practices (Rumford 2006).

The Promises and Limits of Cross-Border Cooperation as Conflict Transformation

Emerging from the EUBORDERSCAPES research Project, funded under the EU Framework Programme 7,[2] the collection is part of a larger and sustained effort that contributes to conceptual change in our understanding of borders, their shifting and dialogical nature and their centrality in processes of cultural encounters, the everyday, transnationalism, conflict, and securitization (Amilhat Szary et al. n.d.). The articles presented here offer a critical analysis of EU sponsored cross-border cooperation as an instrument of conflict transformation that examines the configurations of bordering processes in specific localized geopolitical and social contexts (Brambilla et al. 2015). A key strength of the collection lies precisely in revealing the complexity of bordering processes at stake in different case studies. These shift across the EU space and its external frontier to include negotiations of borders in the shadow of the EU and the accession process, borders in the Neighbourhood, as well as borders between member states and disputed territories. The issues considered by our contributors are as diverse as cross-border cooperation in light of the historical memory of genocide, *cartopolitics*, the role of cultural interventions and cultural institutions (e.g. literature, cinema, festivals), and the implications of Brexit for the future of cross-border cooperation policies. The papers' focus varies from contexts of relative peace shaped primarily by the legacy of WWII (Poland/ Ukraine), cases shaped by post-Soviet geopolitical transformations (Turkey/ Armenia), to broadly defined 'post-conflict' scenarios (Cyprus, Bosnia–Herzegovina, Northern Ireland). The contributions illustrate the ways in which concepts and top-down policies of cross border cooperation intersect, both historically and in the current moment, with specific institutional and political scenarios. Moreover, the papers illuminate how these concepts and policies resonate (or fail to do so) for a range of different actors, such as "ordinary" citizens, grass roots activists, filmmakers, in particular spaces (e.g. cities, regions, borderlands) and as a result of *global* dynamics (e.g. post-WWII, post-Cold War, post-9/11). Some contributions explore how bordering practices and identities are enacted and performed through specific artefacts such as maps, films and literature, as well as cultural interventions (film and music festivals). Read together, the collection mobilises a borderscaping perspective as a critical tool. That is, it examines existing practices of cross-border cooperation through detailed contextual evidence, whilst proposing alternative sites of border politics and perspectives which might otherwise be overlooked.

This collection provides a critical interdisciplinary exploration of the promises and limitations of cross-border cooperation as an instrument of conflict transformation by bringing together concepts and practical evidence from within the EU and in the context of its neighbourhood. Read together, papers offer an examination of practices and discourses of EU sponsored cross-border cooperation and its challenges from multiple perspectives. Geographically, contributions address a diversity of bordering processes shifting across the EU internal boundaries, its external borders, as well as disputed borders and borders involving third countries. Thematically, the collection foregrounds the negotiation of bordering processes enacted at the level of governance, devolution and international intervention on the one hand, and intersecting with grass roots and civil society efforts, cultural cooperation and artistic production on the other hand. In each paper, the analysis is inflected with the specific history of conflict and with wider geopolitical scenarios that shape and affect contemporary reverberations of border politics in the case studies under examination. The collection itself thus offers a kaleidoscopic view of border politics and conflict that zooms in and out of the EU external frontiers and its geopolitics of peacebuilding, security and cooperation.

The section opens with a particularly topical contribution (Komarova and Hayward) which explores the potential effects of the UK's exit from the EU on the nature of the land border between Northern Ireland (as part of the UK) and the Republic of Ireland. Drawing on the notion of the EU external border regime as a fragmented politics, the paper outlines differentiated scenarios for the changing hierarchies of rights and treatment on the two sides of the Irish border that might affect the movement of people across it. In doing so the authors highlight an interesting site of tension between different bordering scenarios resulting from Brexit and conclude that the emerging new 'border regime' will be shaped by the multiple interests and political divisions within Britain, Northern Ireland and the EU, and by the ways in which these might gain representation in the negotiating process. More broadly, what the *problématique* of Brexit and the Irish border demonstrates is how regulation of all kinds of movement across the border is intricately interwoven with key aspects of multi-level governance and regional devolution. Integral to the latter, and a central tenet of the 1998 Peace Agreement is the concept and practice of cross-border cooperation. The post-Brexit possibility of a return to modes and practices of border governance that involve stricter controls of movement threatens to reopen the old contestation over the legitimacy and existence of the border itself.

This is followed by a paper on the *micropolitics* of border-cities partnership (Nowicka, Sagan and Studzińska). Here, the authors examine the role of city-twinning and cultural initiatives in processes of 'bottom-up diplomacy' along the Polish and Ukraine border in the shadow of the long-standing violent legacy of WWII. Drawing on interviews with a range of local actors, the paper highlights possibilities and constraints in the process of EU-supported grass-root forms of cross-border cultural cooperation. Illustrating how the memories of WWII violence and conflict still shape cross-border interactions and city-twinning partnership between Poland and Ukraine, the authors stress the promise and strength of such cooperation where it builds on shared orientation to European/global contemporary culture that unites young people in particular. This shared broader global context helps to zoom out of and transcend local historical conflicts. At the same time, the paper cautions of the limitations imposed by the institutional and legal setup operating at the EU's external borders which limits basic freedom of movement, actively hampering the aims of the EU's own programmes for cross-border cooperation.

Other papers set the investigation within global geopolitical dynamics. Bueno-Lacy and Van Houtum draw on the prism of *cartopolitics*, understood as a political technology of cartographically defining and imbuing political territories with meaning, to question the very ethno-national foundation of Cyprus' Green Line which underpins efforts to resolve the conflict. Cartographically organized imaginations, the authors contend, have historically 'woven a dense web of local and worldwide interests', including those of the EU in more recent times, which 'have constructed and protracted the divide among Cypriots', failing to ameliorate or counter it. It is further argued that in accepting Cyprus as an EU member, to the exception of the Turkish Republic of Northern Cyprus, the EU has effectively abdicated its position as a neutral arbiter, laying bare its own complicity in perpetrating divisions.

Another couple of authors – Doğangün and Karadağ – offer an assessment of EU-led cross-border cooperation which promotes the development of mutual relations and dialogue between both sides of the Turkish-Armenian border. The article provides a compelling overview of the multi-level challenges and opportunities for conflict transformation in both the local historical and present-day contexts to this border, and against the wider geopolitical dynamics of the European eastern neighbourhood. The authors argue, the reconciliatory potential of EU-sponsored cross-border cooperation is limited in cases such as the Turkish-Armenian 'sealed border' since neither can they exert leverage by promising EU membership to the associated countries, nor do they provide a comprehensive regional framework for cooperation and stability. Ultimately, the 'soft power' of EU geopolitics of cooperation in the regional context of post-Soviet transformation, where nationalism and ethno-territorial conflicts over borders are thriving, leaves room for instability, insecurity and suspicion.

Another set of papers explore different reverberations of border politics in the post-Yugoslav space. Trkulja provides an original perspective on bordering and border-crossings through an analysis of literary texts and literary debates among Croatian and Post-Yugoslav intellectuals from the 1990s to the present time. The author demonstrates how the literary sphere acts as an alternative space for a critical articulation of national identity and borders, both reflecting and bearing upon regional socio-political realities. By mapping the ways in which literature and literary criticism reproduce ethno-nationalist tropes, as well as offer more complex, nuanced understanding of regional border(ing) themes, the paper confirms 'the historically intriguing relationship between national, regional and European influences'. Croatia's accession to the EU in 2013 serves as the most recent landmark among these.

Finally, Deiana focuses on post-conflict dynamics that bring into sharp focus the EU's largely rhetorical commitment to conflict transformation and its complicity in producing Post-Dayton Bosnia as a space of impasse. The paper argues that existing approaches to cross-border cooperation overlook important bottom-up dynamics emerging in the Post-Dayton borderscape that can open opportunities for border-crossings. In doing so, it highlights the creative – yet fragile – potential of cultural cooperation, cinema-mediated encounters and grass roots initiatives revolving around the Sarajevo Film Festival as practices that both reproduce and attempt to outlive the divisive legacy of conflict. Once again the paper demonstrates, along the EU external boundaries, cross-border co-operation is a 'double-edged instrument of EU border politics', which 'in the ensuing context of enlargement fatigue and security concerns, is devoid of the transformative value it might had originally assumed in the heyday of European integration'.

The collection of papers presented here provides a timely and critical discussion that is framed through the prism of bordering and builds upon the critical potential of the 'borderscape' concept. From this starting point, it offers new insights into the relationship between theories and practices of conflict transformation, including the perspectives of 'peacebuilding from below', 'everyday peace' (Mac Ginty 2014), territoriality, memory and emotion. In this way, not only do the papers explore and critique the potential, evolution and limits of EU cross-border cooperation, but offer both empirical and conceptual contributions to the critical debates surrounding the significance of the EU, its shifting configurations as a political space and global actor, and its inherent contradictions between border consolidation and cross-border cooperation. Ultimately, the collection explores new openings and opportunities for future paths that might be taken if the EU is to stay true to its original peacebuilding vision and uphold its transformative aspirations.

Notes

1. One example of how this logic is mobilised in the context of the Former Yugoslavia is Federica Mogherini's poignant speech on the Visa liberalization process for Kosovo available at http://eeas.europa.eu/statements-eeas/2016/160505_05_en.htm accessed 10 May 2015.
2. See project details at www.euborderscapes.eu.

ORCID

Maria-Adriana Deiana (iD) http://orcid.org/0000-0003-4310-1728

References

Anderson, J., and L. O'Dowd. 1999. Borders, border regions and territoriality: Contradictory meanings, changing significance. *Regional Studies* 33 (7):593–604. doi:10.1080/00343409950078648.

Balibar, É. 2015 November. Europe at the limits. *Interventions* 1–7. doi:10.1080/1369801X.2015. 1106966.

Bhambra, G. K. 2015 November. Whither Europe?: Postcolonial versus neocolonial cosmopolitanism. *Interventions* 1–16. doi:10.1080/1369801X.2015.1106964.

Bialasiewicz, L., ed.. 2011. Europe in the world: EU geopolitics and the making of European space. In *Critical geopolitics*, ed. L. Bialasiewicz. Farnham, Surrey, England; Burlington, VT: Ashgate.

Brambilla, C. 2015. Exploring the critical potential of the borderscapes concept. *Geopolitics* 20 (1):14–34. doi:10.1080/14650045.2014.884561.

Brambilla, C., G. Bocchi, J. Lane, and J. W. Scott. 2015. *Borderscaping: Imaginations and practices of border making*. Farnham, UK: Ashgate Publishing, Ltd.

Burke, J. 2015. Deep anxiety pervades brussels as lockdown continues. *The Guardian*, 23 November 2015, sec. World news. http://www.theguardian.com/world/2015/nov/23/ deep-anxiety-pervades-brussels-as-lockdown-continues.

Butler, J. n.d. Mourning becomes the law. Judith butler from Paris. *Instituto 25M Democracia* (blog). Accessed 28 November 2016. https://instituto25m.info/mourning-becomes-the-law-judith-butler-from-paris/.

Hayward, K. 2016 'The spectre of a hard border is not just an irish problem, it looms across Europe'. The Conversation. Accessed 27 October 2016. http://theconversation.com/the-spectre-of-a-hard-border-is-not-just-an-irish-problem-it-looms-across-europe-67409.

Hayward, K., C. McCall, I. Damkat, and M. Power. 2011. Building peace and crossing borders: The North/South dimension. In *Building peace in Northern Ireland*, ed. M. Power, 191–208. Liverpool: Liverpool University Press.

Johnson, C., R. Jones, A. Paasi, L. Amoore, A. Mountz, M. Salter, and C. Rumford. 2011. Interventions on rethinking "the Border" in border studies. *Political Geography* 30 (2):61–69. doi:10.1016/j.polgeo.2011.01.002.

Klatt, M. 2018. The so-called 2015 migration crisis and Euroscepticism in border regions: Facing re-bordering trends in the Danish–German borderlands. *Geopolitics* 1–20. doi:10.1080/14650045.2018.1557149.

Kolossov, V., and J. Scott. 2013. Selected conceptual issues in border studies. *Belgeo. Revue Belge de Géographie* 1 (November). doi: 10.4000/belgeo.10532.

Lederach, J. P. 2005. *The moral imagination: The art and soul of building peace*. Vol. 3. Taylor & Francis. http://www.tandfonline.com/doi/full/10.1080/09614520500296740.

Mac Ginty, R. 2014. Everyday peace: Bottom-up and local agency in conflict-affected societies. *Security Dialogue* 45 (6):548–64. doi:10.1177/0967010614550899.

Mac Ginty, R., and O. P. Richmond. 2013. The local turn in peace building: A critical agenda for peace. *Third World Quarterly* 34 (5):763–83. doi:10.1080/01436597.2013.800750.

McCall, C. 2013. European union cross-border cooperation and conflict amelioration. *Space and Polity* 17 (2):197–216. doi:10.1080/13562576.2013.817512.

McCall, C. 2014. *The European Union and peacebuilding: The cross-border dimension*. New York: Palgrave/McMillan.

McCall, C. 2018. Brexit, bordering and bodies on the Island of Ireland. *Ethnopolitics* 17 (3):292–305. doi:10.1080/17449057.2018.1472425.

Nielsen, N. 2015. 'EU internal borders may be reimposed for two years'. Accessed 28 November 2016. https://euobserver.com/justice/131364.

Pelerin, Agence France-Presse on Mont. 2016. 'Cyprus reunification: Leaders leave Switzerland without deal'. *The Guardian*, 22 November 2016, sec. World news. https:// www.theguardian.com/world/2016/nov/22/cyprus-reunification-leaders-leave-switzerland-without-deal.

Popescu, G. 2008. The conflicting logics of cross-border reterritorialization: Geopolitics of Euroregions in Eastern Europe. *Political Geography* 27 (4):418–38. doi:10.1016/j.polgeo.2008.03.002.

Rajaram, P. K., and C. Grundy-Warr. 2007. *Borderscapes: Hidden geographies and politics at territory's edge*, Vol. 29. Minnesota, MN: U of Minnesota Press.

Rumford, C. 2006. Theorizing borders. *European Journal of Social Theory* 9 (2):155–69. doi:10.1177/1368431006063330.

Rumford, C. 2010. Global borders: An introduction to the special issue. *Environment and Planning D: Society and Space* 28 (6):951–56. doi:10.1068/d2806ed.

Rumford, C. 2013. Towards a vernacularized border studies: The case of citizen borderwork. *Journal of Borderlands Studies* 28 (2):169–80. doi:10.1080/08865655.2013.854653.

Scott, J. W. 2012. European politics of borders, border symbolism and cross-border cooperation. In *The Blackwell companion to border studies*, ed. H. Donnan and T. M. Wilson, 83–99. Oxford: Wiley-Blackwell.

Scott, J. W. 2015. Bordering, border politics and cross-border cooperation in Europe. In *Neighbourhood policy and the construction of the European external borders*, ed. Celata, F., and R. Raffaella, 27–44. Cham, Switzerland: Springer. http://link.springer.com/chapter/10.1007/978-3-319-18452-4_2.

Scott, J. W., and H. Van Houtum. 2009. Reflections on EU territoriality and the 'Bordering'of Europe. *Political Geography* 28 (5):271–73. doi:10.1016/j.polgeo.2009.04.002.

Szary, A., V. Anne-Laure, I. L. Kolossov, D. Newman, J. Pertii, N. Yuval-Davis, S. Rosiere, and J. W. Scott. n.d. 'The Evolving Concept of Borders State of the Debate Report I'. http://www.euborderscapes.eu/fileadmin/user_upload/EUBORDERSCAPES_State_of_Debate_Report_1.pdf.

Tocci, N. 2016. The making of the EU global strategy. *Contemporary Security Policy* 37 (3):461–72. doi:10.1080/13523260.2016.1232559.

Väyrynen, T. 2019. *Corporeal peacebuilding - mundane bodies and temporal transitions.* Rethinking Peace and Conflict Studies. Palgrave Macmillan, London. https://www.palgrave.com/gp/book/9783319972589.

Wilson, T. M. 2015. *A companion to border studies*. Oxford, UK: John Wiley & Sons.

Wilson, T. M., and H. Donnan. 1999. *Borders: Frontiers of identity, nation and state.* New York: Berg publishers.

Yuval-Davis, N., G. Wemyss, and K. Cassidy. 2017 May. Everyday bordering, belonging and the reorientation of British immigration legislation. *Sociology* 003803851770259. doi:10.1177/0038038517702599.

The Irish Border as a European Union Frontier: The Implications for Managing Mobility and Conflict

Milena Komarova and Katy Hayward

ABSTRACT

The 1998 Good Friday (Belfast) Agreement defined the conflict in Northern Ireland as being over the border between this part of the United Kingdom (UK) and the Republic of Ireland. This article defines and understands the Agreement as one of a number of 'border regimes' that operate between the two jurisdictions on the island of Ireland and, in doing so, seeks to explain how it is that Brexit has such significant implications for the management of conflict and mobility here. Against the backdrop of the European Union's (EU's) external border regimes, we argue that the most significant point about border regimes is not inclusion/exclusion across a state border but hierarchies of rights and treatment *within* a jurisdiction. This helps illustrate why it is that the UK's withdrawal from the EU holds such significance for the peace process in Northern Ireland and for mobility within and across the islands of Ireland and Great Britain more broadly.

Introduction

The Brexit debate in the United Kingdom (UK), especially in the run-up to the referendum, focused on the movement of people. In particular, Leave campaigners emphasized the desire to 'take back control of borders', by which they meant 'to reduce immigration'. This logic quickly ran into difficulties after the referendum in the face of two main obstacles: first, the European Union's (EU's) insistence that the four 'freedoms of movement'[1] are inseparable, which means that there could be no freedom of movement of goods without freedom of movement of people; and second, the problem of the border on the isle of Ireland between Northern Ireland (as a part of the UK) to the north and the Irish Republic to the south. This is a border across which the UK government is keen to see continuation of free movement of British and Irish citizens but which would become, post-Brexit, an external border of the EU. What is more, if the UK as a whole left the Single Market without providing for bespoke arrangements for Northern Ireland, the Irish border would become a border that the EU would have to manage and reinforce as a boundary to the four freedoms. Thus, the same rights and movement – people, goods, services, capital – could not then be enjoyed on the northern side of the UK–Ireland border as on the southern side.

The UK government has approached the Brexit negotiations as if it were the task for a singular, undifferentiated state; this is entirely reasonable at one level, seeing as the referendum created a slim UK-wide majority for Leave, given the size of the English population compared to the Remain-voting Scotland and Northern Ireland. The rationale for the UK government's 'One Nation' approach is entirely compatible with the nationalism that propelled the Leave vote in the first place. Such Anglo-centric nationalism sees borders as lines of inclusion/exclusion that can be quite straightforwardly managed. This reflects a conception of the British people as being an 'island race', surrounded by sea and with clearly demarcated boundaries to the nation (Whittaker 2017). Such a form of nationalism sits very uneasily with the experience of other regions of the UK and, more specifically, with the existence of a UK land border and with the realities of the 1998 Good Friday (Belfast) Agreement (GFA), which maintains a very different version of sovereignty and border management – one that comes from the tradition of EU rather than British Empire. In this EU/1998 Agreement approach, national borders are not so much sharp lines of division but meeting places between states. The best way of understanding the UK–Ireland border is as a site of integration and cooperation, not as a crossing point between jurisdictions that can be easily managed.

In what follows, we first introduce the kind of popular understanding of borders that formed the backdrop to the 2016 UK Referendum on exiting the EU. We then position our own use of the concept of 'border regimes' within the broader field of border studies and explain its relevance to the paper's focus. Since we borrow this concept from Berg and Ehin (2006), we detail their understanding of its three analytical elements, i.e. function, governance and openness. Using these elements, we demonstrate that, despite recent efforts towards close coordination, the EU external border regime is characterized by inconsistency and variation; this variation may serve as a precedent for the model of the transformed UK–Ireland border as an external EU border. We then outline the layers of concentric border regimes that have shaped this border historically.

Border regimes demonstrate the diffuse operation of borders as networked systems of rules that regulate behaviour and are activated by the mobility of people and things at a variety of scales. The border regimes of the UK–Ireland border also show that the internal UK political and legal space is already characterized by differentiation. On this basis, we discuss the implications of Brexit for the future of these 'Irish border regimes'. In our conclusions, we maintain that the concept of 'border regimes' illuminates the multilayered complexity of borders in contemporary Europe, and why it is that a simplistic understanding of the UK–Ireland border is dangerously inadequate. Our analysis builds upon our academic and policy research work on Brexit and the Irish land border in which we have been engaged since the 2016 UK Referendum on leaving the EU.

Popular Discourses of Borders as Sites of Sovereignty and Barriers to Mobility

Contemporary border studies understand and describe borders not in terms of barriers but in terms of mobilities across borders (Pickering and Weber 2006; Mountz, Coddington and Catania 2012; Richardson 2013). Kolossov and Scott (2013, 7), for instance, write:

> While state-centredness remains an important way of conceptualizing borders and their significance (...) the world is increasingly composed of relational networks rather than only fixed spaces (...) fluidity of movement along global networks, takes little account of fixed borders.

Within this context of increasing flows (not least in terms of digital communications and financial transactions), Latham (2014) conceives borders as 'striking sites' where bodies, mobility and information intersect. Public attention on this intersection is often preoccupied with how the movement of people across state borders is governed.

The pro-Brexit movement in the UK was but one manifestation of an increasing tendency for populist rhetoric on 'stronger borders' to find fertile soil in the mainstream media and political parties. In a European context, official, public and media discourses on the pan-European 'migration crisis' appeared to reach new heights in 2015, after a period of particularly intense conflict and refugee flight from Syria. These discourses reflect stark assumptions in the public mind that the purpose of 'borders' is to constrain 'mobility' – and that failure to do so poses a risk to state cohesion and security. While the migration crisis is broadly viewed as both a practical and humanitarian problem, media discourses tended to focus on the points where the mobility of people is managed, controlled and restricted (including at border fences, sea ports, deportation centres) as a means of illustrating 'a crisis of sovereignty' in the modern nation-state. In the UK, the June 2016 referendum to leave the EU could be interpreted as the manifestation of this same sense of sovereign impotence, exacerbated by concerns about the inability to take single-handed decisions on erecting borders; indeed, it was dubbed as a 'by-election on immigration' (ITV 2016; Travis 2016).

Borrowing McCall's (2013, 2) words from a different context, public opinion on EU membership (and Brexit) was thus shaped by:

responses to features of 'dark' globalization – 'global terrorism' and illegal migration – and resulting discourses of threat and insecurity, which have turned the page in political, media and academic understandings of state borders.

'Borders', in such rhetoric, are lines of defence and distinction between what 'belongs' and what is 'foreign'. The fact that such discourses rely on a clear sense of 'the other' and the 'external threat' is evident in the ways in which British discourses about hardening borders were, up until recently, almost entirely blind to the existence of the UK's land border with the Republic of Ireland, with whom it joined the then-EEC in 1973. Brexit – the process of the UK's exit from the EU – was envisaged by Leave campaigners as an exercise in separation and selective treatment of different types of flows. The Brexit debate and *problematique* is thus quite clearly one *not* of EU per se but of national sovereignty. National sovereignty 'presumes and justifies an alignment between territory, identity and political communities': an alignment that literally comes together at the borders of the state (Kolossov and Scott 2013, 6). However, as any borders scholar will point out: it is not that simple. The greater the flow of goods and trade in services, the greater the need for people to be mobile too.

Multiperspectival Analyses of Borders

State borders are, fundamentally, traversable frontiers – even the most inaccessible and autocratic countries allow for some entry/exit. Rather than in their overall 'impenetrability', the power of a state's borders can be best seen in the enforcement of differential treatment *within* the jurisdiction of the state. As such, borders should be conceptualized as 'practices ... situated and constituted in the specificity of political negotiations as well as in the everyday life performance of them' (Andersen and Sandberg 2012, 6). Such approaches elucidate borders, and European borders in particular, as 'not a static, geographical phenomenon, but [a] dynamic [one], consisting of political power, technological practices and knowledge-production' (Lemberg-Pedersen 2012, 36). Understanding the UK–Ireland border as both an edge and a fissure in such a dynamic and multilayered process presents a fascinating case study because it demonstrates the entanglements and contradictions in the ways in which different groups are treated within these islands of Britain and Ireland.

In this article, we build upon Rumford's (2012) 'multiperspectival' approach to understanding borders. Such an approach effectively espouses both the 'practice' and 'mobility' turns in border studies. Its main propositions centre on the idea that borders are produced and 'performed' through a multiplicity of border practices and 'borderwork' (Rumford 2006). Borders, in other words, 'are not pregiven but [are] rather to be seen as effects of the practices through which they are made' (Andersen and Sandberg 2012, 3). Second, Rumford claims that bordering processes happen at and away from borderlines, and are enacted through the work of political and social institutions (e.g. parliaments, central and local governments, civil society organizations), the bureaucratic practices associated with these, and the application of different legislation and policies (e.g. on citizens' rights, immigration or trade) at various points within and without a state's territory. Third comes the recognition that, to be effective, borders do not have to be either consensual, visible or constructed by state and political actors. Institutions outside the domain of formal political authority, as well as ordinary people, also construct borders through mundane social practices, forms of cultural representation, symbolism and emotion. As such, borders are mobile and diffused since they can be found 'in every instance when/where a legal, political or socio-cultural regulation is applied to different types of flows[2] (Johnson et al. 2011, 64). Needless to say, however, the functions, the effectiveness and the effects of borders at these different levels of production will vary.

Much of this understanding of borders is encoded in the notion of 'borderscapes' (Dell'Agnese and Amilhat Szary 2015), which Brambilla (2015, 19) interprets as expressing:

> the spatial and conceptual complexity of the border as a space that is not static but fluid and shifting; established and at the same time continuously traversed by a number of bodies, discourses, practices, and relationships that highlight endless definitions and shifts in definition between inside and outside, citizens and foreigners, hosts and guests across state, regional, racial, and other symbolic boundaries.[3]

Elsewhere, the concept of 'borderscapes' is referred to by those studying the dynamics of European borders as 'multidimensional abstractions' of knowledge, practice and technologies which capture the dynamic nature of European border control as shaped by political and administrative processes (Lemberg-Pedersen 2012, 35).

Whilst embracing the shared 'multiperspectival' and 'borderscapes' proposition that borders cannot be properly understood from a single perspective, we want to zoom more precisely on the politico-legal and policy-produced order of borders. To do so, we borrow Berg and Ehin's (2006, 54) concept of 'border regime' defined by the authors 'as a system of control, regulating behaviour at the borders'; we understand, however, that such border regimes also control behaviour far removed from the borderline itself. Berg and Ehin's conceptualization of 'border regime' is clearly foregrounded by the process of EU enlargement in the early 2000s. However, their understanding of the concept as the outcome of complex intersecting policy and political practices 'reflecting interests, perceptions, norms, structures and procedures at various levels of authority (supranational, national, local) and in different policy sectors' (2006, 53) lends us the analytical tool for understanding the unprecedented case of withdrawal from the EU, discussed in this article.

For the purposes of this discussion, we define 'border regimes' as particular constellations of knowledge and (technologically assisted, spatially situated) practices which constitute the politico-legal and administrative order in border production and management. Specifically, we are interested in how the legal and policy regimes which have constituted the Irish border historically will change through the process of Brexit. If we understand Brexit in this light – not as building a barrier between the UK and Ireland – but as instigating a change in, and a different relationship between, the border regimes that apply in both jurisdictions we can appreciate the potential damage caused to movement across the border.

Key Features of 'Border Regimes': Functions, Governance, Openness

Berg and Ehin (2006, 55) identify three consistent and important characteristics (dimensions) of a border regime, equally applicable to the EU internal and external borders: (i) the functions attributed to it; (ii) the mode of governance associated with border management (including division of competences among various levels of authority); and (iii) its degree of openness. We can expand these out to consider more broadly the nature of any particular border regime, allowing for the overlapping of operational and normative purposes of borders themselves.

First, in terms of the functions of a border regime, the process of 'permissibility' or permeability is critical: what can cross the border freely and where there are restrictions. The concept of mobility, (and the associated notion of 'flows') understood as the relationship between 'the spatiality of social life' and forms of 'actual and imagined movement' (Sheller and Urry 2006, 8; Cresswell 2011), is useful here. We can think about mobility in very wide terms, such as to include, for example, flows of people, objects, animals, interaction, digital data and economic transactions. The 'four freedoms of movement' in the EU encapsulate four different types of flows. There is a fifth flow that, as suggested by Latham (2014) and more recently by some within the EU institutions,[4] is very important: that of information. Communication technologies demonstrate that border crossings of information need no longer have any physical manifestation. Therefore, this area is one of growing threat to the security of border regimes (as seen in the Wikileaks releases, for example).

A critical manifestation of the function of a border regime can be seen in the question of citizenship. At a very crude level, citizenship demarcates who is foreign; and what rules separate 'us' from 'them'. More generally, citizenship is fundamentally about core human social needs of belonging, acceptability and connectivity. This is a live area of debate in relation to immigration – a phenomenon that has been taken as the driver of major change to the external border regime discourses and practices in the EU, especially since its enlargement in the early 2000s. As Barbero (2012) argues, citizenship 'has become a set of guidelines, discourses, practices and policies for the governance of migration'. Through these guidelines 'neoliberal globalization liberalizes the free movement of citizens and 'westernized' foreign persons while deploying technologies of citizenship and border control against [those] regarded as eternal outsiders, or even aliens' (Barbero 2012, 751).

This relates to the second element of a border regime, i.e. that of a mode of governance. The broad concept of governance refers to the 'self-organized steering of multiple agencies, institutions, and systems that are operationally autonomous from one another yet structurally coupled due to their mutual interdependence' (Jessop 1998, 29). It encapsulates the manifestation of power, law, rights, regulations, and public institutions and administration at work to make manifest the divisions and distinctions that the border represents. This need not only be state power, but it can be power divested down from the state (for example, to a private corporation to enact the border regime) or released up by the state (for example, to a collective transnational agency, such as Europol). More specifically, Monar (2011) describes *modes* of governance as 'the different types of instruments (legislative or non-legislative) used for steering and coordination of interdependent actors through institution-based internal rules systems'. These rules systems can be legally binding or maintained through collective target-setting. Either way, a border regime relies heavily on the interdependence of actors and on their coordination via various means. Rumford (2006) makes the crucial point that the EU as a 'network state' connects different levels of governance 'in a novel non-territorial arrangement'; denial of access to that network – not just denial of access to the territory of the EU – is, he argues, 'a formidable form of bordering'.

Finally, the degree of openness is essential to defining any border regime at any one time. Security is of paramount concern in this respect, not least because the ability to enforce the 'permissibility' or otherwise of crossing a border is essential to the integrity of a border regime. Securitization has been an important aspect of the European border regime in response to both the momentum of the integration process itself in the 1980s and 1990s (Van Munster 2009) and the perceived threats to internal stability and security arising from the flows of people. The very existence of border regimes depends on their ability to police flows at the edge of, and throughout, the territory of a state. Different rules of movement and the associated entitlements may apply across different categories of people, goods and services – the hierarchies within such regimes are enormously complicated (Faist 2013).

Inconsistency and Variation in the EU External Border Regime

Building on the above understanding of the key features of border regimes, Berg and Ehin (2006, 53) reflect on the multilevel and complex nature of the functions, governance and permeability of the EU external border regime. They conceptualize it as:

> a composite policy [...] shaped by policy-making across [...] diverse areas [in which] different policy paradigms [...] prescribe different modes of governance and diverse patterns of openness and control.

The resulting fragmented policy process manifests 'in a differentiated and uneven border strategy' (Berg and Ehin 2006, 53). Furthermore, the weakly coordinated and incoherent process of allocating funding for migration and cooperation policies at the external edge of Europe reflects a wide array of social and political struggles (Den Hertog 2016). Although the enhancement of the European border security policy has developed at a rapid pace since 2015 – especially in the field of shared IT systems and databases, and common means of response, e.g. the European Border and Coast Guard Agency – it appears that national policies still determine the specific effect and shape of EU directives in relation to border security. This relates to the diverging immigration rules, ideological use of the concept of border security and participative structures of governance in each member-state (see, Celata and Coletti 2015; Müller 2014). The often conflicting internal logics of the policies and practices shaping the external European border regime are manifest in the varied controls exercised over different types of flows.

This is seen in the fact that the free movement of citizens to work was restricted for most accession countries – which indicates, as O'Neill (1991)[5] comments, that the dismantling of immigration laws is much more difficult than the dismantling of barriers to trade. It also shows that the permeability of borders depends primarily on the will of member-states, and the fear of immigration is perhaps the strongest incentive for hardening borders. In this process, notions of mobility and security intersect, albeit complexly, as exemplified in the rhetoric regarding 'facilitating business mobility, securing tourist mobility, or blocking illegal mobility' (Vukov and Sheller 2013, 229).

As a response to the 'migration crisis', the EU's border-governing approach has taken a more obvious turn to treating different types of movement differently. Hierarchies of movement that had been establishing within the increasingly securitized and externalized EU border policies for more than a decade (Huysmans 2006; Van Munster 2009) were further consolidated in the development of the 'security union' in this context. The legitimating discourse for these security measures was concerned with hardening the external borders of the EU in order to preserve the particular openness of the market within. On the one hand, such a mode of governing borders is supported by 'a heightened and militarized set of muscular enforcement measures at Europe's southern and eastern borders coordinated through such agencies as Frontex' (Vukov and Sheller 2013, 230). Geographers, political scientists and sociologists alike have stressed that one part of such bordering practices stretches far beyond the external spatial borders of the EU, and includes

> the creation of 'buffer zones', of 'smart borders' able to 'filter' rather than simply block out flows of people and goods, and the increasing use of military technologies for border enforcement, as well as 'layered' border inspection/policing approaches that move customs and immigration inspection activities away from the actual territorial border (Bialasiewicz 2012, 844).

On the other hand, it is crucial to note that border regimes are not just performed at or away from a territory's edge but also *within* the territory of the state through the 'expansion of data-gathering and surveillance' which deepen the effects of a border regime throughout its jurisdiction (Vukov and Sheller 2013, 231). Across Europe,

> all routes of regional infrastructure, such as train connections [...], major urban metro stations, overland bus stations, inter-state highways, and public city plazas, are now [...] subject to intensified border enforcement (Euskirchen, Lebuhn and Ray 2007, 3).

For such reasons, Euskirchen, Lebuhn and Ray claim that the polarized notions of European borders – as either 'porous' or 'Fortress' like – are analytically weak because they conceive of the border as a territorial demarcation between two political entities. Instead, the EU itself has generated new forces for bordering, with 'new institutions, actors, rules and techniques' that act as means of constraint on the mobility of people within and into its territorial area.

All the above have resulted in the EU's border practices being described as 'fluid,' loose' and even 'virtual', 'since there appears to be 'no there'; no single institution, no single set of actors that can be identified as the bordering 'State" (Bialasiewicz 2012, 845).

Another thing which is important to consider is that much of the ground-level EU border policy is flexible and *customized for each member-state's conditions.* The growing trend towards a hardening of borders with respect to the movement of people within the EU (as well as between EU member-states and their non-EU neighbours) has not weakened the sovereignty of member-states in determining their border controls. Again, Berg and Ehin (2006, 66) point out that '[p]airs of countries, including Estonia and Russia, Romania and Moldova and Spain and Morocco, have each invented ways to provide for greater openness of the border than the *acquis* envisions'. The European Neighbourhood Policy allows for conditions within which the countries concerned can decide how to interpret the function of the EU external border in a way that gives them flexibility to govern and control their borders (Celata and Coletti 2015). As a result, 'diverse implementation practices and specific national arrangements continue to produce differentiated outcomes [where] stretches of the external border [are] marked by varying degrees of openness' (Berg and Ehin 2006, 67).

In sum, differentiation and variation characterize the EU's external border. The existing diversity of the EU neighbourhood context, as well as the associated 'tailor-made' measures and bilateral initiatives that constitute border governance, is therefore important to consider in the context of the re/emerging UK–Ireland border after Brexit.

In the remainder of this article, we turn to our case study. In the following section, we outline the historical constitution of the Irish border through a series of crisscrossing border regimes, i.e. different systems of rules and practices that define and regulate its functions, its governance and its degree of openness. Specifically, we discuss the Common Travel Area (CTA), EU membership and the GFA as such border regimes. Both the historical and socio-political background to the development of these border regimes, and their gradually produced and complexly overlapping working and effects explain the uniqueness of the Irish case and make a compelling argument for the need to adopt another 'tailor made' approach to the UK–Ireland land border post-Brexit – a matter that we address in the last section of this article. We base our analysis on past and ongoing research work, conducted in the period since the 2016 Referendum, for a number of projects and organizations, including the Borders in Globalization international research project (funded by the Canadian Social Sciences and Humanities Research Council), the Centre for International Borders Research (Queen's University Belfast) and the Centre for Cross Border Studies (Armagh). This work has included: reviews of the academic literature, media coverage of Brexit and the question of the UK–Ireland land border, policy and position papers (published by each of the EU, the UK and the Irish governments), analysis of academics' and practitioners' oral and written evidence given to the House of Commons' Northern Ireland Affairs Committee, and a series of policy and academic seminars on Brexit and the future of the border which we have co-organized and participated in.

Border Regimes Defining the UK–Ireland Border

The meandering UK–Ireland land border runs for just under 500 km across the northern part of the island of Ireland. It divides the independent state of the Republic of Ireland from the six counties of Northern Ireland, a region of the UK. The island was first divided into two separate jurisdictions by The Government of Ireland Act (1920) which envisaged partition as an internal UK matter and as a temporary answer to the thorny question of contested sovereignty across the island. However, in 1922, after a year of civil war in the south, the unionist-dominated government of Northern Ireland exercised its right not to be included in the Irish Free State, and the border officially became an international border. Over time, it steadily took a more concrete form as a customs barrier and security frontier, as well as a political and symbolic divide. By 1949, when the Free State was reconstituted as the Republic of Ireland and left the British Commonwealth, differences between the two jurisdictions had been deeply exacerbated.

Overall, relations between the two parts of Ireland in the twentieth century were characterized by 'back to back' development, with each jurisdiction acting in almost wilful ignorance of the effects of its policies and laws on the other. With the start of 'the troubles' at the end of the 1960s, divergence between the two sides of the border became manifest in the militarization and securitization of the entire border region in response to the rise of violent conflict concentrated in Northern Ireland. This process was the clearest demonstration of the conflict and division represented by the border. Within Northern Ireland, the border, in the experience of local unionist and nationalist communities, was defined and governed through mutual estrangement, suspicion, fear and instances of violence effectively translating into immobility. Still, three major legal and policy developments that we understand as forming the border regimes constituting the UK–Ireland border of today have stood at odds with the above-described understanding and operation of the border as a line of separation.

The Common Travel Area (CTA) as a Border Regime

The first of those border regimes is the CTA, which was originally created in 1922 with the establishment of the Irish Free State, reflecting a mutual understanding (if not formal agreement) between the British and Irish governments of the need to minimize disruption to the movement of people between these islands. On the one hand, it is fundamentally a set of rules and practices that reduce the need for passport controls for travel between the UK and Ireland. At another level, however, the CTA places the UK, Ireland and the Crown Dependencies[6] together in a border regime that sees hierarchical treatment of British and Irish citizens in comparison to others (including EU). This means that British and Irish citizens are free to 'move between the two jurisdictions, and thereby reside and work in either jurisdiction, without the need for special permission' (ROI Government 2017, 2).

This is important as it demonstrates how a border regime can regulate movement (not so much as a technical process but in its wider relationship to residence, labour market and place) through the differential definition and application of citizens' rights *within* the jurisdiction of a state. Even more pertinently, as the CTA has enabled Irish nationalists in Northern Ireland to avail of many British citizenship rights without having to claim British citizenship, it shows that in cases of contested sovereignty, a border regime can act as a form of conflict management. The CTA has thus created a degree of openness to the border, especially where the movement of British and Irish citizens is concerned.[7] In principle, this movement is not subject to passport checks, but in practice, due to the security situation created by 'the troubles', security checks and close monitoring of movement were regularly experienced by travellers between these islands until the peace process of the late 1990s.

The regime of the CTA is the reason why the UK and Ireland are outside the Schengen Zone – the European equivalent of a border control-free area. The UK decided not to enter the Schengen Agreement when it was first created in 1985 and has remained outside the core developments of it since. The UK's self-exclusion from the initiative was as a result of its wariness of lifting all border checks for other EU citizens (Wiener 1999). Its embroilment in the CTA (and the associated implications for border crossings) meant that the Republic of Ireland had little choice but to also opt out of Schengen. One of the primary motivations for choosing to align with the CTA rather than with Schengen was the desire to avoid the imposition of passport checks at the Irish border.

The Border Regime Associated with European Union Membership

Secondly, the UK and Ireland have been part of a common border regime within the EEC since 1973 and within the EU[8] since 1993. This was reflected in abolishing barriers to trade (e.g. to the mobility of goods, services and capital) at the UK–Ireland land border and, more broadly, in the two countries' shared subscription to the *acquis communautaire* representing a discourse of borders as enablers, rather than as barriers to movement. As a result, and crucially for present-day debates over the effects of Brexit on the UK–Ireland border, customs checks between Britain and Ireland, and between Northern Ireland and the Republic of Ireland were removed since the early 1990s, thus effecting a further degree of openness of the border. Hayward, Komarova and Butazzoni (2016) point to the importance of common EU membership for facilitating, at least in some sectors, advanced market integration, some policy integration, networks and collaboration across the UK-Ireland border.

Participation in the common EU border regime has gone a long way to improve bilateral relations between the Irish and UK governments, as well as between the Irish government and the Northern Ireland devolved administration.[9] As such, it has shaped the peace process on the island in practical and symbolic terms, as well as in terms of rights and entitlements. This has meant the following for the Irish border: strong scope for shared governance over issues of mutual concern (including those that are best addressed at the supranational level); freedom of movement (customs free, visa free) for services, goods, capital and people; common citizenship as members of the EU by virtue of being national citizens of an EU member-state; and some co-operation for security (primarily in terms of information sharing).

The 1998 Good Friday (Belfast) Agreement (GFA) as a Border Regime

Another all-island border regime was created by the 1998 GFA. A critical aspect of the Agreement is its definition of citizenship and sovereignty as it recognizes 'the birthright of all the people of Northern Ireland to identify themselves and be accepted as Irish or British, or both' and 'their right to hold both British and Irish citizenship' (The Belfast Agreement 1998, 4). The Agreement also affirms 'the legitimacy of whatever choice is freely exercised by a majority of the people of Northern Ireland with regard to its status' either as part of 'the Union with Great Britain or a sovereign united Ireland' (GFA, 3). No change to the status of Northern Ireland can thus occur without a majority referendum vote on both sides of the border.

In addition, the Agreement has formalized north/south and east/west (i.e. between Northern Ireland as a constituent part of the UK and Great Britain) institutional governance, and enabled all-island cooperation in specific sectors (e.g. waterways, food safety). When, after the signing of the GFA, security checks at the border also ceased, the UK–Ireland land border all but disappeared from view – a fact of weighty symbolic importance, particularly cherished by Irish nationalists and one which has meant that the legacy of fear, suspicion and restricted mobility in and around the border region, resulting largely from 'the troubles', has been given the chance of transformation. The GFA has thus cemented the openness of the border not only symbolically and politically but also socially.

Finally, within the 1998 Agreement, of no small significance is the fact that there is a border regime that sees differential experience within the UK itself. Northern Ireland has competency on different devolved matters compared to Scotland and different legal, policy and governance environments between Northern Ireland and the other regions in the UK have significant implications for a post-Brexit scenario, especially considering that many policy areas currently decided by the EU may, post-Brexit, well fall under the rubric of devolved competence (e.g. agriculture, environment, trade).

The Implications of Brexit for the Border Regimes on the Island of Ireland

It is essential to emphasize that the present-day functions, governance and degree of openness of the UK–Ireland border is a result of the historical over-layering of the different border regimes introduced above. Its apparent invisibility and openness is much cherished not only by Irish nationalists but is also defended by pro-Brexit unionist politicians in Northern Ireland. All this considered, the challenge of adjusting the differing border regimes that meet at the UK–Ireland land border once the UK leaves the EU is quite enormous. At the very minimum, it inevitably affects and entails the Irish state and the EU as well as the UK itself. An equally complex aspect of the task is the relational nature of the different types of flows that border regimes manage. Overall, the balance between differently functioning and governed border regimes is going to be disturbed by one state leaving the EU, with particular implications for the kind of border management and control that each regime maintains. The final part of our rticle considers these implications.

Avoiding a Hard Border

It is worth noting here that while in June 2016 the UK as a whole voted to leave the EU (with 53% voting Leave and 47% voting Remain), the majority vote in each Scotland (62% Remain and 38% Leave) and in Northern Ireland (56% Remain and 44% Leave) was in favour of remaining part of the EU (The Electoral Commission 2016). Crucially for our case study, while the vote in Northern Ireland largely aligned with 'ethno-national' identifications and the associated constitutional preferences, it did not do so unequivocally. In the analysis of Garry (2016, 3) 'Catholics overwhelmingly voted to stay by a proportion of 85 to 15 while Protestants voted to leave by a proportion of 60 to 40. Similarly, two thirds of self-described 'unionists' voted to leave while almost 90 percent of self-described 'nationalists' voted to remain'. Thus, it must be borne in mind that neither Brexit nor the possibility of a hard border on the island of Ireland as a result of Brexit (particularly in a scenario where the UK exits from each of the Single European Market and the customs union)[10] enjoys popular legitimacy in the region. It is notable that even politicians in Northern Ireland most in favour of the UK's exit from the EU – specifically, the Democratic Unionist Party (DUP) on whose votes in Westminster the present minority Conservative government is vitally dependent – do not wish to see a hardening of the border between the two parts of the island (DUP 2017; Hayward and Whitten 2018).

In recognition of the critical economic, political, symbolic and practical importance of the 'invisible and open' (HM Government 2017a, 3) Irish border, all parties to the Brexit negotiations have repeatedly stated and agreed on the view, first articulated by the European Council (2017, 6), that 'the unique circumstances on the island of Ireland' require 'flexible and imaginative solutions..., including with the aim of avoiding a hard border'. In turn, the UK government, have called for 'devising new border arrangements [that] respect the strong desire... to avoid any return to a hard

border and to maintain as seamless and frictionless a border as possible'
(2017, 7).

Yet, while 'all have requested that the specific needs of Northern Ireland
(particularly arising from the land border) be addressed in the withdrawal
process' (Phinnemore and Hayward 2017, 7), the political difficulty hinges on
differing views regarding how this task can be achieved (Murphy 2018). The
Irish state has stressed that the answer to this question lies either in the UK
remaining in both the single market and the customs union or in agreeing on
a special arrangement for Northern Ireland that would effectively retain its
membership in the single market and customs union (Connelly 2018). The
UK government on the other hand (vociferously urged by the DUP) has been
firm in rejecting both of these suggestions, the latter on grounds of being
potentially threatening to the constitutional and economic integrity of the
UK itself.[11] Key to a UK–EU agreement on the future of the UK–Ireland
border is thus not simply the question of how closely aligned Northern
Ireland's trade-associated regulations will be with those of the Republic of
Ireland and the rest of the EU, (in order to avoid a 'hard' border for goods)
but the fact that trade regulation alignment itself is intricately interwoven
with the devolutional, legal and other regulations pertaining to citizenship
and the movement of people, all issues which are highly politically charged in
the UK domestic context.

Specifically, the problem that has emerged is the UK's desire to restrict
the movement of non-Irish and non-UK citizens across the Irish border,
while remaining close to the status quo with regard to its openness to
other types of flows (goods, services, capital). While the disentanglement
of different forms of regulation has variously been referred to as 'squaring
the peg' or 'magical thinking', the approach to it taken by the UK
government can be discerned in a series of position papers published in
the summer of 2017. Even if the UK government's position paper on
Northern Ireland and Ireland remains rather vague on the detail, what it
makes clear is an underlying understanding that movement across the
Irish border will be managed not through checks at the point of entry
but in terms of rights and entitlements enjoyed once within the jurisdiction of the state. As the government explains:

> immigration controls are not, and never have been, solely about the ability to
> prevent and control entry at the UK's physical border. Along with many other
> Member States, controlling access to the labour market and social security have
> long formed an integral part of the UK's immigration system (2017, 11).

Such point-of-contact controls can entail landlords, doctors, university lec-
turers, employers, bank workers performing checks on individuals to see
whether they are 'legally' resident/working/accessing provisions in the country. At the moment, they are used to check on the status of non-EU citizens;

after Brexit, the range and frequency of such checks can be expected to increase exponentially, and the work of ordinary citizens as 'border guards' of the UK's border regime – to become increasingly normalized (Rumford 2009; Vaughan-Williams 2008; Weber 2006; Wemyss, Yuval-Davis and Cassidy 2017).

Any immigration controls at points of contact would centre upon the ability to distinguish between British and Irish citizens, other EU citizens and those from outside the European Economic Area.[12] Such measures would seek to protect the special status of British and Irish citizens in these islands, while avoiding the imposition of constraints on the movement of people across the Irish border.

Maintaining the Common Travel Area and Associated Rights

That Irish citizens are subject to immigration controls in the UK has been obscured both by EU freedom of movement of labour and by CTA arrangements (as per 1972 Immigration Order, which only deals with entry from the ROI). In fact, border controls already vary among the members of the CTA (Ireland, the UK and the Crown Dependencies) and across different types of borders be they land, sea or air. Since the late 1990s, immigration officers in Irish ports have had the capacity to examine the identity documents of travellers from elsewhere in the CTA. This takes the form of fixed controls at air and sea ports and targeted controls along the Irish border. It is a tactic that means passengers are more conscious that they are being scrutinized, although their freedom of movement is not restricted. Thus, although the UK government refers to the CTA as 'a special border-free zone' (HM Government 2017a, 7), it is not always experienced as such and, that it can be, depends on a system of legal rules and practices that extend far beyond the borderline, applying throughout the territories of each of the UK and Ireland. It has been suggested, in this respect, that since 'most economic and social entitlements of Irish citizens in the UK currently arise from their position as EU citizens', the continuation of a special status for Irish citizens in the UK after Brexit will not be automatic. Instead, there will be a need to *ensure* this status by revising current CTA legislation, amending the Immigration Act of 1971, and introducing further legislation to protect the social and economic rights of Irish citizens (de Mars et al. 2017; Ryan 2016).[13]

Originally, the 'non-foreign' status of Irish citizens in the UK was to give them the same status as those from the Commonwealth states. Such rights have since, of course, been dramatically enhanced by EU membership (particularly in relation to economic and social rights). After Brexit, Irish citizens' status as non-alien will supersede their position as EU citizens in the UK. The question is how this will be done; much will fall on (a) what counts as evidence of eligibility for these rights and (b) on the status of the CTA, following the conclusion of the Withdrawal negotiations. The advantage Irish citizens currently have over other EU/EEA citizens already centres upon what counts as residency. Residency anywhere within the CTA counts as habitual residency in the UK (e.g. for the purposes of assessing rights relating to non-contributory benefits, or application for settled status).

In practice, there will also need to be clarity on what counts as valid documentation for Irish citizens to prove right to work/reside, etc. At present, this is already different for them compared to other EU citizens, in that (since in the UK, ID cards or passports are not habitually used in order to demonstrate entitlements) Irish citizens can prove their right to work with a birth certificate. In terms of social security, these rules are coordinated rather than harmonized, so there is differentiation already. A particular concern in this regard centres on the rights of cross-border workers, or the obstacles put in the way of cross-border work if there is growing disparity between social security rules north and south of the UK–Ireland border. The question of coordination of social security rules is one thing; the recognition of contributions (e.g. towards pension funds) made elsewhere is another. Again, the status of the territory of the CTA could be vital here, but would have to be carefully negotiated as it would necessitate a significant enhancement of its importance (and some particular concessions by the EU).

Crucially, of course, the CTA does not apply to citizens who are neither Irish nor British, nor does it apply to any other type of movement beyond that of people. The latter is of critical importance and is something yet to be resolved since the freedom of movement of other (non-Irish and non-British) EU citizens will depend on the reciprocal arrangements that negotiators are able to achieve with respect to British citizens in the EU. Having never joined the Schengen Agreement, the UK has continued to operate control of the movement of EU citizens at its airports and sea borders. In practice, however, at present there are no border check points at the UK–Ireland border to control the movement of such citizens between the two jurisdictions on the island. Early indications are that one way to avoid the imposition of such border checks for other (non-Irish) EU citizens is to continue allowing visa-free travel/entry into the UK for a limited period of time while tightening regulations with respect to rights to reside, work and use public services in the country. Thus, much will depend on the future distinction between those EU citizens in the UK with registered residence rights (a certification of which under the name of 'settled status' has been proposed by the UK Government (2017)) and those without such status, as well on what the rights guaranteed by such a residence status will be.[14] Another problem arises from the fact that if the Irish border becomes a customs border for the movement of goods (if the UK leaves the single market and customs union), some restrictions will have to be imposed on the freedom that individuals have to cross the border and purchase goods (or work, offer services or run businesses). It remains unclear how this can be achieved without introducing custom checkpoints and thus additional degrees of friction or visibility to the experience of the border for those crossing it.

Finally, one of the issues concerning citizens' rights after Brexit, partly but not entirely associated with the future of the CTA, is that of the rights of British citizens in Ireland and Europe. As discussed above, entry into Ireland from Britain/Northern Ireland will continue to rely on reciprocal CTA arrangements. However, difficult questions may arise with respect to the new European Travel Information and Authorisation System being introduced by the EU for all visa-free non-EU arrivals at the Schengen border. This means pre-authorization of entry for non-EU citizens and will surely apply to UK nationals after Brexit. Ireland, however, is not a Schengen country and so this new arrangement should not affect the travel of British citizens between UK and Ireland. This is one example of differential rights and entitlements between British and Irish citizens when it comes to travel outside the CTA. The potential for a growing disparity between Irish and British citizens' rights and entitlements after Brexit has weighty implications for the population of Northern Ireland – the equality of the two being a fundamental tenet of the Good Friday Agreement (Centre for Cross Border Studies 2017, 2018).

Conclusion

Attempts to understand the effects of Brexit on the UK–Ireland border in terms of its future function(s), modes of governance and permeability – particularly for the movement of people – must both take into account the overall EU border regime framework and consider the specificity of British–Irish relations and the particular position of Northern Ireland therein. As discussed, this border can be understood historically as produced by layers of concentric border regimes within and without the British isles. Irrespective of the gradually diminishing over the past number of years visibility and symbolic significance of the Irish land border as a result of both common British and Irish participation in the single market, customs union and the peace process, it is crucial to remember that the very existence of this border reflects and manifests the enduring *problematique* of state sovereignty. Advances in peacebuilding notwithstanding, at the macro-political level ethno-national conflict in Northern Ireland can still be described as conflict over the very existence and legitimacy of the border. The debates prior to and since the Brexit referendum in both Britain and Northern Ireland demonstrate unequivocally the return and the enduring conflict potential of this crudely narrow definition of state borderline as the bulwark of sovereignty.

The mode of governance that will determine the new border regime's treatment of different types of movement is, to a degree, beholden to political divisions and interests within Britain and Northern Ireland – divisions that are ultimately structured by the sovereignty question. This will shape not only the substantive definition of Northern Ireland interests vis-à-vis UK's Brexit negotiations but also the degree and form of representation of these interests.

The debates surrounding Brexit and the very concept of 'border regime' tease out the extent to which sovereignty itself is challenged within and without the state. They help to demonstrate the entanglement of different forms of movement and the associated right within and across state jurisdictions, and reveal that borders operate not so much as lines of division but as meeting places and sites of integration and cooperation. Thus, the European border regime, already the result of 'numerous conflicting interests, principles, and "imaginaries", mediated through various political representations and procedures' (Euskirchen, Lebuhn and Ray 2007, 16) is about to undergo yet another transformation. Located at the edge of a new EU external frontier, the implications could not be starker for the conflict-scarred region of Northern Ireland.

Notes

1. These include the free movement of goods, services, capital and workers as part of the European Union's *acquis* (enshrined in the 1957 Treaty of Rome). They are not to be confused with the more commonly known outside of Europe four fundamental freedoms (of speech, worship, and from want and fear) proposed by President F. D. Roosevelt in his 1941 State of the Union address.
2. Example of people, goods, services, information or capital.
3. Here, the author discusses Perera's (2007) use of 'borderscapes'.
4. For instance, former European Commissioner for Science and Research Janez Potočnik has called for the 'freedom of knowledge' (dubbed by some 'knowledge mobility') to be achieved with the free movement of data. More recently, Estonia has made the case for the free movement of data in a 'Vision Paper on the Free Movement of Data – the Fifth Freedom of the European Union' (2017).
5. Cited in Koeppen (2015, 12).
6. As the Ministry of Justice (n.d., 1) explains, 'The Crown Dependencies are the Bailiwick of Jersey, the Bailiwick of Guernsey and the Isle of Man... [They] are not part of the UK but are self-governing dependencies of the Crown. This means they have their own directly elected legislative assemblies, administrative, fiscal and legal systems and their own courts of law. The Crown Dependencies are not represented in the UK Parliament'.
7. The fact that the CTA was maintained at the same time as the Anglo-Irish Trade War shows how different types of flows can be treated very differently within a single border regime.
8. Established through the Treaty of Maastricht (1993) and interlinked with the completion of the European single market through the implementation of the Single European Act (1993).

9. Between 1921 and 1972, Northern Ireland was governed through a unionist-dominated local devolved parliament and government. The onset of 'the troubles' (1969) and an increasingly fragile political and security climate led to the suspension of local parliament in 1972 (and to its formal abolishment in 1973). Thus, for the first 25 years of UK's and Ireland's EEC/EU membership, Northern Ireland was governed through direct rule from Westminster. In 1998 the Good Friday (Belfast) Agreement re-established devolution in Northern Ireland. Though the devolved institutions (parliament and government) in the region operated successfully and without interruption between 2007 and 2017, since then regional power sharing has collapsed as a result of a breakdown of relationships between the main political parties.

10. An intention which the UK Prime Minister Theresa May first announced in January 2017.

11. As confirmed by PM Theresa May in her speech in Parliament on 28th February 2018, broadcast by the BBC.

12. Especially since the UK Government has indicated that the country would not remain a member of the EEA.

13. Also, with respect to possible changes to how the CTA regulates the status of British and Irish citizens in each-others' territories, de Mars et al. (2017, 6) point out that since '[t]he main tenet of the CTA is that UK nationals in Ireland are treated as equivalent to Irish nationals in Ireland in almost all respects, and vice versa', without changes to the CTA post-Brexit, UK citizens would be granted 'EU-level rights… in an EU-member state'. The authors further suggest that 'while the EU has no automatic competence over third country migration policy in the Member States who are not party to Schengen… there is no EU Member State that offers nationals from *outside* of the EU a better status in an EU Member State than EU nationals have'. This may be among the reasons why, by contrast to the recurrent (since the EU Referendum in 2016) news coverage of a surge in Irish passport applications by citizens living in Northern Ireland and Britain, there has been very little public discussion of potential migration of UK citizens to Ireland.

14. The 'Joint report from the negotiators of the European Union and the United Kingdom Government on progress during phase 1 of negotiations under Article 50 TEU on the United Kingdom's orderly withdrawal from the European Union' (on 8th December 2017) states that 'The UK and EU27 Member States can require persons concerned to apply to obtain a status conferring the rights of residence as provided for by the Withdrawal Agreement and be issued with a residence document attesting to the existence of that right'. In this regard, advocacy groups such as 'the3million' (2018) have been extremely critical of the proposed by the UK Government 'settled status' (eligibility for which includes 5 years of lawful residence in the UK prior to the date of withdrawal), suggesting that it does not deal with issues such as the aggregation of pensions, healthcare or benefits from EU countries, provides no reciprocity with British citizens in Europe, proposes systematic criminality checks (illegal under EU law), and altogether represents a reduction of status, compared to the presently applying permanent residence.

Funding

This research was supported by the Social Sciences and Humanities Research Council of Canada with funding from the Borders in Globalization research programme (http://www.biglobalization.org/), led by the Centre for Global Studies, University of Victoria in British Columbia.

References

Andersen, D., and M. Sandberg. 2012. Introduction. In *The border multiple*, eds. D. Andersen, M. Klatt, and M. Sandberg, 1–22. Farnham: Ashgate.

Barbero, I. 2012. Orientalising citizenship: The legitimation of immigration regimes in the European Union. *Citizenship Studies* 16 (5–6):751–68. doi:10.1080/13621025.2012.698504.

BBC. 2018. Theresa May: No UK PM could ever agree with EU draft. Accessed March 1, 2018. https://www.bbc.co.uk/news/av/uk-politics-43228485/theresa-may-no-uk-pm-could-ever-agree-with-eu-draft.

Berg, E., and P. Ehin. 2006. What kind of border regime is in the making? Towards a differentiated and uneven border strategy. *Co-Operation and Conflict* 41 (1):53–71. doi:10.1177/0010836706060935.

Bialasiewicz, L. 2012. Off-shoring and out-sourcing the borders of EUrope: Libya and EU border work in the Mediterranean. *Geopolitics* 17 (4):843–66. doi:10.1080/14650045.2012.660579.

Brambilla, C. 2015. Exploring the critical potential of the Borderscapes concept. *Geopolitics* 20 (1):14–34. doi:10.1080/14650045.2014.884561.

Celata, F., and R. Coletti, eds. 2015. *Neighbourhood policy and the construction of the European external borders*. New York: Springer.

Centre for Cross Border Studies (CCBS). 2018. Citizens' rights and the UK-Ireland border. Briefing Paper 2. Brexit and the border series. Accessed January 30, 2018. http://cross border.ie/centre-cross-border-studies-publishes-new-briefing-paper-citizens-rights-uk-ireland-border/.

Centre for Crossborder Studies (CCBS). 2017. Response to HM Government position paper on Northern Ireland and Ireland. Accessed August 18, 2017. http://crossborder.ie/?s=northern+ireland+and+ireland+position+paper.

Connelly, T. 2018. *Brexit and Ireland. The dangers, the opportunities and the inside story of the Irish response*. Ireland: Penguin.

Cresswell, T. 2011. Race, mobilities and the humanities: A geosophical approach. In *Envisioning landscapes: Making worlds*, eds. S. Daniels, D. Delyser, J. N. Entrikin, and D. Richardson, 74–83. London: Routledge.

De Mars, S., C. Murray, A. O'Donaghue, and B. Warwick. 2017. Policy paper. The common travel area: Prospects after Brexit. Accessed January 13, 2018. http://dro.dur.ac.uk/20869/1/20869.pdf?DDC71+DDD19+DDC108+dla0ao.

Dell'Agnese, E., and A. Amilhat Szary. 2015. Introduction. Borderscapes: From border land-scapes to border aesthetics. *Geopolitics* 20 (1):4–13. doi:10.1080/14650045.2015.1014284.

Den Hertog, L. 2016. Money talks. Mapping the funding for EU external migration policy. CEPS paper in Liberty and Security in Europe, N. 95. Accessed August 13, 2017. https://papers.ssrn.com/sol3/papers.cfm?abstract_id=2965981.

DUP. 2017. Standing strong for Northern Ireland. The DUP manifesto for the 2017 Westminster election. Accessed June 5, 2018. http://dev.mydup.com/images/uploads/pub lications/DUP_Wminster_Manifesto_2017_v5.pdf.

Estonian Ministry of Economic Affairs and Communications. 2017. Vision paper on the free movement of data – the fifth freedom of the European Union. Accessed November 27, 2017. https://www.eu2017.ee/sites/default/files/inline-files/EU2017_FMD_visionpa per.pdf.

European Commission. 2017. Joint report from the negotiators of the European Union and the United Kingdom Government on progress during phase 1 of negotiations under Article 50 TEU on the United Kingdom's orderly withdrawal from the European Union.

Accessed December 9, 2017. https://ec.europa.eu/commission/sites/beta-political/files/joint_report.pdf.

European Council. 2017. Guidelines following the United Kingdom's notification under Article 50 TEU. Accessed August 20, 2017. http://www.consilium.europa.eu/media/21763/29-euco-art50-guidelinesen.pdf

Euskirchen, M., H. Lebuhn, and G. Ray. 2007.From borderline to borderland: The changing border regime, transnational labor, and migration struggles in Europe. *Monthly Review: An Independent Socialist Magazine* 59 (6). Accessed October 17, 2016. http://monthlyreview.org/2007/11/01/from-borderline-to-borderland-the-changing-european-border-regime/.

Faist, T. 2013. The mobility turn: A new paradigm for the social sciences? *Ethnic and Racial Studies* 36 (11):1637–46. doi:10.1080/01419870.2013.812229.

Garry, J. 2016. The EU referendum vote in Northern Ireland: Implications for our understanding of citizens' political views and behavior. Knowledge Exchange Seminar Series Report. Accessed December 1, 2017. https://www.qub.ac.uk/brexit/Brexitfilestore/Filetoupload,728121,en.pdf.

Government, R. O. I. (2017, 2) Common travel area. Information note from Ireland to the Article 50 Working Group. Accessed September 8, 2017. https://merrionstreet.ie/Brexit/Info%20Note%20CTA%20FINAL.docx.

Hayward, K., and L. Whitten 2018. What is Northern Ireland saying about Brexit – Key slides. Accessed June 5, 2018. http://qpol.qub.ac.uk/northern-ireland-saying-brexit-key-slides/.

Hayward, K., M. Komarova, and M. Butazzoni. 2016. Brexit and the border: Managing the UK/Ireland impact. Report. Accessed October 10, 2016. https://thewonk.eu/reports/brexit-and-the-border-managing-the-uk-ireland-impact__r2132.html.

HM Government. 2017a. Northern Ireland and Ireland position paper. Accessed August 16, 2017. https://www.gov.uk/government/uploads/system/uploads/attachment_data/file/638135/6.3703_DEXEU_Northern_Ireland_and_Ireland_INTERACTIVE.pdf.

HM Government. 2017b. Technical note: Citizens' rights – Administrative procedures. Accessed December 3, 2017. https://www.gov.uk/government/publications/citizens-rights-administrative-procedures-in-the-uk/technical-note-citizens-rights-administrative-procedures-in-the-uk.

Huysmans, J. 2006. *The politics of insecurity: Fear, migration and asylum in the EU.* Routledge: London, UK. New international relations series.

Jessop, R. 1998. The rise of governance and the risks of failure: The case of economic development. *International Social Science Journal* 50 (155):29–45. doi:10.1111/1468-2451.00107.

Johnson, C., R. Jones, A. Paasi, L. Amoore, A. Mountz, M. Salter, and C. Rumford. 2011. Interventions on rethinking 'the border' in border studies. *Political Geography* 30 (2):61–69. doi:10.1016/j.polgeo.2011.01.002.

Koeppen, B. 2015. The EU's internal market paradigm as de-bordering tool and dominant vision for Europe? EUROBORDERSCAPES Working Paper 11. Accessed October 22, 2016. http://www.euborderscapes.eu/index.php?id=working_papers.

Kolossov, V., and J. Scott. 2013. Selected conceptual issues in border studies. EUROBORDERSCAPES Working Paper 4. Accessed October 22, 2016. http://www.euborderscapes.eu/index.php?id=working_papers.

Latham, R. 2014. The governance of visibility: Bodies, information, and the politics of anonymity across the US-Mexico borderlands. *Alternatives: Global, Local, Political* 39 (1):17–36. doi:10.1177/0304375414560279.

Lemberg-Pedersen, M. 2012. Forcing flows of migrants: European externalization and border-induced displacement. In *The border multiple*, ed. D. Andersen, M. Klatt, and M. Sandberg, 35–53. Farnham: Ashgate.

McCall, C. 2013. European Union cross-border co-operation and conflict amelioration. EUROBORDERSCAPES Working Paper 1. Accessed October 22, 2016. http://www.eubor derscapes.eu/index.php?id=working_papers.

Ministry of Justice. n.d. Fact sheet on the UK's relationship with the Crown Dependencies. Accessed October 16, 2016. https://www.gov.uk/government/uploads/system/uploads/attachment_data/file/361537/crown-dependencies.pdf.

Monar, J. 2011. Modes of EU governance in the justice and home affairs domain: Specific factors, types, evolution trends and evaluation. In *The dynamics of change in EU governance*, ed. U. Dietrichs, W. Reiner, and W. Wessels, 180–209. Cheltenham, UK: Edward Elgar.

Mountz, A., K. Coddington, and R. T. Catania. 2012. Conceptualizing detention mobility, containment, bordering, and exclusion. *Progress in Human Geography* 37 (4):522–41. doi:10.1177/0309132512460903.

Müller, A. 2014. *Governing mobility beyond the state: Centre, periphery and the EU's external borders*. Palgrave Studies in European Political Sociology. New York: Springer.

Murphy, M. 2018. *Europe and Northern Ireland's future*. Newcastle upon Tyne: Agenda Publishing.

Perera, S. 2007. A Pacific Zone? (In)security, sovereignty, and stories of the Pacific borders-cape. In *Borderscapes: Hidden geographies and politics at territory's edge*, ed. P. K. Rajaram and C. Grundy-Warr, 201–27. Minneapolis: University of Minnesota Press.

Phinnemore, D., and K. Hayward 2017. UK withdrawal ('Brexit') and the Good Friday Agreement. Study. European Parliament. Directorate General for Internal Policies. Policy Department for Citizens' Rights and Constitutional Affairs. Accessed March 3, 2018. http://www.europarl.europa.eu/RegData/etudes/STUD/2017/596826/IPOL_STU(2017) 596826_EN.pdf.

Pickering, S., and L. Weber. 2006. Borders, mobility and technologies of control. In *Borders, mobility and technologies of control*, ed. S. Pickering and L. Weber, 1–19. Netherlands: Springer.

Richardson, T. 2013. Borders and mobilities: Introduction to the special issue. *Mobilities* 8 (1):1–6. doi:10.1080/17450101.2012.747747.

Rumford, C. 2006. Theorizing borders. *European Journal of Social Theory* 9 (2):155–69. doi:10.1177/1368431006063330.

Rumford, C. 2009. *Citizens and borderwork in contemporary Europe*. Abingdon: Routledge.

Rumford, C. 2012. Towards a multiperspectival study of borders. *Geopolitics* 17 (4):887–902. doi:10.1080/14650045.2012.660584.

Ryan, B. 2016. Written evidence. Submission to House of Lords European Union Committee inquiry on Brexit: UK-Irish relations. Accessed October 5, 2017. https://www.parliament. uk/documents/lords-committees/eu-select/Brexit-UK-Irish-Evidence-Volume.pdf.

Sheller, M., and J. Urry. 2006. The new mobilities paradigm. *Environment and Planning A* 38 (2):207–26. doi:10.1068/a37268.

The 3 million. 2018. 150 unsettling questions to the home office. Accessed May 15, 2018. https://www.the3million.org.uk/questions.

The Agenda. (25 October 2016). ITV. Accessed October 26, 2016. http://www.itv.com/hub/the-agenda/2a1635.

The Belfast Agreement. 1998. https://www.gov.uk/government/publications/the-belfast-agreement

The Electoral Commission. 2016. EU Referendum results. Accessed November 20, 2017. https://www.electoralcommission.org.uk/find-information-by-subject/elections-and-referendums/past-elections-and-referendums/eu-referendum/electorate-and-count-information.

Travis, A. 2016. Fear of immigration drove the Leave victory – Not immigration itself. *The Guardian.* June 24.

Van Munster, R. 2009. *Securitizing immigration. The politics of risk in the EU.* Basingstoke: Palgrave Macmillan.

Vaughan-Williams, N. 2008. Borderwork beyond inside/outside? *Space and Polity* 12 (1):63–79. doi:10.1080/13562570801969457.

Vukov, T., and M. Sheller. 2013. Border work: Surveillant assemblages, virtual fences and tactical counter-media. *Social Semiotics* 23 (2):225–41. doi:10.1080/10350330.2013.777592.

Weber, L. 2006. The shifting frontiers of migration control. In *Borders, mobility and technologies of Control,* eds. S. Pickering and L. Weber, 21–43. New York, NY: Springer.

Wemyss, G., N. Yuval-Davis, and K. Cassidy. 2017. 'Beauty and the beast'. Everyday bordering a 'sham marriage' discourse. *Political Geography.* doi:10.1016/j.polgeo.2017.05.008.

Whittaker, N. J. 2017. The Island race: Ontological security and critical geopolitics in British parliamentary discourse. *Geopolitics* (published online: 10 November 2017). doi: 10.1080/14650045.2017.1390743.

Wiener, A. 1999. Forging flexibility – The British no to Schengen. *European Journal of Migration and Law* 4 (1):441–63. doi:10.1163/15718169920958702.

Small Diplomacy: Cultural Cooperation As a Factor Alleviating Societal Tensions — The Case of Lviv and Its Polish Partner Cities

Klaudia Nowicka ⓘ, Iwona Sagan ⓘ, and Dominika Studzińska ⓘ

ABSTRACT
Poland and Ukraine share a long and complicated history with some really dramatic events which still overshadow relations between both nations, especially those which took place in Volhynia and other areas with a mixed Polish–Ukrainian population during 1943–1945 when soldiers of the Ukrainian Insurgent Army (UPA), the military wing of the Organisation of Ukrainian Nationalists – Bandera faction (OUN-B), planned and carried out the extermination of the Polish population. What is more, the nationalists killed several hundred Ukrainians as all manifestations of friendliness towards Poles were regarded as acts of collaboration with the enemy and a betrayal of national ideas. The main difference between the approach of Polish and Ukrainian historians is the terminology which they use to describe and evaluate those events. The endless public discussions, often accompanied by negative emotions, continues to heat up the historical debate. The Volhynia massacre, as it is often called in Poland, or the Volhynian tragedy, the term used by more moderate Ukrainian researchers, still overshadows Polish–Ukrainian relations. The echoes of this historical conflict (some historians claim that the Volhynian events were a continuation of the Polish-Ukrainian war of 1918–1919 for control over Lviv and Eastern Galicia) also exert a significant influence on the political decisions made by both countries with regard to commemoration of the victims – for indeed, they have become an element of the Polish–Ukrainian conflict of memory. During the communist period, there was no opportunity to talk openly about the history and conflict that divided the two nations. Nowadays, there are many initiatives aimed at reconstructing the past and building a new future. Many of these are inspired by culture and take advantage of its various forms. This article discusses detailed research on how city twinning and cultural cooperation can become a tool of small diplomacy. The case of Ukrainian Lviv and its six Polish partner cities has been studied.

Introduction

Various forms of cross-border cooperation have been recognised as a kind of a 'trademark' of the integration processes taking place in Europe. They are supported by different European Union (EU) structural founds and many community initiatives and organisations (Scott 2012). What is more, McCall (2013) argues that cross-border cooperation remains central to the process of ameliorating ethno-national territorial conflicts and social tensions since it promises to open the territorial cage of the state to enable development of inter-communal relations and intercultural dialogue with 'the others' living on the other side of the border. Borders analysed as socially constructed distinctions and as a social formation directly refer to the cultural dimension and its role in shaping the identities in neighbouring countries (Berg 2000; Newman 2006). While sharing these arguments, the article is an attempt to assess to what extent cultural cooperation between the selected Ukrainian and Polish partner cities contributes to alleviating the societal tensions between Ukrainians and Poles, to determine the main forms and dimensions of this cooperation and to verify whether the fact that Poland is a member state of the European Union facilitates the cooperation or not. Moreover, the present unstable political and social situation in Ukraine makes the efforts to alleviate this historical conflict even more important than ever as modern grievance-driven nationalism gaining more and more supporters both in Poland and Ukraine can provide an ideological driver for conflict reoccurrence. Cross-border cooperation in the cultural dimension strongly shapes the nature of borderscapes. Sometimes shared and properly promoted intangible values and ideas can result in tangible effects, transforming the cultural landscapes of borderlands, like in the case of the European Days of Good Neighbourhood which will be mentioned in the article.

The article is divided into five main sections. The first one presents the research methods implemented and provides detailed information on the fieldwork done in Poland and Ukraine in the period of 2013–2015. Section two introduces the idea of partner cities as a way of bringing together societies divided by boundaries as well as providing a brief history of twining. It also explains the case study selection. In third section, the authors explain the social and historical background of the Polish–Ukrainian conflict which still overshadows relations between the two nations. The last two sections present the outcomes of the fieldwork. Section four deals with the dimensions and forms of cultural cooperation between the selected partner cities and section five highlights one example of successful cooperation involving Lviv and Przemyśl – the case of the European Days of Good Neighbourhood.

The Idea of Partner Cities as a Way of Improving Relations Between Nations

Cooperation between nations at a local level constitutes 'small diplomacy' which exemplifies many decisions made at national level. The idea of partner cities, twin towns or sister cities, as this form of cooperation is called in different countries, can be perceived as a first step to integrate not only countries but above all nations. According to Bollens (2007), cities can be critical agents in the development of multi-ethnic tolerance. Nowadays, alongside diplomatic relations between countries, direct relations between local authorities have become an essential feature. European Union policy assumes that the idea of partnership, no matter its level, is one of the most basic concepts underlying the Union itself. The sense of European unity should be built on the basis of tolerance and with respect to the cultural diversity of the member states. The Council of European Municipalities and Regions is an advert advocate of twinning since its establishment in 1951 (Hałas and Porawski 2003).

The origin of city associations is derived from the Greek *poleis*. Later, in the 14th century, some spontaneous associations of cities also emerged in a form of the Hansa – a trade group or confederation of merchant guilds and their market towns. At the time of its splendour, the Hanseatic League comprised 160 cities. However, the associations of communes and cities in northern France and southern England established after the First World War can be considered the first prototypes of the modern partner cities. The idea behind these associations was to reduce the post-war gap between nations. Again, after the Second World War, European society had two choices: eternal hatred or creation of a new order. Obviously, the tragic consequences of the war showed that it is necessary to build a partnership in order to prevent such dramatic events in the future. At that time, the people of Europe wanted one thing above all – peace. Europeans took up the idea of partnership and twinning very quickly. The 1950s brought a real explosion in the number of newly concluded partnership and twinning agreements, especially between French and German cities (Ciok, Dołzbłasz, and Raczyk 2006; Kalitta 2008). Moreover, from the 1950s, town twinning become one of those means that were used in the competition for cultural and political influence during the Cold War. In the West, town twinning with western partners was encouraged in order to reinforce its cultural legacy against communism. Along with this kind of bonding model of twinning, a so-called bridging model appeared as many forms of cooperation between East and West block towns developed during the Cold War (Mikkonen and Koivunen 2015). For instance, Communist-run Yugoslavia was unique in Europe in relation to twinning as it established intense twinning with western, and later also eastern, towns (Unkovski-Korica 2014). Even though East–West twinning activities were obviously characterised by the Cold War spirit of rivalry, they enabled encounters between people living on the opposite sides of the Iron Curtain (Ahonen 2013). In 1956, President Dwight D. Eisenhower proposed a people-to-people, citizen diplomacy initiative in the US called the National League of Cities. However, two years later, due to the growth and popularity of the US programme, it became a non-profit corporation called Sister Cities International (Zelinsky 1991). The Sister Cities programme is designed as a means for cultural exchange. A community of any size decides to join with a community of another nation to learn more about each another. The organisation's mission is to 'promote peace through mutual respect, understanding, and cooperation – one individual, one community at a time' (Sister Cities International 2017).

After the Communist bloc had broken-up, the countries of Central and Eastern Europe joined in the twinning process. Partners from developed countries sought to encourage the growth of democracy and free market economy in the region (Handley 2001). Many of twinning initiatives between Polish and western cities were undertaken at that time.

The cooperation between Polish and Ukrainian cities started during Soviet times although it was not a people-to-people initiative. The cooperation involved only the largest cities of both countries: Kiev, Kharkiv, Odessa and Lviv on the Ukrainian side, and Warsaw, Cracow, Poznan and Gdańsk on the Polish side. Until 1989, in both countries, all the international contacts were controlled and restricted for ideological reasons by the communist administration of the state (Furmakiewicz 2001). Spontaneous and voluntary development of real cooperation between Polish and Ukrainian cities started in 1991 when Ukraine became an independent country. The largest number of partner agreements (15) were concluded in 2006 as a reaction to the Proclamation of the Verkhovna Rada of Ukraine made on 20 June 2002. The Proclamation to the parliaments, governments and peoples of the United Europe was a call for support of Ukraine's efforts to join the process of European integration. At present, Ukrainian–Polish cooperation is very intense. In 2014, there were 193 twin city agreements in force (Bogorodecka 2015).

Nowadays, the concept of twinning is one of the most intense forms of international cooperation at a local level. Until now, over 6,000 twinning agreements have been concluded by the cities in the European Union (Local and Regional Europe 2016). Nonetheless, twinning is a dynamically changing process. Both fields of cooperation as well as types of partnership agreement are being constantly modified. The traditional concept was based on the idea that interactions between people are the most important issue. That is why, at the beginning, the main areas of cooperation were sport, culture and students exchange. It is not a coincidence that most activities in the scope of partnership agreements were addressed to young people who are the least prejudiced as they have not witnessed the cruelty of nations involved in the conflicts. Currently, the extension of cooperation fields is observed. Economic cooperation and exchange experiences in local governance have become a common platform for cities' twinning. In the case of Polish and Ukrainian cities, all types of cooperation are observed, both traditional and modern. Undoubtedly, an additional benefit of twinning is the European Union funding opportunities allowing partner cities to implement joint projects strengthening the cooperation.

Using this relatively small-scale cities' cooperation tool seems to be a good solution in the process of alleviating conflicts between nations. Partner cities have a trust-based knowledge of each other. Partners perceive each other as credible as both sides of a twinning agreement enter into it voluntarily with no top-down pressure. This trust creates favourable conditions not only for cooperating and sharing ideas but also for solving problems. As the idea of twinning is to bring people to a closer understanding of each other, it can be a tool used for alleviating social conflicts, such as the one between Poland and Ukraine.

The Polish–Ukrainian border is an external border of the EU and the border regime makes Ukrainians obtain a visa to enter Poland's territory which hinders cross-border cooperation and networking. Therefore, in the investigated case of partner cities, local cooperation is of special meaning. It makes the border less permanent, enabling European values to spread to the Eastern European countries.

In this context, a border separating two countries can be perceived as a resource as, according to Warschawski (2005, 18) it 'is not merely a place of separation where differences are asserted; it can also be a place of exchange and enrichment where pluralist identities flourish'. Assuming that borders co-create cultural diversity, they can be used as gateways, zones of contact and communication, not an obstacle hampering cross-border cooperation. The latter is 'integral to conflict amelioration because it promises to open the territorial cage of the state to enable the development of intercultural dialogue and inter-communal relations across the border' (McCall 2015, 7). The idea of partner relations between cities takes advantage of this resource and some cities located near state borders use them to provoke joint activities as will be exemplified in a later part of the article.

Social Background of the Tense Relations Between Poland and Ukraine

The antagonistic relationship between Poland and Ukraine can be traced to its roots as far as seventeenth century (Davis 2001, 2003; Hud 2013). This relationship eventually evolved into an intense religious, social, ethnic and military conflict that lasted for over 300 years and into the twentieth century. Although there are many initiatives aimed at reconstructing Ukrainian–Polish relations, the conflict still overshadows many different aspects of Ukrainian–Polish cooperation.

When explaining origins of the Polish–Ukrainian tensions, some authors, such as Serczyk (1990), Wapiński (2002), Bakuła (2003), Beauvois (2011) or Hud (2013) use the sociological theory of conflict between two interest groups: farmers and peasants (usually Ukrainians) and nobility and landowners (usually Poles). Polish–Ukrainian conflicts concentrated in Dnieper Ukraine, Volhynia and West Galicia are perceived to be a result of relations and social divisions which were established in sixteenth and seventeenth centuries during the Kingdom of Poland and the

Grand Duchy of Lithuania (cf. Figure 2) and later in the eighteenth century when the Russian Empire consolidated the feudal system in which farmers and peasants were oppressed like slaves. What is more, in the discussed region, social division coincided with religious and cultural divisions. The elites consisted of Catholic Poles while the masses were mostly Ruthenians (Ukrainians) of mainly orthodox religion. As the Ukrainian peasants possessed low national consciousness, the conflict between them and the Polish nobility was a conflict of a socio-ethnic nature (Hud 2013) and, as Beauvois (2011) claims, it was a fight for land and freedom. It is also worth adding that the Polish–Ukrainian antagonisms were skilfully fuelled first by the Russian Empire, then by Soviet Russia.

This tragic conflict between two completely different worlds of wealth and poverty smouldered for several centuries and its history can be divided into five periods determined by the following events: (1) Polish November Uprising of 1830; (2) Polish January Uprising of 1863; (3) the Russian Revolution of 1905; (4) the Ukrainian Revolution of 1917–1921; and (5) the Second World War with the deadliest events in 1943 – the massacre of Poles in Volhynia and Eastern Galicia where soldiers of the Ukrainian Insurgent Army killed thousands of civilian Poles living there. During this last period, social, cultural and religious factors intertwined with national and political ones and this 'infernal mixture' led to the brutal and bloody culmination of the conflict.

Even today the conflict overshadows many different aspects of Ukrainian–Polish relations. The historical guilt perception still significantly differs between the two nations. Figure 1 presents results of the survey by the Institute of Public Affairs in summer 2013 in Poland and Ukraine. The survey was representative of the countries' adult populations. The interviewees were asked which nation bears the guilt of the historical events dividing Poles and Ukrainians in the past.

However, the years of cooperation and many initiatives aimed at reconstructing the history of Poland and Ukraine have ameliorated the conflict. A half-century after the Second World War, 50% of the interviewed Poles and 33% of Ukrainians claim that 'both nations are guilty'. What is more, a relatively small percentage of the interviewees blame only one side of the conflict – 18% of Poles blame Ukrainians and 14% of Ukrainians blame Poles. Obviously, people try to understand the past more deeply.

According to the nationwide survey of 2013, about half of both Ukrainian and Polish respondents claim that people living in their countries are similar to one another and share the same values and way of life. For the Ukrainian respondents, cultural similarities were very important when asked about their associations with Poland. Additionally, Poland was associated with economic growth and successful political transformation. The same survey showed that the Poles were focused on the shared history, however, they also emphasised cultural similarities. In this context, cross-border cooperation based on cultural closeness and similarities can be an essential instrument of conflict amelioration.

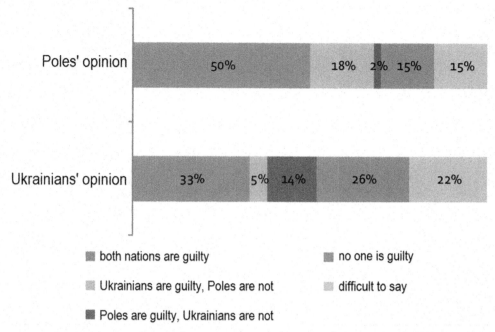

Figure 1. Historical guilt perception. Source: Fomina et al. (2013, 71)

Methods of Researching Small Diplomacy at the Polish–Ukrainian Border

For detailed research on how cultural cooperation between partner cities can alleviate conflicts and improve relations between nations, Ukrainian Lviv, with a population of approximately 700,000, and its six Polish partner cities have been chosen. The partner cities are: Wrocław (population of approx. 600,000), Lublin (approx. 300,000), Rzeszów (approx. 200,000), Łódź (approx. 700,000), Przemyśl (approx. 60,000) and Kraków (approx. 750,000) (Figure 2). The selected cities have a long-lasting tradition of cooperation as their partner agreements were signed at least 12 years ago (Lublin). Rzeszów and Lviv have the longest partner relationship as their agreement was signed in 1992.

The selection of Lviv was not accidental as it is a city of special meaning for both Poles and Ukrainians. For centuries, the border areas of Poland and Ukraine have shared a common history and the border has changed its position several times (Figure 3) (Davis 2003). Finally, in 1945 when the entire area was divided for the last time, Lviv, the most significant urban centre of pre-war South-East Poland became a Soviet city, and, then a Ukrainian city (Krok and Smętkowski 2006). Moreover, the city of Lviv cooperates mainly with Polish cities. Although it has some partner cities

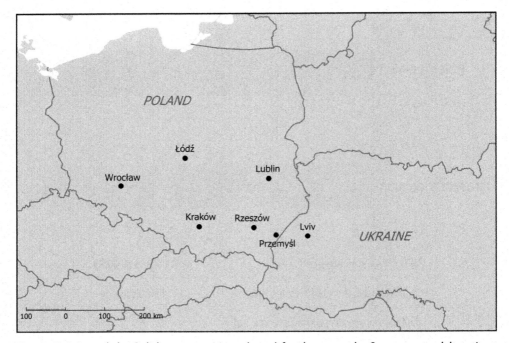

Figure 2. Lviv and the Polish partner cities selected for the research. Source: own elaboration

from the US, Sweden, Germany, Russia, Great Britain, Serbia, Bosnia and Herzegovina, Canada and Georgia, only in the case of Poland is there more than one city cooperating.

Once Polish, now Ukrainian, Lviv is still a main centre of Polish culture and social life in Ukraine. As the interviewed employee of the Polish Consulate General in Lviv states, the majority of numerous Polish tourists visit Lviv in order to contemplate and find some signs of Polish identity as well as to take part in a sentimental journey to find their roots. There are still many Polish accents in the city's space, such as: monuments commemorating Poles (e.g. Adam Mickiewicz, Jan Zeh, Jerzy Franciszek Kluczyckior, Ignacy Łukasiewicz), buildings designed by Polish architects (e.g. the National Academic Opera and Ballet Theatre designed by Zygmunt Gorgolewski) or inscriptions in Polish on the facades of old tenement houses. As Berezin (2003) states, such objects being part of particular cultural practices 'serve to steep a territory in national communal memory' and this Polish national memory is still vivid. At the same time, Lviv is also perceived by Ukrainians as 'the cultural capital of Ukraine' like one of Lviv's City Hall representatives said.

What is more, the report on social attitudes of Poles and Ukrainians issued by the Polish Institute of Public Affairs (Fomina et al. 2013) confirmed that

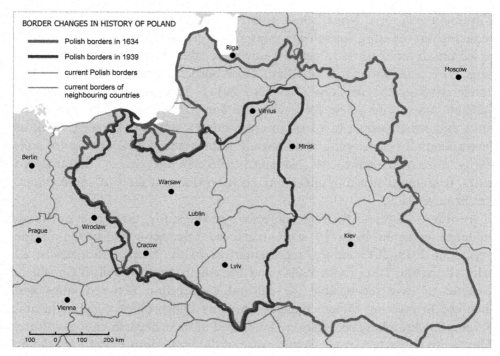

Figure 3. Selected border changes in the history of Poland. Source: own elaboration based on Atlas Historii Polski (2016)

cultural ties are the strongest between Poland and Western Ukraine with Lviv as the main urban centre – 36% of Ukrainians living in Western Ukraine have visited Poland at least once, while in other regions this percentage does not exceed 15%.

Cooperation between Lviv and its Polish partner cities is facilitated by the fact that approximately 66% of Ukrainians living in Western Ukraine declare that they speak Polish. The same report states that for 36% of all Ukrainians visiting Poland and 66% of all Poles visiting Ukraine cultural tourism was the main motive.

Lviv is also a city where history unifies and divides people at the same time. It unifies people as many Polish tourists visit Lviv in order to find their roots. This sentimental tourism brings people together, refers to hundreds of years of a common history and is economically profitable for the city and its citizens. It divides them, as Poles easily think that it is their city and their heritage which makes the tensions related to the historical conflict between Poland and Ukraine even more visible there.

Direct contacts diminish the distance between nations. This clear correlation observed in the authors' study has been also confirmed by the outcomes of the research conducted by the Institute of Public Affairs regarding Polish–

Ukrainian relations. Nonetheless, this is true when these contacts lead to reducing the existing knowledge gaps or to establishing real relationships based on an inner thirst to get to know each other. Otherwise, the antagonisms grow and, in such a situation, cross-border cooperation may lead to acceleration of the tensions (Newman 2011). The border may become a valuable asset only when used with the good intention of tightening the links and when people involved in cross-border activities perceive them as instruments for developing authentically human social relationships of solidarity, trust and reciprocity (Nadalutti 2015). In the case of the analysed cities, it seems that a tool alleviating such tensions, at least to some extent, has been revealed.

In order to address the main objectives of the study, the article draws on evidence gathered from 19 semi-structured interviews conducted in the period of 2013–2015 among representatives of the local authorities of all selected partner cities (both Polish and Ukrainian) and the Polish Consulate General in Lviv responsible for cultural cooperation between cities and involved in creating foreign policies. In some Polish cities, e.g. Lublin and Przemyśl, Ukrainian specialists are employed in their departments of culture. They were also interviewed. Being aware of the limitations that ethnographic methodology has when used to analyse foreign policies and other political issues (Kuus 2013), the research was supplemented by a series of interviews with representatives of organisations promoting Polish culture in Lviv and Ukrainian culture in Lviv's Polish partner cities, e.g. representatives of honorary consulates of Ukraine in Rzeszów and Lublin, the Polish Tourist Society in Lviv, the Polish Association for the Care of War Graves in Lviv, 'Lwowskie Spotkania' – monthly, Ukrainian 'White Eagle' Association and the Polish Scouting and Guiding Association. Additionally, Ukrainian and Polish scholars and border guards were interviewed. Moreover, several unstructured interviews with citizens of Lviv were done during the study visit to Lviv in August 2013.

The interview's basic scheme comprised nine questions covering the most important issues connected with the role of cultural cooperation in the process of peace building, the main forms and dimensions of cultural cooperation between Ukrainian and Polish partner cities and the meaning of the fact that Poland is a member state of the EU in the context of cultural cooperation and culture sharing. The questions were divided into three thematic groups: (1) cultural cooperation as part of small diplomacy influenced by both institutionalised and bottom-up initiatives (organisation, legal aspects, funding, stakeholders, barriers, limitations, forms of cooperation, events, evaluation, etc.); (2) elements of Polish and Ukrainian culture which are widely promoted during organised cultural events (visual arts, sports, folk or contemporary culture); (3) social perception of the events and the cultural content itself (attendance, people's opinions, reviews and feedback received from spectators as well as from the people involved in the organisation of the events). Importantly, there was no direct question about the conflict itself in order to check whether this issue has any connection with the present cultural cooperation between the cities and the people. Most of the Ukrainian interviewees did not agree to being recorded and they refused to justify their decision, too. It may be due to political reasons and the fact that the political party ruling the city ('Svoboda') in 2013 is a far-right nationalist party and does not support cultural cooperation with Poland and Western Europe. However, most of the interviewed people were open and eager to talk and answer all the questions. During the interview they shared their own opinions and observations as well as providing some additional data, mostly connected with organisational issues and attendance derived from official documents, reports and evaluation sheets.

Cooperation Inspired by Culture – Dimensions and Forms

Bogusław Bakuła (2003) argues that the initial breakthrough in the Polish–Ukrainian conflict was achieved only through dialogue in the scope of culture, especially literature, art, cinema and music. These cultural confrontations created a unique atmosphere of change although, at first, they had not been recognised as a contributing factor. Deeply nostalgic Polish borderland literature is an example of inspiration and dialogue, although this dialogue still has some negative connotations in Ukraine. After the Second World War, the historically rooted Polish culture of this land was the opportunity for sovietised Ukraine to establish some contact with Western Europe. Since the systemic transformation of Poland and the gaining of sovereignty by Ukraine in 1991, cultural contacts between the two countries have been flourishing. One year later, in 1992, Rzeszów and Lviv entered a partnership agreement. Then, in 1995, another two Polish cities became Lviv's partners – Kraków and Przemyśl. The remaining three cities under investigation (Wrocław, Lublin and Łódź) started cooperation after 2000.

Polish culture has occurred to be sensitive to the values of Ukrainian literature, painting and music. With their absorption it has become richer in new experiences and forms of artistic expression. Still, Poland is the largest foreign market for widely understood Ukrainian art. The fact that Ukrainian culture is rather hermetic is not a result of its pure reluctance to external contacts or influences. It is the expression of its internal problems of a postcolonial nature (Bakuła 2003). However, the level of openness has been constantly increasing over the years and year after year cultural cooperation between Poland and Ukraine has been tightening and involving new institutions, organisations and people.

In the years of cultural partnership development, numerous different forms of cooperation have been established as one of the interviewees claims,

'[...] it is good to know that we [Poles and Ukrainians] are so similar and that it is so easy to mix our cultures and values. It seems so natural.'

The outcomes of the fieldwork, taking place from August 2013 to February 2015, allowed determination of the dimensions of the cooperation taking place between the partner cities as well classifying the cities in groups reflecting the level and advancement of the partnership. Table 1 presents examples of the most important initiatives and events organised in cooperation with partner cities or those in which partner cities take part. They are divided into two groups. The first one is organisational – it is internal as its initiatives are mainly for people involved in cultural projects. Such forms of cooperation build strong foundations for future projects and, as one of the interviewees said,

'sometimes it is possible to create some unconventional solution to procedural or legal barriers hampering the cooperation'.

The second dimension comprises all events and initiatives aimed at popularising culture – they are called external ones as they are for people – citizens.

As for the external dimension of cooperation, partner cities collaborate in many different ways. There are concerts, exhibitions, festivals, competitions and sporting events organised every year in almost every partner city, as is presented in Table 1. There are implemented projects, some of them co-funded by the EU, which allow their participants to become familiar with the culture of the other nation. It would not be extraordinary, there are many partner cities in the world which take up such cooperation, but in this particular case – so historically complicated – it seems that the core of all these events, which is contemporary culture, constitutes a way to overcome the tensions between the nations. The cooperation between the partner cities is mainly based on contemporary art, music (particularly jazz music), cinema and other modern ways of artistic expression (e.g. graffiti). There are a few events promoting traditional folk, so tightly linked to the past and history. Thanks to this, people, especially the young, are able to build a new type of relation between each other which, as has been mentioned, is the most effective way to eliminate the conflict. As McCall mentions, 'it is now generally accepted by peace-building theorists that the engagement of the "grassroots" is an essential component of a peace-building endeavour' (McCall 2013, 206). He also adds that this is particularly important in a situation where borderlanders are on the periphery of the state and geopolitically remote from central government, as in the analysed case. Many bottom-up initiatives arranged by the 'grassroots' like, for example, exhibitions organised by the 'Black and White' group in Lviv, were observed. An interesting example is a rock group called 'Enej'. It is a band of Polish and Ukrainian musicians who derive inspiration from Ukrainian folk and mix it

Table 1. The most important examples of cooperation between Lvis and its Polish partner cities.

Cooperation dimension	Cooperation form/ issue	Example	Partner cities involved
organisational/ sharing good practice [internal]	Tourist infrastructure	Underground Cities project	Lviv, Lublin, Rzeszów
	Restoration and conservation of monuments	Conferences, study tours and workshops organised by the city of Cracow for Ukrainian city hall employees	Lviv, Cracow
	Erecting monuments	A monument erected in Wrocław in 2011 to commemorate the murder of Lviv's professors	Lviv, Wrocław
	Workshops	EU fund raising	Lviv, Łódź
		Monument conservation	Lviv, Cracow
		Tourism development	Lviv, Rzeszów
	Conferences	Culture for the Eastern Partnership (2013)	Lviv, Lublin
	Seminars	A report on the condition of culture and NGOs in Ukraine (2012)	Lviv, Lublin
	Publications	Strategy of cross-border cooperation 2007–2016 (2007)	Lviv, Lublin
		Experiences in implementing cultural projects in Lublin, Lviv, Łuck and Ivano-Frankivsk (2015)	Lviv, Lublin
popularising culture [external]	Concerts	European Days of Good Neighbourhood	Lviv, Przemyśl
		FortMission	Lviv, Przemyśl
		Jazz Bass	Lviv, Przemyśl
	Exhibitions	Fashion Philosophy Fashion Week Poland	Lviv, Łódź
		Europe Day [graffiti]	Lviv, Lublin, Rzeszów, Przemyśl
	Large events	Cultural Market	Lviv, Łódź
		Festival of Partnership	Lviv, all Polish partner cities
	Festivals	Review of Current Polish Cinema	Lviv, selected partner cities
		International Festival of Ukrainian Theatre	Lviv, Cracow
		International Dance Festival – Folk Inspirations	Lviv, Łódź
	Competitions	Carpathia Festival	Lviv, Rzeszów
	EU projects	Eastern Partnership Culture Programme	Lviv, Lublin
	Other projects	Closer to each other. Three cultures, one Europe.	Lviv, Lublin
		Open Lviv	Lviv, Lublin
	Sporting events	Rzeszów-Lviv Bridge of Cooperation	Lviv, Rzeszów
	Cultural education	International Bridge Tournament: student exchange programmes	Lviv, all Polish partner cities

Source: own elaboration

with Polish elements. Such spontaneous forms of collaboration reflect the level of trust and openness to dialogue when ordinary people do not need top-down stimulation or funds to do something together.

Patrick Buckley, Takahashi, and Anderson (2015) argue that great value can be derived from city-to-city exchanges through social capital development. The representatives of city halls take part in many different training, workshops and study tours (Table 1). When asked about the main field of cooperation, the interviewees could not definitely choose only one, as the cooperation with Lviv is multidimensional and multi-layered. The interviewed representatives of the Mayor's Office in Lviv admitted that they usually learn from their Polish colleagues, while in Lublin only, the respondents said that they learn from Ukrainians how to obtain funds from the private sector.

When analysing cooperation intensity, three groups of the Polish partner cities of Lviv can be distinguished: the so called 'big players', real partners and 'small players' – cities that take part only in initiatives at a local level (Figure 1).

Wrocław, Łódź and Kraków can be classified as the 'big players'. They are mostly in a position of 'teachers' but they usually undertake cooperation with Lviv when they need an eastern partner in projects co-funded by the EU – that is why it is understandable why, for example, in Wrocław the interviewee claimed that she is not capable of determining a clear field of cooperation and that it *'depends on the project'*.

The real partners, as it is possible to call Lublin and Rzeszów, cooperate with Lviv in many different dimensions – they share good practice, they are open to learning from each other and they have citizens and culture in mind. It may be stated that Lublin is the leader of cooperation with Lviv and, generally, with Ukraine.

Przemyśl, having only 62,500 residents, represents the last considered group. Although it is a city located almost on the border and, despite it being a partner city of Lviv, it actually does not cooperate with Lviv in a way that is comparable to Lublin or Rzeszów. It cooperates mainly with the small towns and villages situated in the vicinity of the border, organising concerts and other events. However, many of these activities are supported and co-organised by the authorities of Lviv (e.g. the European Days of Good Neighbourhood).

Obstacles and barriers to cultural cooperation have also been determined in the studies. Most of the interviewees of both countries agreed that the impediments are mainly on the Ukrainian side and they are as follows:

(1) Lack of systemic solutions and long-term planning in Ukraine;
(2) Ukrainian partners have no experience in applying for external funds;
(3) Lack of modern and effective programmes for children and young people in Ukraine (lack of proper cultural education);
(4) Lack of cooperation between NGOs and national bodies in Ukraine;
(5) Complicated procedures for obtaining visas;
(6) Centralised budgetary system of Ukraine – lack of money for cultural projects.

The above-listed barriers are in line with the arguments raised by critical voices saying that EU cross-border cooperation involves excessive bureaucracy, artificiality and that it is dominated by the public sector (Newman 2006; Scott 1999). Almost all the impediments are, more or less, connected with EU regulations and demands, including the border regime which was mentioned by all the interviewees as one of the most important barriers to cooperation. However, of significant meaning for the subject of study, none of the interviewees mentioned that the conflict between Poland and Ukraine hampers cultural cooperation.

The cooperation in the scope of culture is developing intensively in all of the selected cities. It takes many different forms and is multidimensional. Each Polish city has managed to establish unique relations with Lviv and some kind of specialisation in cooperation fields can be observed, e.g. Kraków and Lviv cooperate mainly in the field of restoration and conservation of monuments, while Lublin and Rzeszów are into the creation of tourist infrastructure. However, it is not possible to determine one clearly defined field of cultural cooperation as cities cooperate on many different levels and in many different scopes. What can be stated, though, is that turning to contemporary culture has allowed building relations based on the shared present rather than on the past – relations which do not force the old generation to forget, but which allow the young to get to know each other without hatred or prejudice. This kind of peace-building process, like the one taking place in the selected cities of Ukraine and Poland, based on shared European/global contemporary culture uniting young people, partly by its accessibility and 'ubiquitousity' in media and every-day life, may be perceived as a promising strategy, being part of the larger processes of conflict transformation and alleviation, especially in cases of old (historical) conflicts and in a situation when there is a generation of young people who did not take part in or witness the (usually cruel) reality of the conflict. The cooperating cities benefit from the processes and mechanisms of knowledge diffusion and mutual learning which indirectly contribute to normalisation of cross-border relations (Adaelli 1999).

The Light of Successful Cooperation and the Shadow of Conflict

The wide range of different activities undertaken by the partner cities results in easing the tensions between Poles and Ukrainians. The strategy to promote contemporary culture and emphasise cultural similarities has turned out to be very successful. Another key element of the cooperation success is localness of the events organised. Most of them are not planned to be events at a national level like, for instance, the Rise of Eastern Culture project. The organisers do not aim for them to be attended by people from all over Poland or Ukraine. They are mainly for local people living in the borderland as they are the key actors who shape the relations in the first place. Nonetheless, the importance of nationwide events should not be underestimated.

The case of the European Days of Good Neighbourhood taking place at the Malhowice–Niżankowice border-crossing point is a good example of the regional and small-scale cooperation in which Przemyśl and Lviv are involved. It is a case that proves that cultural cooperation may have a strong physical effect, too. Malhowice–Niżankowice is a closed border-crossing point with almost no infrastructure. But during the European Days of Good Neighbourhood (co-organised by the city of Przemyśl, the authorities of the Lviv district and the authorities of the city Lviv), a stage was placed actually ON the border, in a small area between two borderlines (a 'no man's land' area), so people could listen to concerts together and take part in different cultural events without the necessity of actually crossing any border (Figure 4). In 2014, 2,000 people took part in the event. It has become clear that cultural cooperation can change the space significantly for the moment of an event, but some lasting results may also appear. The plans to open this cross-border point have started to be developed. People have been struggling for many years to do so and the scope of this event has shown that people living on both sides of the border want to communicate and share the

Figure 4. Malhowice–Niżankowice border-crossing point during (a, b) and after (c, d) the European Days of Good Neighbourhood in 2014. Source: own collection

CROSS-BORDER COOPERATION 53

common space. However, the interviewed border guard remains rather sceptical that it will happen as, like he said,

'*opening of this cross-border point has been planned for 20 years and nothing has happened yet*'.

On the other hand, the representative of the city of Przemyśl claims that the money has already been assigned in the budget and that the Malhowice–Niżankowice border-crossing point will be reopened soon.

Similar events are organised across the Polish–Ukrainian border involving other cities and regions (e.g. Kryłów, Zbereże). These small-scale events integrate local people and they have the bottom-up power to build new, friendly relations between Poles and Ukrainians.

When contemplating the bright side of Polish–Ukrainian relations, it is obvious that many things have changed over the years and the efforts of people involved in cultural cooperation resulted in creation of a 'cultural bridge' joining the two nations, no matter the real physical or/and mental barriers dividing them. However, the shadow of conflict is still present. Although during the interviews there were no direct questions about the conflict, it was always mentioned, yet not in the context of cultural coopera-tion. Sometimes it was just a little remark, sometimes the respondents felt an urgent need to talk about it for a long time. Although it is not perceived as a barrier to cultural cooperation, it is an unsettled matter which is still on people's minds. Nowadays, both in Poland and Ukraine, there are organisa-tions and political parties fuelling the conflict. They organise exhibitions and events during which they astound onlookers with brutal pictures document-ing the massacres carried out by the Ukrainian Insurgent Army and the Polish Home Army in Volhynia during the Second World War. The inter-viewed people involved in cultural cooperation claim that such events do not affect their activity. They believe that the cultural ties between Poles and Ukrainians and the years of fruitful cooperation cannot be destroyed by such political provocations, as the confrontational type of activities result from the frustration and willingness of some people to gain political capital.

For cultural cooperation, the fact that Poland is a member of the European Union facilitates the cooperation. On the basis of the conducted study results, it may be stated that it is much easier for Ukrainians to accept European cultural values than purely Polish ones as their national character have been slightly diminished. Nowadays, in Ukraine, Poland is associated with '*the great and mighty West*' (three interviewees used this wording) and, therefore, it represents the global culture shared by the European Union – the com-munity which Ukraine wants to be part of. Being an EU member facilitates cooperation, not only in the above-mentioned mental dimension, but also in a practical one. So far, EU funds have allowed the implementation of many projects in the scope of culture, e.g. the Eastern Partnership. However, to achieve better results, the EU's institutional and legal cooperation framework should be revised as in the contemporary form it hampers some forms of cooperation, especially between countries separated by the EU's external border with the visa regime in force.

Conclusions

In the difficult post-war European reality, the different forms of partnership and twinning between cities has become one of the most effective instruments of the policy of conflict amelioration. Cooperation in the sphere of culture has especially high potential for the process of healing historical wounds. The investigated case of cooperation under the partner city scheme of Ukrainian Lviv and six Polish cities verifies the thesis that cooperation in the sphere of culture is the first and most reliable form of activity possible between historically antagonistic nations. Despite different types of cooperation between the partner cities being identified, in all of them cultural cooperation is present and occupies an important position.

Although the role of cultural cooperation in alleviating the conflict between Poland and Ukraine is difficult to measure by simple means, it is definitely a contributing factor. Undoubtedly, cultural cooperation between Polish and Ukrainian cities results in many positive effects – some of them have a strong real-life representation, like the case of the European Days of Good Neighbourhood and its effects. There is a will to cooperate on both sides and many interviewees mentioned that, through small-scale events, ordinary people have a chance to get to know each other and this is the most important goal of cultural cooperation. The fact that a successful event was organised by provincial Przemyśl and small locations on the other side of a border once more verifies the observation that bottom-up initiatives, organised at the very local level, are highly effective in the process of bridging communities.

Another aspect of cooperation in culture mentioned in Lviv is that *'politicians are not involved in it'*; this sphere is managed by people who are really into culture and who are focused on cooperation, not on building political capital. Although the present political situation, both in Poland and Ukraine, is very tense as a result of the very recent changes (Law & Justice government in Poland, the civil war in Ukraine and the re-actualisation of the fascist heritage of Ukrainian nationalism), it does not affect the level of 'small diplomacy' and cultural cooperation between Polish and Ukrainian cities is being continued.

Polish membership of the European Union exerts a positive influence on the cultural cooperation between the selected Polish cities and the Ukrainian city of Lviv. Contemporary Polish culture and cultural events are perceived by Ukrainians, and especially by a young generation, as a part of a bigger phenomenon of Western European culture rather than national – Polish – events. Thus, acceptance of Polish culture is much easier as it is associated with a vaguer entity of western culture. It evokes the tendency to be identified and included in the western stream of culture rather than to be separated and rejected from it.

One thing that can be stated clearly, and that was commonly admitted, is that the chance to change the attitude of the old generation is very weak or does not exist at all. The long-lasting conflict is so deeply rooted in their minds that no one believes that it can be changed. However, the representatives of the old generation do not stimulate or provoke cultural cooperation and do not take part in it, so they do not negatively affect the practice of cultural cooperation. Young people are eager to share culture and even to create a new mutual one, like the above-mentioned rock group 'Enej'. Their work is a good example that Polish and Ukrainian cultural roots are similar enough to be successfully combined.

There are also some promising signs for the future and as one of the interviewed Poles working in Lviv said: *'the shadow of this historical conflict will still be with us, as still lots of old people remember the events of 1943 and we celebrate them every year, however a great step has been made for the last 20 years as both sides do not demonize each other anymore and nowadays in the scope of cultural cooperation the conflict is not a barrier.'*

The provided analysis presents the cultural cross-border cooperation, although being irregular and to some extend ephemeral phenomenon, significantly influences the process of building a positive, long-lasting social memory of joint events. Cultural events importantly intensify the cross-border contacts. According to the social psychological contact theory encounters between members of different social groups positively influence the relations between them (Allport 1979). The cross-border contacts are of a particular importance in historically difficult borderlands like Polish–German (Grix and Knowles 2002) or Czech–German (Mirwaldt 2010). In such cases the frequency and the character of the contacts have a crucial meaning for mutual understanding and reconciliation. However, in the case of Polish–Ukrainian cooperation the fact that two countries are separated by the EU external border and that Ukraine is not an EU member state changes the cooperation environment completely and makes this case an extraordinary one. On the one hand, such a situation makes Polish culture more attractive for Ukrainians, as it is perceived part of a greater European whole, as it has already been mentioned. On the other, the border regime, current political situation and different legal systems makes the institutional cooperation very demanding and the fact that the analysed cities cooperate on so many different levels only proves the strength of their motivation and the willingness to create a true cultural bridge between Poland and Ukraine.

With no doubt it can be stated that culture provides an especially fertile ground for contacts that alleviate historical tensions and open a platform for a dialogue. The presented case of Polish–Ukrainian cross-border cooperation is a great example of that.

Funding

This work was supported by the Project EUBORDERSCAPES, financed though the EU's 7th Framework Programme for Research and Technological Development 290775.

ORCID

Klaudia Nowicka ⓘ http://orcid.org/0000-0002-2961-4634
Iwona Sagan ⓘ http://orcid.org/0000-0001-6363-3831
Dominika Studzińska ⓘ http://orcid.org/0000-0002-9779-223X

References

Adaelli, C. 1999. *Technocracy in the European Union*. London: Longman.
Ahonen, K. 2013. Town twinning in the Cold War World. *Geopolitical Magazine* 1:85–90.
Allport, G. 1979. *The Nature of prejudice*. Reading, MA: Addison Wesley.
Atlas Historii Polski. 2016. *Atlas Historii Polski, collaborative work*. Warszawa: Demart.
Bakuła, B. 2003. *Polska – Ukraina: Partnerstwo kultur*. Poznań: Wydawnictwo Naukowe UAM.
Beauvois, D. 2011. *Trójkąt ukraiński. Szlachta, carat i lud na Wołyniu, Podolu i Kijowszczyźnie. 1793-1914*. Lublin: Wydawnictwo Uniwersytetu Marii Curie-Skłodowskiej.
Berezin, M. 2003. Territory, emotion and identity. In *Europe without borders: Remapping territory, citizenship and identity in a transnational age*, ed. M. Berezin and M. Schain, 1–30. Baltimore: John Hopkins University.
Berg, E. 2000. Border crossing' in manifest perceptions and actual needs. In *Borders, regions, and people*, ed. M. van der Velde and H. van Houtum, 154–65. London: Pion.
Bogorodecka, O. 2015. The peculiarities of Poland and Ukraine's twin cities' cooperation progress. *Historia i Polityka* 13 (20):171–82. doi:10.12775/HiP.2015.011.
Bollens, S. A. 2007. Urban Governance at the Nationalist Divide: Coping with group-based claims. *Journal of Urban Affairs* 29 (3):229–53. doi:10.1111/j.1467-9906.2007.00341.x.
Buckley, P. H., A. Takahashi, and A. Anderson. 2015. The role of sister cities' staff exchanges in developing "learning cities": Exploring necessary and sufficient conditions in social capital development utilizing proportional odds modelling. *International Journal of Environmental Research and Public Health* 12:7133–53. doi:10.3390/ijerph120707133.
Ciok, S., S. Dołzbłasz, and A. Raczyk. 2006. *Dolny Śląsk. Problemy rozwoju regionalnego, Studia Geograficzne 76*. Wrocław: Wydawnictwo Uniwersytetu Wrocławskiego.
Davis, N. 2001. *Heart of Europe*. Oxford: Oxford University Press.
Davis, N. 2003. *God's playground*, Vols. 1,2. Oxford: Oxford University Press.
Fomina, J., J. Konieczna-Sałamatin, J. Kucharczyk, and Ł. Wenerski. 2013. *Polska – Ukraina. Polacy – Ukraińcy. Spojrzenie przez granicę*. Warszawa: Instytut Spraw Publicznych.
Furmakiewicz, M. 2001. The international partnership relations of Polish municipalities – An example of Lower Silesia. In *Changing role of border areas and regional policies*, ed. M. Koter and H. Heffner, Vol. 5, 105–14. Łódź: Region and Regionalism.

Grix, J., and V. Knowles. 2002. The Euroregion and the maximization of social capital: Pro Europa Viadrina. *Regional and Federal Studies* 12 (4):154–76. doi:10.1080/714004770.

Hałas, K., and A. Porawski. 2003. *Twinning – Współpraca miast bliźniaczych. Stare wyzwania – Nowe szanse*. Warszawa: Urząd Komitetu Integracji Europejskiej.

Handley, S., ed. 2001. *The links effect – A good practice guide to transnational partnerships and twinning for local authorities. International Report 3*. London: Local Government International Bureau.

Hud, B. 2013. *Ukraińcy i Polacy na Naddnieprzu, Wołyniu i w Galicji Wschodniej w XIX i pierwszej połowie XX wieku*. Zalesie Górne: Pracownia Wydawnicza.

Kalitta, E. 2008. Rola miast partnerskich w budowaniu przyjaźni między narodami. Przykład Chojnic. *Samorząd Terytorialny* 12:52–63.

Krok, K., and M. Smętkowski. 2006. *Cross-border co-operation of Poland after EU enlargement. Focus on Eastern Border*. Warszawa: Scholar.

Kuus, M. 2013. Foreign policy and ethnography: A sceptical intervention. *Geopolitics* 18 (1):115–31. doi:10.1080/14650045.2012.706759.

Local and Regional Europe. 2016. Accessed April 04, 2016. http://www.twinning.org.

McCall, C. 2013. European union cross-border cooperation and conflict amelioration. *Space and Polity* 17 (2):197–216. doi:10.1080/13562576.2013.817512.

McCall, C. 2015. *The European Union and peacebuilding. The cross-border dimension*. London: Palgrave Macmillian.

Mikkonen, S., and P. Koivunen, eds. 2015. *Beyond the divide: Entangled histories of Cold War Europe*. New York, Oxford: Berghahn Books.

Mirwaldt, K. 2010. Contact, conflict and geography: What factors shape cross-border citizen relations? *Political Geography* 29:434–43. doi:10.1016/j.polgeo.2010.10.004.

Nadalutti, E. 2015. Is EU cross-border cooperation ethical? Reading cross-border cooperation through the 'needs for roots' by Simone Weil. *Geopolitics* 20 (3):485–512. doi:10.1080/14650045.2015.1016155.

Newman, D. 2006. Borders and bordering – Towards an interdisciplinary dialogue. *European Journal of Social Theory* 9:171–86. doi:10.1177/1368431006063331.

Newman, D. 2011. Contemporary research agendas – Border studies. In *The Ashgate research companion to border studies*, ed. D. Wastl-Walter, 33–47. Farhkam: Ashgate.

Scott, J. W. 2012. European politics of borders, border symbolism and cross-border cooperation. In *Companion to border studies*, ed. H. Donnan and T. M. Wilson, 83–99. Oxford: Wiley-Blackwell.

Scott, W. 1999. European and North American contexts for cross-border regionalism. *Regional Studies* 33 (7):605–17. doi:10.1080/00343409950078657.

Serczyk, A. W. 1990. *Historia Ukrainy*. Wrocław-Warszawa-Kraków: Zakład Narodowy Imienia Ossolińskich.

Sister Cities International. 2017. Accessed June 30, 2017. http://www.sister-cities.org.

Unkovski-Korica, V. 2014. The Yugoslav Communists' special relationship with the British Labour Party 1950-1956. *Cold War History* 1:23–46. doi:10.1080/14682745.2013.765864.

Wapiński, R. 2002. *Polska na styku narodów i kultur. W kręgu przeobrażeń narodowościowych i cywilizacyjnych w XIX i XX wieku*. Gdańsk: Stepan Design.

Warschawski, M. 2005. *On the border*. London: South End Press.

Zelinsky, W. 1991. The twinning of the world: Sister cities in geographical and historical perspective. *Annals of the Association of American Geographers* 81 (1):1–31. doi:10.1111/j.1467-8306.1991.tb01676.x.

∂ OPEN ACCESS

The Glocal Green Line: The Imperial Cartopolitical Puppeteering of Cyprus

Rodrigo Bueno-Lacy and Henk van Houtum

ABSTRACT

Cyprus has been divided for more than four decades by a cease fire line known as "the Green Line". This long-standing partition has made the island infamous for the seemingly unsolvable antagonism between its "Turkish" and "Greek" inhabitants. In this article, we argue that, in order to better understand why this division has remained obstinately meaningful for Cypriots, we need to "delocalise" the Green Line that separates them. We contend that the foundation upon which the conflict between Greek and Turkish Cypriots has been built—and consequently also the location of the Green Line keeping them apart—does not lie in an indigenous hostility between the Greek-speaking and Turkish-speaking communities of Cyprus. Instead, we argue that this is the result of imperial puppeteering: Cyprus' Greco-Turkish enmity is largely based on perceptions of space, heritage and identification that were first introduced during the British colonisation and have been persistently—if not always deliberately—reinforced by chronic external intrusions and counter-productive conflict-resolution initiatives. We claim that a succession of British imperialism, Hellenic irredentism, Turkish nationalism, Cold-War geopolitics, UN conflict resolution and EU expansion have created, inculcated and reinforced cartographically organized perceptions of space, history and culture—a *cartopolitics*—that have invented the *Turkish Cypriots* and *Greek Cypriots* as identitary categories and perpetuated their antagonism. Thus, rather than an essentially local and binary play, the Cypriot conflict should be regarded as a *glocal* drama in which outside actors have been pulling the strings of the island's politics. The readjustment of the historiographical and geographical limitations to which the Cypriot conflict has been confined so far has decisive implications for the island's reunification: merely to zoom in on the hostile dichotomy at work is insufficient. Rather, to understand the persistence of the Green Line fracturing the island we need to zoom out from Cyprus.

A Glocal Genealogy of Cypriot Segregation

To walk alongside Nicosia's Green Line today implies walking along a lingering past that uncannily refuses to fade away. A succession of sandbags, dilapidated

---

This is an Open Access article distributed under the terms of the Creative Commons Attribution-NonCommercial-NoDerivatives License (http://creativecommons.org/licenses/by-nc-nd/4.0/), which permits non-commercial re-use, distribution, and reproduction in any medium, provided the original work is properly cited, and is not altered, transformed, or built upon in any way.

façades pockmarked with bullet holes and a scatter of slouching soldiers cut through Cyprus' capital as unassuming reminiscences of the murderous conflict that started to unfold between the island's Turkish-speaking and Greek-speaking communities back in the 1950s. The peak of their interethnic violence, in 1974, led to Cyprus' partition along the "Green Line": the UN-guarded buffer zone that has separated the island in two halves and largely severed the interaction between Greek and Turkish Cypriots ever since (see Figure 1).

This territorial partition has been replicated in many everyday borders that divide the lives of Cypriots—from political identity to collective memory—and, most recently, in the Turkish North's exclusion from the Greek South's membership to the EU. We claim that by conceptualizing the Green Line as part of the bigger picture of EU border making we can better understand it: not as a stand-alone exception but as a fragment of a larger cartographical imagination with geopolitical implications for the wider European context. The Green line can be seen as a scale replica of the physiographical convention that invents discontinuity between "Europe" and a vaguely defined "East" along the Bosporus, the Ural Mountains or even, oddly, the Mediterranean (Dunn 2010, 15; Bueno-Lacy 2011, 64). These borders are the expression of the widely held misconception of almost essential incompatibility between "East" and "West" and the long-standing and recurrent prejudice that it begets: the portrayal of Semitic people in general—and Muslims, Arabs and Turks in today's political context—as Europeans' most antagonistic others (Al-Azmeh 2003; Allen 2004;

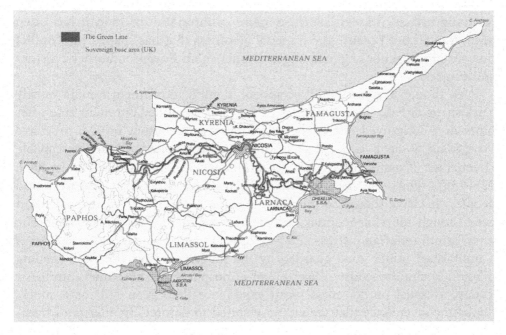

Figure 1. Ceci n'est pas la Ligne Verte. Based on: http://www.globalsecurity.org/military/world/europe/cy-green-line.htm

Born, Dziewulski and Messling 2015; Bulliet 2006; Khaf 1999; Vaughan and Vaughan 1997; Bayraklı and Hafez 2016).

However, neither the Green Line nor Europe's physiographical borders are self-evident testaments of spatial, ethnic and civilisational splits between Europe and *the Orient* but rather proof that power can rupture otherwise seamless communities, cultures and geographies (Said 1978). Cyprus offers an inestimable scale model to study how the borders of Europe have been made by concealing the sustained historical contact between East and West that has left profuse traces of cross-fertilization in what today is considered as quintessentially European heritage—from the gothic cathedrals and Renaissance art to cuisine, science and philosophy (Al-Azmeh and Fokas 2007; Brotton 2002; Bulliet 2006; Goody 2004; Raquejo 1986). Thus, studying the Green Line might provide as many insights into the interethnic conflict between Greek and Turkish Cypriots as into the growing anxiety towards Muslims across the EU (Goodwin and Raines 2017).

The very *Greekness* or *Turkishness* that nationalists on both sides of the Cypriot Green Line persist to represent as a threat to one another, just like the very *Europeanness* that mushrooming demagogues purport to defend from Islam in the rest of the EU, betray a fundamental historical ignorance about the very identity that they are anxious to shield. The consanguinity between Greek Cypriots and Turkish Cypriots as well as between Europeans on the one hand and Arabs/Muslims on the other runs much deeper than Cypriot ethno-nationalists and Eurocentrists would like to admit. Therefore, in this paper we want to focus on the stubbornness of the Cypriot Green Line not only because its persistence is more counterintuitive than it has often been granted but because the imperial aloofness that has shaped the conflict that sustains it echoes a much larger dispute about European borders, history and future.

Even though Cypriots' ethno-national identification might remain mostly Turkish or Greek, their 300 years of *convivencia* under Ottoman rule offer hints of a long-lived shared heritage—however rebutted by the pervasive evocations of deep and ancient differences embedded in the inescapable Green Line (Cassia 1986, 3–28; Kitromilides 1977, 35–70; Brambilla 2009, 121–138).[1] Thus, the specific question that drives this paper is: Why would people who have shared so much for so long keep eschewing reconciliation even though the violence that caused their separation has faded away? The inter-communitarian distress and geopolitical tension one would expect from a militarized buffer zone guarded by the longest-serving UN peacekeeping mission is simultaneously offset by an atmosphere of sheer uneventfulness. Today, a casual border-crosser can experience the Green Line as a superfluous inconvenience that seems more suited to enforce the inertia of tradition rather than as a border keeping at bay any impending security concerns.

What then has kept the island's communities apart and the approaches to the resolution of its conflict going amiss for over 40 years now?

By way of an answer to this question, a great deal of the literature on the Cypriot conflict has conceptualized it as a "protracted conflict" stemming from *longue durée* incompatibilities between Cyprus' culturally discordant Greek and Turkish communities—an animosity often postulated to be rooted in a mutual ethnic animosity dating back hundreds or even thousands of years (e.g., Azar 1985, 68; Fisher 2001; Coleman 2003, 4; for a notable exception see: Kontos et al. 2014).[2] Although we do not dispute that Cypriots' own agency has played a role in stoking and perpetuating their conflict, we are wary to assume that ethnic bad blood between Turkish-speaking and Greek-speaking Cypriots has caused a spatial, social and political fracture for as long as Turks and Greeks have inhabited the island.

Moreover, the very assumption that Greek Cypriots and Turkish Cypriots have always thought of themselves as such is anachronistic. For most of Cypriot history, *Greek* and *Turk* have been inexistent or unstable categories of either ethnic self-identification or division (on the historical instability of words see: Foucault 1971, 152). Accordingly, we explore how these very categories of ethnic identification have acquired their meaning and how they have persistently precluded the formation of a Cypriot nation state with its own identitary mythology (Foucault 1982; Hobsbawm 1990, 20–22).[3]

In what follows we contend that imperial intrusions have largely determined Cypriots' inimical politics through either strategic or cavalier impositions that have been persistently puppeteering their identities and digging an entrenched *cartopolitical* fracture across the island. As we will make clear, the very meaning of "Turkish Cypriot" or "Greek Cypriot", by association to the nation states that they refer to, evoke a cartography of antagonistic Greek and Turkish political myths. This geopolitical cartography, in turn, is associated to an entire system of thought that has constructed the history, culture, space, politics and even people from East and West, Europe and Turkey, Greek Cypriots and Turkish Cypriots as inherently different. However, the Bosporus is as questionable a civilisational split between Europe and *the Orient* as the Green Line is between Greek Cypriots and Turkish Cypriots (Said 1978).

Imperial Cartopolitics

The imperial impositions in Cyprus that we aim at identifying in this article follow a broad understanding of empire derived from its classical etymological root in the Latin *imperare*: to command. In this article, we understand this imperial command as *a centre's pre-eminence to rule over a subordinated periphery* (Hardt and Negri 2000; Hobsbawm 1987; Kumar 2017; Münkler 2005). Thus, the empires and imperial attitudes whose influence on Cyprus we discuss belong to an imperial political technology that, historically, has been characterized by the hierarchical duality between a metropole that rules and colonies that obey.[4] We pay attention to the political organizations (i.e., states as well as international and supranational organizations) whose relations with Cyprus can be captured by what Edward Said described as the "high-handed executive attitude of nineteenth-century and early twentieth-century European colonialism" (Said 1978, 2).

Our angle to study the imperial imprints on the island is what we have called *cartopolitics* (van Houtum 2012, 412).[5] With cartopolitics we mean "the visual imposition of control and meaning over space as well as over its inhabitants, their behaviour and ideologies [...] It is a political technology that consists in cartographically defining political territories and empowering them with meaning" (Bueno-Lacy and van Houtum 2015, 485; Strandsbjerg 2012, 827). Although cartopolitics are often related to maps and visualized by them, they are by no means limited to them: they are *geopolitical imaginations that evoke a map*, like "the Orient", "The Muslim World", "the West", "the Global South", etc. We are interested in how Cyprus has been bordered and ordered within a structure of geopolitically meaningful hierarchies. Geopolitical metaphors that, for example, as ancient Greece and thus a gateway to the cradle of European civilisation for British imperialists in the nineteenth century or a threatening Mediterranean Cuba for the US during the Cold War. Contrary to their ambition to provide an objective representation of the world, cartopolitical notions predominantly derive from neither dispassionate history nor first-hand experience (Gregory 1994, 70; Derrida 1982, 307–330; Critchley 1999, 31–44; Ó Tuathail 1996, 58–86) but rather from a piecemeal of geographical signs edited and promoted by power and reproduced by the inertia of "common sense" (Eco 1976). These manipulated signs create a "cartography of identities" (Gregory 1995, 447), an imagined geographical distribution and historical belonging that tell us where we are, who we are and, in consequence, who are like us and who are different from us. These notions of space and history and the borders they engender form the basis of grand geopolitical strategies and imperialist interventions.

The cartopolitical b/ordering of spaces as well as the coinciding process of othering is often done via *heterotopias* and *chronotopes* (Bakhtin 2004; Foucault 1986). Heterotopias are "places within places": notions of spatial connection or transmission between a *here* and an *elsewhere*, such as ideas of cultural connection between a colony and a motherland.[6] Chronotopes— which literally mean "temporal locations"—are time-space distortions which national identities typically configure to celebrate, ritualize and invent the spurious longevity of a political myth (Renan 1997[1882]). Through both these spatio-temporal imaginary mechanisms, members of a political community mutually construct notions of themselves as part of anachronic and thus fictitious groups bound by a common geography and a shared history (Basso 1984, 44–45). Nation states have traditionally tapped into these representational techniques to craft a mythology of their polity as pre-existent and even *essential* (Anderson 2006[1983]; Bottici 2007).

In what follows we will analyse the imperial cartopolitics—or what could be termed *cartocolonialism*—that various imperial meddlers have shipped into Cyprus. We will pay particular attention to the heterotopias and chronotopes that have configured Greek Cypriot and Turkish Cypriot identities. Our aim is to explore how politically meaningful and cartographically organized imaginations of Cyprus, both within the island and beyond, have woven a dense web of local and worldwide interests which, we argue, have constructed and protracted the divide among Cypriots. Chronologically, we focus on the British Empire's pursue of its colonial interests in the Middle East; the post-colonial antagonism between Greek and Turkish national myths; the US concerns about a latent strife between crucial NATO allies in the Cold War context; the Greek-supported coup followed by the Turkish invasion and lastly the failed reunification plans brokered by the EU and the UN.

Brutish British Sophistication

As the sluggish collapse of the Ottoman Empire threatened to splinter the Balkans into many nationalisms and endanger the delicate balance of power in the region, the British Empire occupied Cyprus in 1878 to safeguard its endangered commercial and military interests in the Near East (Hopkirk 1990, 328–329). Cyprus came into the British radar as a convenient location from which their empire could ward off the expansionist ambitions of the Russian Empire in the eastern Mediterranean, watch over Egypt and protect the Suez Canal as well as the passage to India—the "pearl" of the empire's colonies (Varnava 2005).

Although a mix of imperial wantonness and strategic geopolitical interests drove the British to colonize Cyprus, the fortuitousness of their colonisation eventually acquired the more calculated character of a civilising mission (a *mission civilisatrice*). The British government's ignorance about Cyprus together with its distinctively Anglocentric understanding of history and civilisation heavily influenced the colonial policies with which they transformed the island (Pollis 1973; Varnava 2005, 175).

As the British settled in Cyprus, they found in their new and exotic Mediterranean colony two heterotopias that would guide their colonial administration and lay the grounds of today's Cypriot conflict. The first was the glory of ancient Greece that their philhellenic imperial upbringing had taught them to idealize. The second was an orientalist vision of Ottoman Turks that had been taking shape in Britain since the times of Shakespeare (Vitkus 1999, 224; Ross 2012, 7). It is worth emphasizing that, although the British set foot in Cyprus at a time when every corner of Europe seemed to belong—and was certainly being reclaimed—by a Romantic project of nation-building, Cyprus was isolated from this nationalist trend sweeping the European continent. In the absence of a Cypriot national project that no one had yet cared to invent, the British cavalier identification of Cyprus' inhabitants as an extension of already existing nationalities flourished unimpeded: they saw Greeks and Turks instead of Cypriots and their misperception went unchallenged (Pollis 1973; Varnava 2005, 175).

The British philhellenic imagination imprinted an ironic duality on Cypriots: it invested them with the grandeur of yore yet simultaneously justified their colonisation. The first impressions of Robert Hamilton Lang —a leading British diplomat at the time—articulated the ambiguity of this colonial gaze: "There are no modern wonders in the Cyprus Court [...] but things of which you read in ancient Greek literature [...] which seems to tell us how little has been the progress in such arts in Cyprus during the past two thousand years [...] But the clouds are breaking, and British rule will soon dispel them altogether" (Lang 1887, 186-187). As these lines reveal, as far as the Victorian colonial elite was concerned, nothing had changed in Cyprus since the times of Aristotle. Paradoxically, the very patina of ancient venerability that made Cypriots part of Antiquity's unsurpassed pinnacle of intellectual sophistication also made them primitive people in need of enlightenment. The British felt uniquely qualified to civilise Cyprus and by extension ancient Greece—of which they thought it was a relic—the cradle of the European civilisation which they fancied themselves leading in the nineteenth century (Byron 1823; Mikhail 1979, 107–108; Ross 2012).

The ambiguous philhellenic yet orientalist overtones of this British imperial gaze were also captured by an old image published in the Illustrated London News of 1895 (see Figure 2). The British are depicted as sophisticated surveyors and aloof guards who scrutinize their Cypriot subjects from positions of authority. In contrast, Cypriots are portrayed as an arrange of stereotypical mannequins inhabiting a museum's showcase. Their dress, actions and artefacts suggest some sort of primitive rural eccentricity set against a background strewn with exotic minarets and oriental decorative elements. Cypriots are exposed to the dissecting stare of British colonial officers—and, by extrapolation, to the eyes of the British public to which this publication was addressed. Overall, this representation makes Cypriots seem "quaint" and less modern, perhaps even less refined than their British masters: they are rendered as colourful but simple people from a remote island's countryside.

This picture's composition condenses the main interpretation that the British made of Cypriots at the time: rural, corporate people with an uncivilized loyalty for their kind—a character that the British assumed was a hindrance to their development (Bryant 2003, 247). Stemming from their "popular anthropology of Cypriots' nature", the British enshrined in law what they saw as Cypriots' tribal barbarism by introducing a legal system

Figure 2. Cypriots through imperial eyes: "Native Types of Cyprus", image of Cyprus from the Illustrated London News of 1895. Source: Illustrated London News Historical Archive: http://find.galegroup.com/iln/start.do?prodId=ILN&userGroupName=acd_iln&trialParam=PcaUEOQ22QvXwa0Z8Knerby2NagyHDpZ

that made the Turkish and Greek ethnic groups the basis of public administration and legal redress. They "civilized" Cypriots by replacing what they dismissed as a cumbersome system of Ottoman village authorities with a clear-cut system of island-wide ethnic leaders (Bryant 2003, 261). This modernization ripped apart multi-ethnic and multi-confessional village politics, thus provoking an island-wide political reconfiguration that is still felt today: in their ambition to simplify Ottoman complexity, the British bordered and ordered Cypriots according to the *mainly Turkish* and *mainly*

Greek populations that they thought to "recognize" in the island (van Houtum and van Naerssen 2002). The British colonial administration broke down a Cypriot society that had been slowly brewing over centuries of intermingling and replaced it with a new managerial reality of spatial, political and legal order (Scott 1998).

Before the British reorganized Cypriots along Greek and Turkish ethnic lines, Christian Orthodox and Muslim Cypriots inhabited the same neighbourhoods and homes without the intercommunal hatred later found during the twentieth century (Brambilla 2009, 123; Pollis 1979, 49–50; Nevzat 2005, 69–72). However, the British re-oriented Cypriots' local allegiances and placed them in the hands of their ethnic representatives (the "ethnarcs"). Everyday problems that in Ottoman Cyprus had been solved by non-ethnic village politics became matters to be treated by mono-ethnic, island-wide representatives. Muslim–Christian syncretism gradually unstitched as the administrative—and later territorial—border imposed by the British started to pull apart newly invented groups of "Turkish Cypriots" and "Greek Cypriots". Ironically, rather than breaking down corporatism, the British manufactured it (Bryant 2003, 263).

Language was another crucially divisive border carved by British imposition. A common set of languages was already spoken by both Muslim and Christian Orthodox Cypriots when the British arrived (Pollis 1973, 586–587; Hobsbawm 1990, 110–111). However, the rapid proliferation of newspapers and schools that followed the British occupation dealt a fatal blow not only to the common Cypriot languages—for multilingualism was a common feature of Cypriot life for most of its history (Hadjioannou, Tsiplakou and Kappler 2011)— but also to other symbolic commonalities that could have served as the foundation of a proto-national and unhyphenated Cypriot identity (Pollis 1973, 586–587).

The national identities of Greece and Turkey were inculcated into Cypriots' minds through an educational system set up by the British who "began to encourage the importation of teaching personnel from Greece and Turkey" (Pollis 1973, 589). As consequence of these policies, the print cultures of mainland Greece and Turkey became the print cultures of Cypriots, who began to acquire a collective consciousness of themselves as either Orthodox Christian, Greek-speaking Greeks or Muslim, Turkish-speaking Turks. By extension, they learned to see Cyprus not as the land of Cypriots but as the incomplete, adulterated, even contaminated version of an unfulfilled M/Otherland corrupted by the presence of either Greek or Turkish neighbours, who they learned to regard not as compatriots but as a misplaced national community.

These caveats about the emergence of modern Cypriot consciousness are critical for the analysis and resolution of the Cypriot conflict. Contrary to what often has been claimed, the Cypriot conflict did not acquire "significant international dimensions" after the Turkish invasion of 1974 (Nugent 1997). Although Cyprus was an isolated province of the Ottoman Empire, international politics has shaped today's Cypriot conflict ever since the British occupied it in 1878. Their colonial policies dug a trench between Christian Orthodox and Muslim Cypriots with the import of foreign sensibilities. A telling imperial cartopolitical artefact evoking the ideology that percolated all spheres of life in the island as a result is the British colonial map of Cyprus (see Figure 3).

This was the first detailed modern map of the island—made by Herbert Kitchener, a senior British army officer. The scrupulous mapping of a new colony belonged to the standard procedure that the British colonial administration used to turn the unknown complexity of faraway colonies into manageable subjects (Given 2002). The British imperial obsession with the demarcation of space (maps, surveys and censuses) created a colonial knowledge that not only cast light on topographical details but which also invented sociopolitical realities that were later taken as incontrovertible facts by the bureaucracies who relied on them to govern the island. British governmentality surveyed, drew, codified and ultimately invented a Cyprus where ethnicity and religion were the main politico-territorial divisions (Constantinou 2007). Maps and their borders took

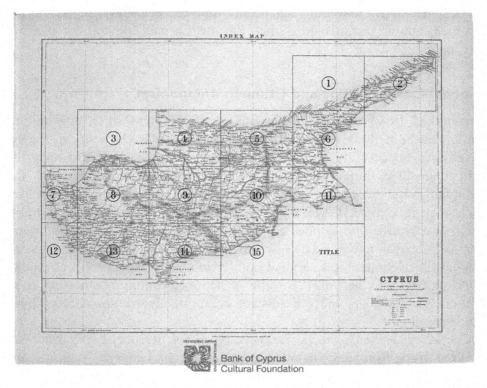

Figure 3. Herbert Kitchener's map of Cyprus, 1885. Source: Bank of Cyprus Cultural Foundation, http://www.boccf.org/museums-and-collections/cyprus-map-collection/collection-Items/C/001-100/C-085/

power away from communities and deposited it in a state that had little knowledge of the population it set itself to manage (Bryant 2003).

This cartocolonialism laid the basis for the future understanding of Cyprus' internal borders, which were replicated until they found their most dramatic expression in the establishment of the Green Line—the product of crude British military conflict resolution after Cyprus became an "independent" country. The process that led to the conflict that remains unsolvable today has recurrently relied on the British colonial presupposition that the island is naturally divided in two ethnic groups. This simplistic assumption—whose continuity can be traced from the British colonisation of Cyprus in the nineteenth century to today—persuaded Major General Peter Young, a British military officer leading the peace forces deployed to appease the inter-communal clashes of 1963, to draw a line with a green chinagraph pencil on a map as a sensible measure to quench the interethnic strife between Greek and Turkish Cypriots. Although intended as a temporary *cordon sanitaire*, this cartographic sketch would prosaically become known as "the Green Line", the border that still separates Turkish and Greek Cypriots today (Harbottle 1970, 67; Grundy-Warr 1994, 74–75). The imperial intrusions that have followed the British colonisation of Cyprus, from the end of the nineteenth to well into the twenty-first century, have relied on the invented ethnic infrastructure that the British laid down. To this we turn now.

Imperial Clash: Hellenic and Ottoman Antagonism

Encouraged by the British Hellenization of Cyprus—which squarely fit within their increasingly ambitious nationalism—Greek political leaders seized the opportunity to culturally dominate the island. Through the British unedited import of Greece's educational system, the idea of "the Ottoman"—and by extension of "the Turk"—as an intruder found a firm anchorage in Cyprus. Greek Cypriots learned to find their place within a national narrative that extolled the liberation from Ottoman-Turk domination as the Greek nation's date of emancipation (today, Greek Independence Day is still celebrated as a national holiday in Greek Cyprus too). Orthodox Cypriots began to be pulled towards a national community beyond their borders (Bryant 2003, 263), the distant dream of nineteenth-century Greek irredentism.

Greek irredentism was a rare symbiosis of territorial expansionism inspired by a Romantic historiography, a sort of "imperial nationalism" (Kumar 2017, 15–24).[7] It ambitioned to restore the territorial glories of classical Greece and Byzantium by encompassing within Greece's national borders all the Greek-speaking populations along the eastern Mediterranean (Kitromilides 1990, 6; Peckham 2000, 77). Such yearning to create a "Greater

Figure 4. Map of Greater Greece, circa 1919. Source: National Historical Museum of Athens.

Greece"—i.e., "a new Hellenic Empire that would encircle the Aegean Sea"—came to be known as "the Megali Idea" (or "the Great Idea") (see Figure 4) (Finefrock 1980; Walker 1984, 477–478; Kitromilides 1990, 3–17; Stouraiti and Kazamias 2010, 11–34).

This grand geopolitical ambition found a favourable breeding ecosystem in the prevalent imperial ideology of late nineteenth and early twentieth century geopolitics. Shaped by the lens of evolutionary racism (Hobsbawm 1990, 2), the eye driven by such imperial mindset perceived a landscape fractured by frontiers—which in the parlance of the time referred to places of natural confrontation between savagery and civilisation that justified the imposition of a colonising enterprise (Kristof 1959; van Houtum and Bueno-Lacy 2016). These were times when imperialists mixed the "political principle, which holds that that the political and the national unit should be congruent" (Gellner 1983, 1)—i.e., nationalism—, with an idea of the state that, drawing on evolutionary metaphors taken from biogeography (Bassin 1987, 474; Craw 1992) justified the violent expansion of the nation state as the natural necessity of a "geographical-biological organism" (Kristof 1960, 21–22). Whenever such organic notion of the state met the self-righteousness of the civilising mission, violent imperial expansionism and colonisation were justified as the inexorable fate of "better and lesser races" (Turner 1920, 85). In a similar vein, Greek irredentism created a powerful narrative of ultimately tragic consequences.

Through a series of powerful geopolitical and historical metaphors carried by cartopolitical heterotopias and chronotopes—i.e., politically and territorially meaningful distortions of time and space—the independent Greek nation state came to combine "the appetite of Russia with the dimensions of Switzerland" (Peckham 2000, 85).

Greece's political elites found in the Romantic Hellenic nostalgia the geopolitical force to turn scattered Greek-speaking populations throughout the eastern Mediterranean into the possible borders of their grandiose imperialism (Kitromilides 1977, 3–17). As for Greek Cypriots, this Hellenist utopia—a cartopolitical imagination that placed them within the Greek state and its Hellenic and "turkophobic" historiography—exerted a seductive appeal. It created a path for a self-righteous identity-politics. As far as nineteenth century Greek Cypriots were concerned, the Megali Idea turned the characteristics that for centuries had made the Christian Orthodox majority of Cyprus subservient to the Ottomans into a legitimization to exercise their dominance over Turkish Cypriots—i.e., the Ottomans' successors.

Through chronotopes that anchored them to classical Greece and Byzantium, Greek Cypriots nurtured geographical imaginations of a greatness injured by Turkish affronts. They learned to recognize themselves as a group different from Turkish-speaking Muslims in comparison to which they made up a sizeable majority. It was thus, at the end of the nineteenth century, that Greek Cypriots acquired not only a sense of self-identification as an ethnopolitical collective but also the hazardous moral superiority that chauvinism draws between friends and foes and right and wrong (on the friend/foe dichotomy see: Schmitt 1932). In congruence with the imperial nationalism of their contemporary irredentist Hellenic discourse (Kumar 2017, 23–36; 2000, 2003, 30–35), Greek Cypriots learned to feel that their Ottoman and British rulers owed them a redress that should be delivered in the shape of political union with Greece (aka *enosis*), the "fatherland" that the Greek Orthodox church and Cypriot schools modelled on Greece's had taught Greek Cypriots to "remember" and "long for" (Walker 1984).

Greek Cypriots' yearning for a "return" to the Hellenic world intensified as consequence of the war that broke out between Greece and the Ottoman Empire in 1897. In its aftermath Crete gained its independence and in 1913 succeeded in annexing to the Greek nation state. The Cretan experience gave Greek Cypriots a cartopolitical blueprint for enosis: a Mediterranean island with a Greek-identifying majority showed them that it was possible to vanquish the Ottomans, expel the entire Turkish minority and join Greece. Crete's enosis turned the Greek Cypriot dream—and Turkish Cypriots' anxiety—into a very real possibility (Dimitrakis 2008, 377).

Textbook Nationalism

One could say that when Greek Cypriots first approached the national myth of Greece through its schoolbooks and publications, they read in Greek nationalism and prints an archaeology into their own selves where they found ancient sensibilities that previously had been largely unimportant to them. Since then, the textbooks used by Greek Cypriots have followed what in Cypriot historiography is known as the "Hellenization thesis". This posits that, in spite of the many conquests that the island has experienced over the centuries, its inhabitants have recurrently managed to preserve its "original" Hellenic character until today—ever since the Mycenaean culture settled Cyprus in the 12 century BC. It is a discursive strategy that turns Turkish Cypriots into an artificial ethnic group while simultaneously denying them whatever belonging they might claim to the Turkish national history and state (Papadakis 2008).

Before their reform in 2004, the textbooks used by Turkish Cypriots used to be no better. According to them, the history of Cyprus began with the Ottoman conquest in 1571, which ushered a period of progress only interrupted by ungrateful revolts against Ottoman tolerance. These textbooks used in Turkish Cyprus made reference to "Our Motherland Turkey" and Turkish Cypriots were referred to as "Turks of Cyprus", thus making them a mere extension of the larger Turkish nation. At the same time, Greek Cypriots were belittled as *rum*, a nomenclature used during Ottoman times to refer to the Greek Orthodox subjects within the empire, different from Greeks, and thus a term intended to deny Greek Cypriots the connection to continental Greeks that inspired their push for enosis (Papadakis 2008, 134–137).

Until 2004, when Northern Cyprus reformed its textbooks to tell a more reconciliatory history of Cyprus, Cypriots to both sides of the Green Line grew up reading textbooks that promoted some of the most powerful heterotopias and chronotopes through which the antagonism between Greek and Turkish Cypriots infiltrated entire generations (Vural and Özuyanık 2008). The textbooks worked as cartopolitical artefacts that taught Cypriots to find their geo-historical location not in the common past and fate of a Cypriot political community but rather in the histories and fates of either Greece or Turkey while portraying "the other" as a cruel adversary (Christou 2006).

Religious Antagonism

The Hellenization of Cyprus also brought about religious tensions. The religious freedom allowed by the British Empire after 1878—which overlapped an older Ottoman tradition of religious tolerance (Dietzel and Makrides 2009)— gave way to a multiplication of voluntary associations dedicated to the "Hellenization" of Cyprus. This development would later promote intolerance towards Turkish Cypriots as the Orthodox Church—a pillar of modern Hellenism—politicized throughout the twentieth century (Dietzel and Makrides 2009, 80–81). The relatively easy religious coexistence that had prevailed since 1606—when the Ottoman Empire forcibly settled a small Turkish minority in Cyprus—up to the end of Ottoman rule in 1878 (Brambilla 2009, 121)—collapsed when the multi-confessional Ottoman empire was replaced with the bi-nationalist colony manufactured by a British imperialism that, unsuspectingly, became a vessel for Greek ethno-religious irredentism.

Competing Imperial Cartopolitics

A powerful testimony to the growing Hellenic and Ottoman antagonism amidst which Cyprus got entangled at the beginning of the twentieth century can be found in the iconological comparison of competing Greek and Turkish cartopolitical discourses from the time (see Figures 4 and 6). These maps can be seen as illustrations of the larger cartopolitical discourses that shaped the ethnic antagonism of the island in the early twentieth century. Their cartopolitical significance lies in the extent to which they splice into the political, cultural, social, historical context in which they were made. Their visual composition condenses geopolitical imaginations of Cyprus that organize it as an extension of either the Greek or the Turkish national myth (Van Straten 1991, 11; Collini 1992).[8]

Let's first focus on the Greek poster (see Figure 4). This is an illustration of the dominant geopolitical discourse that circulated in Greece after the signing of the Treaty of Sèvres in 1919. It is perhaps the most popular version of the Megali Idea ever to have circulated. The borders of Greater Greece depicted on this cartopolitical artefact represent neither the only nor even the main vision of Greater Greece—a flexible notion of which different versions existed at the time—but merely the borders that Greece was able to agree upon by diplomatic compromise after World War I (Stouraiti and Kazamias 2010, 30). On the upper left corner appears Elefterios Venizelos, the respected Greek statesman who took the Megali Idea as close as it would ever get to its consummation. His dignified expression looks over the territorial ambitions that he held to "restore" the Greek nation's greatness. His face is surrounded by the laurel wreath that ancient Greeks awarded their victors. On the right flank of the map stands a black-maned Athena reminiscent of the one imagined by Eugène Delacroix in his *Greece on the Ruins of Missolonghi* (1826) (see Figure 5): the personification of the Greek nation. She is defiantly coming to the fore brandishing a Greek banner crowned with the cross of Christian Orthodox faith. On her other hand she holds a parchment with the legend "Greece is destined to live and shall live". Although Cyprus is not coloured as part of the territories ambitioned by

Figure 5. The Romantic embodiment of the Greek nation. *Greece on the Ruins of Missolonghi*, by Eugène Delacroix (1826), Musée des Beaux-Arts de Bordeaux.

Greece, it is alienated from its proximity to Anatolia and displaced to a location closer to the core of the Greek state. There is a reason for this. Although Greeks considered Cyprus to be indisputably theirs, they were also aware that they could not realistically claim it yet as part of their expansionist ambitions, for the British were unwilling to give it away during the Paris negotiations of 1919 (Helmreich 1974, 40). Perhaps as a recognition of this international reticence, this map is careful about appropriating Cyprus by

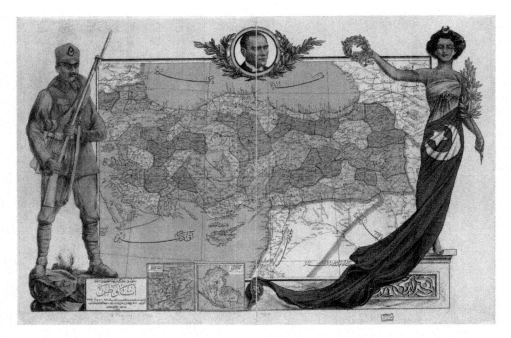

Figure 6. The other side of the Megali Idea. *Map of the Turkish Republic* (1927), by Kitaphane-yi Sûdî. Source: Library of Congress: http://www.loc.gov/item/2010593205/

blatantly colouring it as part of Greater Greece. Instead, the territorial claim is surreptitiously made by detaching Cyprus from its Anatolian context and placing it to the left of the Balkan peninsula: safely within the space of the Greek state.

The counterpart to the previous map is a Turkish map by Kitaphane-yi Sûdî dating from 1927 (see Figure 6). A fascinating aspect of this map is that it shows both how closely Turkish nationalism came to mirror Greek nationalism and in which important aspects it differed. Its centre top depicts Mustafa Kemal Atatürk, whose military and political leadership to defend and found the modern Turkish state is lauded by a wreath of laurels surrounding him. This emblem is granted to him by the Turkish nation which, mirroring the Greek map, is embodied by a woman. She is crowned with the golden crescent of Islam and stands on a pedestal; her body draped in an Ottoman/Turkish flag stamped with the star and crescent, symbols reminiscent of the Ottomans' Byzantine heritage—curiously, the same heritage claimed by Hellenic irredentists (Ridgeway 1908). This Turkish map prominently portrays an explicit military component which the Greek map only indirectly suggests through the colouring of the lands Greece ambitioned to conquer. The Turkish territory is chaperoned by a soldier holding his rifle ready across his chest (perhaps a nod to the central role played by the army in fending off the Greek invaders that allowed Atatürk to rally the Turkish nation around his leadership). The cartopolitical claim upon Cyprus is unambiguous: the island is represented as an integral part of the Turkish territory even though the Ottomans had definitely relinquished Cyprus over to the British in 1922, 5 years before this map was drawn.

A significant aspect shared by the Greek and Turkish maps alike is that they reproduce the mutually constitutive struggle between the Greek and Turkish nation states at the beginning of the twentieth century (Özkırımlı and Sofos 2008). The year of the Greek map's production, 1919, represents the peak of Greece's enthusiasm for the Megali Idea. It was in this year that, spurred by the nationalist hubris that followed World War I, modern Greece carried out its most "inopportune, ill-advised, and suicidal" expansionist attempt. Under the excuse of protecting local Greek minorities in Anatolia, the pan-Hellenist government of prime minister Eleftherios Venizelos—one of Crete's enosis main architects—found support among the vanquishing powers of World War I to invade the Anatolian town of Smyrna (now called Izmir). However, rather than expanding the Greek nation's borders, the incursion of the Greek army in Smyrna "fanned to flames the smouldering fires of Turkish nationalism and gave Mustafa Kemal his chance" to rally the Turkish army behind his command (Penn 1938; Buzanski 1963; Finefrock 1980, 48–49; Helmreich 1974, 44; Millas 1991, 22). In a historical paradox, modern Turkey came to find its foundational drama in Greek post-colonial imperialism—one century after the Greeks had found theirs in their struggle against the predecessor of the Turkish state, i.e., the Ottoman Empire. Ironically for Greek imperialists, the disastrous attempt to resurrect a glorious Byzantine past through force backfired prodigiously. The mutually agreed Greek-Turkish population exchange that followed the Greek invasion of Smyrna amounted to a reciprocal ethnic cleansing that rooted out three millennia of continuous Hellenic existence in Asia Minor (Petropulos 1976, 135).

The tragic fate of Greek irredentism is crucial to understand the Cypriot conflict. The adversities of the 400,000 Turks that were expelled from Greece as well as the plight of the 1,100,000 Greeks that were forced out of Turkey during the population exchange of 1923 remain latent memories for Greeks and Turks alike, both in the mainland and in Cyprus. Their recollections of mutual animosity produced a resounding echo in 1974, when Cyprus' own Greek and Turkish populations underwent a similar odyssey and both the Greek and Turkish states saw a renewed threat posed by their foundational foe. The slow identification with the national identity of either Turkey or Greece that Cypriots had been cultivating since the nineteenth century made them part of the memories of Smyrna, a conflict they had never experienced yet an international trauma that their ethnic clashes repeatedly evoked.

The reciprocal Greek/Turkish ethnic cleansing that followed the disaster of Smyrna reverberated beyond the borders of Greece and Turkey: it foreshadowed the collapse of one of the most influential multinational European empires and its dissipation from a territory it had controlled for over four centuries. Today, the Ottomans' geopolitical losses in the Balkans still give credit to the anachronic cartopolitical fantasy that the Bosporus constitutes a civilizational gap separating East from West, Turkey from Europe and Islam from Christianity. And yet, much of the current instability in the Middle East can be interpreted as a prolonged aftermath of the Ottoman Empire's collapse, which has been characterized by relentless European and American attempts to seize what the Ottomans lost (Fromkin 2009). In what follows we will further zoom into the process that led to the war in 1974, a conflict that has stood fossilized in the Green Line that still stands today.

Decolonisation and Further Glocalisation of the Conflict

After World War II, the cause of self-determination movements was propelled by the wave of anti-imperialism that washed away whatever was left of colonial legitimacy. Encouraged by this international atmosphere, in 1950 the Cypriot Orthodox Church organised a referendum on enosis in which 95% of Greek Cypriot voters favoured union with Greece (Emilianides 2014, 11–13). This result alarmed Turkish Cypriots who, suspecting the revival of enosis, lobbied Turkey to officially state that, should Cyprus head towards independence, Turkey would safeguard Turkish Cypriot interests by partaking in any such settlement (Stefanidis 1999, 211).

Turkish Cypriots' apprehension was not unfounded. The politico-cartographic imagination that bound Greek and Greek Cypriot nationalists was surreptitiously resuscitated in 1953, when their political and military elites secretly gathered in Athens to set up an underground Liberation Committee tasked with enosis. The Greek Cypriots' ethnarch, the archbishop Makarios III, was designated as the movement's political leader (Emilianides 2014, 20), and Georgios Grivas, a retired Greek colonel, became his military counterpart (French 2015, 46).

Once a diplomatic solution to the Cypriot conflict was summarily discarded by the UK and the UN (United Nations 1954, 11; Xydis 1968; Newson 2001, 84). Georgios Grivas, "a fanatical supporter of Enosis" funded and organised by the Greek government and Makarios (French 2015, 88–89; Dimitrakis 2008, 386) disembarked in Cyprus at the end of 1954 to organise an armed rebel group: the National Organisation of Cypriot Fighters (EOKA) (Dimitrakis 2008, 377). While EOKA yearned to emancipate a nation, it ambitioned no Cypriot nation. Rather, its glorification of Hellenism envisioned a Greek Cyprus that would join Greece and thus conjured the Greek irredentism that seemed to have perished at Smyrna more than two decades earlier.

A fervent Hellenist and former Nazi collaborator (Katsourides 2013, 570; Markides 1977, 19; Von Kogelfranz 1985), Grivas modelled EOKA after the fashion of right-wing ultranationalist parties and made the sanctity of EOKA's mission justification enough to trample upon whomever might get in its way (Gunther and Diamond 2003, 181). In a replication of the historical irony that befell Greek nationalism in the nineteenth and early twentieth centuries, the Greek Cypriot struggle for independence became an anti-imperialist yet colonising enterprise. While EOKA rebelled against British rule, it simultaneously aimed at imposing enosis upon the Turkish Cypriot population (Walker 1984; Pollis 1996, 77; Loizides 2007, 176; Dimitrakis 2008, 377–378). Faced with this prospect, Turkish Cypriots became ever more engulfed in the fear that they would undergo the same fate as Cretan Turks—i.e., deportation—should Cyprus become part of a Greek nation that would make no place for them (Bolukbasi 1993, 507).

The barrier between Greek and Turkish Cypriots grew taller when EOKA started targeting Turkish Cypriots. As EOKA infiltrated the island's security personnel, Greek Cypriots' collusion with the organisation—out of either sympathy for EOKA or fear of its ruthlessness—turned them into unreliable elements of colonial law enforcement (Grivas 1964, 149). To solve the Greek Cypriot infiltration, the British colonial government "started hiring Turkish constables en masse" and relying more heavily on Turkish Cypriots for the running of the island's everyday colonial administration (Dimitrakis 2008, 92). This drove a wedge between Greek Cypriots who fought for independence and Turkish Cypriots who supported the colonial government. More divisively still: in order to counterbalance Greek Cypriots' growing power, the British started to promote a *divide-et-impera* strategy that consisted in stressing the Muslim and Turkish identities of Turkish Cypriots in the hope that their preoccupation with enosis would build a bulwark against EOKA's liberation struggle.

In response to the incorporation of larger numbers of Turkish Cypriots into the colonial ranks, EOKA started to provoke clashes with Turkish Cypriots (Novo 2012, 416). As a result, the tension between Turkish and Greek Cypriots acquired an ever more violent dimension. Although Turkish and Greek Cypriots could have fought together against British rule for their own Cypriot nation, they fought one another instead. After decades of imagining themselves as part of nations beyond their borders, the intimate everyday familiarity of living together in the same island turned out to be less powerful than the imagination of belonging to distant nation states beyond their coasts.

Confronted with the growing chaos on the island and burdened with its own imperial decline after the Suez crisis of 1956, the British Empire finally accepted to let go of Cyprus (Wesseling 1996; Sutton 2017, 1–14). The imminent dissolution of British rule from Cyprus unsettled sentiments among Turkish Cypriots and Anatolian Turks alike. Turkey feared that the UK's disposition to grant Cyprus self-determination would open the path for enosis, resurrect the Megali Idea and expose Turkish Cypriots to the brutality of another Smyrna (Bahceli and Rizopoulos 1996/1997, 27). Protecting Turkish Cypriots in the 1960s and 1970s acquired the same urgency as defending Turks in Smyrna had in 1919. Meanwhile, Turkish Cypriots responded to the threat of enosis with the ambition of *taksim* (partition)—a project that received the official backing of Turkey in 1956 (Loizides 2007, 175; Attalides 1977; Bahcheli 1972, 60)—and EOKA's escalating violence with the creation of the Turkish Resistance Organisation (TMT), a counter paramilitary group founded in 1957 (French 2015, 258–259).

In 1958, violence between Greek and Turkish Cypriots broke out in earnest and by 1959 Greece, Turkey and Britain hurried to negotiate Cyprus independence in what became known as the London–Zürich Agreements. In 1960, diplomats of these three countries drafted a constitution for Cyprus that de facto divided its people in two communities on the basis of "ethnic origin", while safeguarding its sovereignty by granting themselves a right to unilateral intervention as guarantor powers. These paternalistic provisions not only perpetuated the colonial division between Greek and Turkish Cypriots but they brought the rivalry between Greece and Turkey closer to an armed conflict by granting them a legal entitlement to intervene in the island's affairs (Adams 1966, 475–476). Paradoxically, Cypriot independence planted the seed of renewed imperial subjugation by giving the "motherlands"—which were supposed to safeguard Cyprus' independence—the very justification to undermine it.

To make it worse, the Cypriot constitution satisfied neither of the island's communities. In the eyes of Greek Cypriots, it granted disproportionate rights to a minority that represented 18% of the island (Theophanous 2004, 26); while Turkish Cypriots thought that the rights of which it deprived them turned them into de facto second-class citizens. In any case, the London–Zürich agreements and the constitution of the newly independent Cypriot state formalized the cartopolitical imagination of separateness that had been promoted by British rule and which had driven Greek and Turkish Cypriots apart, thus not only perpetuating the island's ethnic division but making it part of a broader Greco-Turkish geopolitical antagonism.

The Imperial Logic of the US

Making Greece and Turkey guarantor powers of a Cypriot polity divided along Greek and Turkish ethnic lines did not make Cyprus more stable but precisely the opposite. It gave Greece and Turkey an excuse to keep meddling in the internal affairs of an island whose communities sought their active support to advance their geopolitical goals of hegemony or partition. Moreover, the Cypriot constitution formalized an international dispute between countries that considered each other the most significant national rivals in a history of postcolonial antagonism. Pulled to the island by communities who saw them as champions of their geopolitical objectives—i.e., either enosis or taksim—Cyprus became a heterotopic battlefield for Greece and Turkey to revive chronotopes of old rivalries and a chance to settle past grievances: an assemblage of antagonist memories and perceptions that arguably still constitutes the most solid foundation of the Green Line dividing Cyprus today.

In 1963, 3 years after independence, a combination of Greek hardliners and members of the Greek Cypriot leadership secretly devised the infamous Akritas Plan, which envisaged that a provocation by Turkish Cypriots would provide Greek Cypriots with the best excuse to subdue them into accepting enosis (Boyd 1966, 4; Sertoglu and Ozturk 2003, 58; Constandinos 2011, 18–19).[9] In order to trigger this plan, Makarios made a 13-point proposal to Turkish Cypriots on the assumption that they would reject it and this would give his government domestic and international legitimacy to "[reduce] Turkish Cypriots to minority status by force if necessary and [achieve] union with Greece at a later stage" (Faustmann 2004, 154–159). Inter-ethnic warfare ensued across the island (Adams 1966, 475), and Turkish Cypriots retreated into ethnically Turkish enclaves acting on Ankara's advice (King and Ladbury 1982, 3). As the rumour of war between Greece and Turkey grew—two strategic NATO allies whose confrontation the US deemed "literally unthinkable"—their dispute over Cyprus became Washington's concern (Johnson and Inonu 1966, 391). The US feared that, should Cyprus consummate enosis, Greece's flirtation with the Soviet Union or its incapability to defend Cyprus from Soviet influence would put a strategic Mediterranean island at the brink of communism and thus turn it into a geopolitical liability for Turkey, the US and NATO (Dimitras 1985; Stefanidis 1999, 210). That fear was bolstered by a powerful cartopolitical allegory in the Turkish military that survives until today and which imagines Cyprus as a dagger threatening Turkey's "soft belly" with the sharp blade of its pointy Karpass peninsula (Borowiec 2000, 114).

Although Makarios pursued enosis as leader of EOKA in the 1950s, the convulsions of the 1960s persuaded him that union with Greece had become unfeasible and he finally renounced enosis in 1968. As a consequence, he became a traitor in the eyes of Greek and Greek Cypriot irredentists who had supported him in previous years. Under the auspices of the Greek junta that had seized power in 1967 and revived the Hellenic irredentist goal of enosis (Pedaliu 2011), Georgios Grivas, Makarios' former ally, returned to the island in 1971 as his enemy. He founded EOKA B—"the most extreme right-wing organisation Cyprus has ever seen"—to help Greece's "extreme right-nationalist military dictator" overthrow Makarios (Katsourides 2013, 571; Loizos 1988, 640).

With the help of EOKA B, Greece invaded the island in 1974 and, as foreseen, this move triggered Turkey's invasion. The role of the US cannot be considered a mere footnote in this process. In the cartopolitical worries of the US foreign policy establishment, Makarios' communist inclinations risked turning Cyprus into a "Mediterranean Cuba" that the Soviets could exploit to threaten American interests like they had done in the Caribbean during the Cuban missile crisis of 1962 (Kennan 1947, 575; Hitchens 1997; Constandinos 2011, 21–24). Since the US State Department had long favoured a partition of Cyprus to satisfy both Greece and Turkey with a piece of the island, some commentators have speculated that this is why Henry Kissinger, then the US Secretary of State, let Ioannides, the Greek dictator, go ahead with the coup in 1974—a hypothesis that seems supported by confidential documents from the US State Department published by WikiLeaks. Fully aware that Turkey would tolerate neither a Greek-led putsch nor enosis, Kissinger seems to have misled the Greek dictator Ioannides when he enquired about the US position regarding a possible Greek intervention in Cyprus. Instead of his explicit support, Kissinger seems to have given Ioannides an ambiguous silence only to give Turkey green light to invade Cyprus immediately after the Greek-led putsch had taken place (Hitchens 1997, 146; 2001, 77–89; US Department of State 1974). And so it seems that for a big empire like the US, the little island of Cyprus in the middle of the Mediterranean was a mere bargaining chip in a much larger play on the world map, which is exactly the kind of imperial logic that continued to haunt Cyprus after 1974.

The Green Line After 1974

In the aftermath of the Greek and Turkish invasions of 1974, "an artificial line cut through the island like a cheese-wire" (Grundy-Warr 1994, 79). Tourism, the island's main industry, was severely curtailed and cooperation between the Greek and Turkish communities was brutally severed by the Green Line (Dikomitis 2005, 7–12; Webster and Timothy 2006, 168). In 1975, an independent Turkish Federated State of Cyprus was established and in 1983 the Turkish Republic of Northern Cyprus (TRNC) declared its independence—to this day recognized only by Turkey (Nugent 1997, 55–56). Since the partition of Cyprus, each side started to demonize the other through governmental propaganda (Spyrou 2002; Zembylas and Karahasan 2006). The nationalist indoctrination that has taken place in both Turkish and Greek Cyprus since 1974 is, quite literally, a "textbook" case of ethno-nationalist cartopolitics (Papadakis 2008, 135). The textbooks used by Turkish Cypriots have told the story of Cyprus as an extension of Turkish history while depicting the Ottoman rule as a time of prosperity and freedom that was disturbed by the ungrateful Greek Cypriots' struggle for enosis and then made right by the "Happy Peace Operation" carried out by the "Heroic Turkish Army" in 1974 (Papadakis 2008, 136). For their part, Greek Cypriot schoolbooks have lumped together Turkish Cypriots with Turks not only as the aggressors of 1974 but also as the ones responsible for the interethnic violence of the 1960s. Since 1974, subsequent generations of Greek and Turkish Cypriots have been socialized by an educational system that already at an early age instils a cartopolitical grievance: to remember their lost homes in the other side, thus inheriting the affront of murder and occupation as well as a politics of vengeance against the other Cypriots (Christou 2006, 286). One of the most striking illustrations of this self-victimizing approach is the popular cartographic politicization of the conflict that has been consistently imprinted on Greek Cypriot history books since 1974: the "bleeding island" (see Figure 7).

The long-standing cartopolitical conditioning that has taken root in Greek Cyprus—epitomized by its bloody iconography—can be discerned in the student maps produced a few years ago for an artistic competition organized by the Cypriot Embassy in Greece in collaboration with the Greek Ministry of Education. The title of the competition, "Cyprus 40 years. I don't forget. I struggle. I create", encapsulates the Greek Cypriot exclusionary ethnonationalism: an unforgettable grievance and a heroic endurance to remember in a commendably peaceful manner. On this map (see Figure 8)—which is but one among many showing a similar cartopolitical composition—a Greek student has reproduced the most emblematic cartopolitical account of the conflict made by the Greek Cypriot side. Cyprus stands in the middle of a sea inscribed with legends speaking of the persistence of the imperial ethnonationalist bond linking Greece and Cyprus: "We will never forget this betrayal. Black pages were written with this story. As time keeps passing by the memory keeps growing stronger. We tell you loudly: CYPRUS YOU ARE NOT ALONE". In this cartopolitical rendition of the Cypriot conflict, Northern Cyprus, occupied by Turkey since 1974, is bleeding into the Greek Cypriot side: an allegory of the Greek Cypriot blood spilled during the Turkish intervention of 1974 and a very graphic reminder of the Turkish North's violence towards the Greek South. The tenacity of this geopolitical image is encoded in the movement inherent to the visual motif of dripping blood as well as in a legend right below it: "I don't forget".

EU's Imperial Conflict Resolution

Recently, yet another imperial power made its entrance into the Cypriot stage. In spite of Cyprus' unresolved division, in 1990 the European Community (EC) accepted the Greek Cypriot application for membership

Figure 7. Examples of Greek Cypriot history books with a cover based on the "bleeding island" theme. From left to right and top to bottom: Cyprus is not. I am, by Georgiades Stavros; Cyprus, by Dimitris T. Anallis (2000); We were once shooters, by Nikolaos Skarlatos (2000); The Cypriot Tragedy, by Panayiotis Nastros (2017). Source: http://www.skroutz.gr/books/c.1687.kypros-istoria.html

in representation of the whole island. Aware of the exclusion of the TRNC that this implied, the EC originally conditioned Cypriot membership to the island's reunification. However, in 1995, Greece threatened to veto the entire EU's eastern enlargement should such condition be imposed on the Greek Cypriot government. Pressured by Greece's blackmail (Bryant 2003; Boedeltje, Kramsch and van Houtum 2007, 132; Bourne 2003, 394), the EU

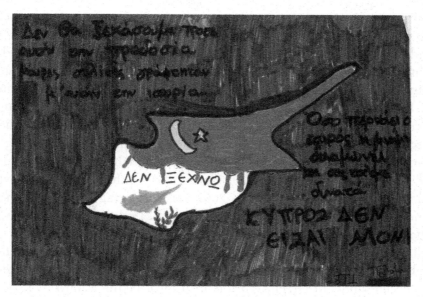

Figure 8. A bloody cartopolitical imagination. Source: http://takshmou.blogspot.nl/2015/02/1974-2014-40.html

dropped the condition and accepted the Greek Cypriot membership application. Since the TRNC and Turkey had been the most adamant opponents of reunification since 1974 anyway (Çarkoğlu and Sözen 2004, 130), the EU tried to lure Turkish Cypriots into a peace settlement with the prospect of prosperity that has characterized much of the EU's power of attraction during its successive enlargements (Christou 2002; Sahin 2011, 586). This coincided with the arrival to power of the Justice and Development Party (JDP) in Turkey which, led by prime minister Recep Tayyip Erdoğan, saw the partition of Cyprus as a major hurdle in the way to its craved EU membership and speedily repudiated a decades-long stance of obstruction regarding Cyprus' reunification and replaced it for a pro-EU course instead.

With the support of the EU and Turkey, the UN took over the peace process and aimed at securing the island's reunification before it was granted EU membership. Kofi Annan, the UN Secretary-General at the time, orchestrated what became known as "the Annan Plan", which provided a blueprint for the reunification of Cyprus and was put to a referendum right before Cyprus accession to the EU (Thompson, Karayanni and Vassiliadou 2004, 283). The result of this concerted action to change the minds of Turkish Cypriots paid off and, in 2004, 65% of them voted for reunification. Although the peace process seemed to have gained an unstoppable momentum, Tassos Papadopoulos, the Greek Cypriot leader, took the EU and UN by surprise when, a couple of days ahead of the referendum, he advised Greek Cypriots against supporting the Annan Plan—which they opposed by an overwhelming 75%. This abrupt change of mind came unexpectedly to the EU and the

UN, who saw the Greek Cypriot last-minute turnaround as a betrayal of the entire peace process (Spiteri 2004).

And yet, when one reads about how the Annan Plan was negotiated and what it stipulated, it is hard to understand how its failure could have come as a surprise to either the EU or the UN (Boedeltje, Kramsch and van Houtum 2007, 130–135). The plan proposed concessions long regarded with suspicion by many Greek Cypriots and its unwieldy 9000 pages were inexplicably drafted mainly by Annan and his foreign consultants without taking into account Cypriot leaders and their communities (Yilmaz 2005). This made Greek Cypriots deeply uneasy. Considering the depth to which the Cypriot conflict had already been studied by 2004, it is staggering that neither the UN nor the EU suspected that Greek Cypriots would find the procedure, content and haste of the Annan Plan unacceptable (Kyriakides 2004).

Tellingly, the EU and the UN expressed outrage after the referendum (Wright 2004). They blamed the fiasco on what EU officials characterised as the deceitfulness of Greek Cypriots instead of taking a hard look at their own ineptitude. Their impatience to push a plan that had been so scantily negotiated with the local population betrayed a patronizing imperial attitude: the expectation that Greek Cypriots would be satisfied with whatever the EU and the UN thought was best for them. This colonial infantilization of Cypriots has been the recurrent cartopolitical attitude towards Cypriots since the times of the British occupation and it goes to the core of the failed attempts brokered by imperial meddlers to solve the island's inter-communal conflict, from the London–Zürich agreements to the referendum of 2004.

The biggest misjudgement should perhaps be attributed to the EU, who held all the cards in the negotiation of Cyprus EU accession and thus in its reunification. By granting membership to the Greek Cypriot side without conditioning it to a settlement with the Turkish Cypriot northern half, the EU froze both the Cypriot conflict and, indirectly, also Turkey's EU member-ship (Tocci 2007, 2–3). Although the EU Council and Turkey agreed to start accession negotiations even after the controversial incorporation of a divided Cyprus to the EU,[10] by the time the negotiations were set to begin, Turkey's incentive to extend the Ankara Agreements—the customs and trade agree-ments between the EU and Turkey—to Cyprus had been offset by a German change of heart towards Turkey. The election of Angela Merkel to the German chancellorship in September 2005 represented an inflection point in both the EU's mood towards Turkey's accession and, consequently, also in Turkey's negotiation strategy regarding EU membership (Ugur 2010, 981). Already as a candidate in 2004, Merkel had proposed to downscale the EU's offer to Turkey: from the long-standing prospect of membership to a mere "privileged partnership" (Deutsche Welle 2004). An unsolvable Cypriot con-flict turned into a conveniently unworkable hurdle for an EU that was no longer interested in offering Turkey a prospect of EU membership.

The EU's insistence on Turkey to extend the Ankara Agreements to Cyprus—notwithstanding the unresolved partition of the island that the EU itself had aggravated—became a handsome excuse to justify the growing opposition to Turkish membership across the EU (Ugur 2010, 979). The EU's hostility towards Turkey (particularly from France, Germany, Greece, Cyprus and Austria) was further aggravated by the EU Commission's recommendation to block the opening of eight crucial chapters in the accession negotiations with Turkey in 2006 (Schimmelfennig 2009, 419), and later by the election of Nicolas Sarkozy to the French presidency in 2007 (Idiz 2010). The foreseeable refusal of Turkey to extend the Ankara Agreements to a divided Cyprus gave the EU a dignified justification to replace Turkey's prospect of EU membership for a privileged partnership—in open contravention to the EU's long-standing international commitment to eventually admit Turkey as a Member State. By insisting on Turkey to extend the Ankara Agreements to Cyprus, the EU was demanding Turkey to fulfil its commitments to the EU even as the EU was increasingly suggesting that it would honour its commitments towards neither Turkish Cypriots nor Turkey. What can hardly be described as anything other than the EU's poorly concealed bad faith towards Turkey's accession left a void in what had been both one of Erdoğan's most successful electoral promises and Turkey's biggest geopolitical ambition since 1963—when the Ankara Agreement between the European Economic Community and Turkey was signed. In the absence of a prospect for EU membership, Erdoğan saw an electoral opportunity to dramatically change the geopolitical strategy of Turkey and ever since he has drifted to an increasingly Islamist-based authoritarianism to cement his base and power (Özbudun 2014).

Seen from the broader perspective of the Cypriot conflict, the EU's admission of a divided Cyprus and its partiality towards the Greek Cypriot government amounted to an oblivious backing of Hellenist irredentism: Cyprus membership to the EU with the exception of its Turkish north constituted an enosis of sorts. EU numismatics tell this story in small but telling visual allegories. On the 1 and 2 euro coins that were minted after the accession of Cyprus to the EU (Bueno-Lacy 2011, 57–58), the EU has emulated the geographical prestidigitation that was contrived by the carto-politics of Hellenist irredentism (see Figure 9 and compare it to Figure 4). Cyprus has been moved away from Anatolia and placed near Greece as a statement of the island's "proper" civilisational belonging (Hymans 2004; Kaelberer 2004; Raento et al. 2004). The European Commission, the self-acclaimed "soft empire", moved the position of the island "hundreds of miles West" and erased Turkey from the map (Walters 2002). Times and forms may have changed, but the EU's approach to the Cypriot conflict shows that the blunt imperialist high-handedness that has fuelled it still exerts a powerful grip on the island.

Figure 9. Snatching Cyprus away from Anatolia. Source: Bank of Lithuania, https://www.lb.lt/n22978/2_eur_reversas.jpg

Today we see once again the imperial cartopolitical puppeteering of Cyprus; this time with the EU and Turkey pulling the most powerful strings. While the EU may have made an unsuspecting alliance with Hellenist irredentism by granting Greek Cypriots EU membership without requiring reunification, Recep Tayyip Erdoğan, Turkey's prime minister, has been using Turkish Cyprus to his advantage. Having found in religious authoritarianism an abundant source of political support (Kaja 2014), Erdoğan has been extending the Islamisation of Turkish society into Northern Cyprus. Today, Koran lessons are being forced upon school pupils in Turkish Cyprus while massive mosques like the Hala Sultan are being erected: the colonial imposition of a politico-spatial piousness that stands in stark contrast with otherwise remarkably secular Turkish Cypriots (Smith 2015, 2018; Yeşilada 2009). Ultimately, more than a century after British colonizers split Cypriots into Greek and Turkish national identities, their puppeteering by centres of power beyond their country's boundaries endures.

Conclusion

In this article, we have studied the persistence of the Cypriot Green Line through an analysis of the geographical imaginations that have framed the conflict between Greek and Turkish Cypriots since the end of the nineteenth century. Our analysis shows that geopolitical (mis)representations of history and heritage, culture and identity, geography and borders construct cartographically organized notions of territory (i.e., people as well as "their" space and culture) and that these notions can have the most dramatic political impact (Elden 2014). Perceptions of geographical closeness and distance organized within a material or imaginary cartographical framework create b/orders and thereby others. These notions have the power to (re)shape the interaction among large population groups. Cultural anxiety, apprehension about migrants and war are just some of the geopolitical phenomena steered by cartopolitical representations which may have no other basis than the representation that gives them credence (Baudrillard 1981). Yet, regardless how unstable or unfounded these ideas might be, they become real once they are accepted to be real by large numbers of people—in particular by political organizations like states that wield the power to turn these representations into a material reality (Branch 2014; Bueno-Lacy and van Houtum 2015).

In the case of Cyprus, a varied collection of centres of imperial power—from the British Empire to Greece, Turkey, the US, the Soviet Union, the EU and the UN—have modelled places and heritages in Cyprus after geographies and legacies that never existed as they were imagined by those who promoted them. They have created imperial perceptions of *distant closeness*—what was in fact far and unrelated, such as the colonial motherland, is constructed as close and familiar—and *adjacent remoteness*—what was historically close and familiar, such as the Greek Cypriot and Turkish Cypriot neighbours, is constructed as distant and alien. Thus, rather than a fracture dug by ancient ethnic incompatibility between Greek and Turkish Cypriots, the Cypriot Green Line should be seen not only as a UN buffer zone or as a territorial division but mainly as a set of borders built over the past two centuries by discursive bricks of global and local provenance. The divisive narratives, practices and representations have entrenched a perception of the Cypriot Self that can be either Turkish of Greek, but never both.

Spanning Ottoman and British empires to the modern states of Greece and Turkey and to international and supranational organisations like the UN and the EU, these imperial meddlers have imported, defined and reinforced the meaning of Turkish and Greek ethnicities in Cyprus. Moulded by the patient hands of ceaseless imperial intrusions, Cypriots have largely internalized otherwise external notions of their own identity and turned them into the chief dimensions of their geopolitical calculations. Thus, rather than an exotic local play, Cypriot politics and ethnopolitical identities should be regarded as a much larger, global geopolitical drama. The scenario may be Cypriot but neither all the characters nor the playwright are native to the island—many of the puppeteers remain concealed behind the dark curtains of surreptitious international politics and the neglect of historical accounts suffering from methodological nationalism (Wimmer and Glick Schiller 2002). Ultimately, a strict local framing of the Cypriot conflict should be considered misleading—i.e., a cartopolitical *idée fixe*, a territorial entrapment (Agnew 1994). The Cypriot buffer zone made of dusty sandbags and abandoned houses dating from 1974 is in fact the result of imperial cartopolitical overstretch. The Green Line dividing the island of Cyprus may be real, but so are its international dimensions and unscrupulous imperial puppeteers. The Green Line is not a local division between two essentially and naturally antagonistic parties, a closer scrutiny makes clear that the line is made of a glocal web of imperial strings.

Notes

1. Convivencia (a word for "living together" in Spanish) is a historiographical term used to refer to the peaceful coexistence among Jews, Muslims and Christians during the Moorish rule of the Iberian peninsula (Al-Andalus), from its conquest by the Umayyad caliphate in 711 to the Reconquista by the Castillian Catholic kings in 1492.
2. European anti-Semitism has been characterized by an aversion to Jews as well as to a loose group of people who have been (derogatorily, more often than not) lumped together as "Muhammadans", "Turks", "Ottomans" or "Moors" without much regard for the ethnic accuracy of these misnomers.
3. According to Hobsbawm, nationalism is the principle that holds that the political and national unit should be congruent. This principle implies a duty that individuals of the same nation owe to one another. In turn, this duty overrides all other public obligations and, in case of war, all public obligations of whatever kind. On the basis of this definition, Cyprus cannot be a congruent political unit because it is not a congruent national unit. Although nationalism has earned a deserved disrepute on the pages of twentieth century history, in the nineteenth century it was considered a revolutionary idea capable of bringing people together by smoothening out their differences.
4. Empires and nation states operate according to completely different operatives and follow entirely different action logics. Although imperialism is hard to define, expansionism as well as the establishment and ruling of colonies seem to be their defining characteristics—especially in comparison to nation states.
5. Cartopolitics is a term that has been coined recently in the fields of critical geopolitics and critical border studies. We use this concept's definition as a sort of "drawing-table politics".
6. Such as La Hispanidad or La Francophonie, which, respectively, join Spain and France with their former colonies.
7. Although "imperial nationalism" might sound as a *contradictio in terminis*, it "is not as contradictory as it sounds", for not only "many early modern states—those which later evolved into nation states—saw themselves as empires" but "most nation-states, or

what became nation-states, are, like most empires, the result of conquest and colonization".

8. To be sure, we do not intend to argue claim that the following maps we present influenced the whole colonisation and resulting ethnic antagonism between Greek and Turkish Cypriots. Instead, we argue that these maps are the crystallization of the larger cartopolitical discourses that have shaped the ethnic politics of the island in the early twentieth century and still exert an impact. Although there is always the possibility of reading too much into iconography—its eternal pitfall as an essentially interpretive endeavour—our iconological analysis can be evaluated by the extent to which it splices into the political, cultural, social, historical context in which it was made.

9. Although there is no proof that Makarios was involved in such a scheme, in 1963, he proposed a 13-point constitutional reform that would have drastically curtailed the prerogatives enjoyed by Turkish Cypriots. After the Turkish Cypriot leadership refused to accept Makarios' amendments, Greek Cypriot EOKA members started killing Turkish Cypriots in Nicosia.

10. Cyprus became an EU Member State on the 1st May of 2004. Afterwards, in December 2004, "the European Council decided that Turkey sufficiently fulfil[ed] the criteria to open accession negotiations". See: http://www.consilium.europa.eu/en/policies/enlargement/turkey/$.

Acknowledgements

Our research for this text has been conducted within the framework of EUBORDERSCAPES funded by European Commission FP7-SSH-2011-1 (290775).

Funding

This work was supported by EUBORDERSCAPES, an FP7 project of the European Commission Research & Innovation [grant number 290775].

References

Adams, T. W. 1966. The first republic of Cyprus: A review of an unworkable constitution. *The Western Political Quarterly* 19 (3):475–76. doi:10.2307/444709.

Agnew, J. 1994. The territorial trap: The geographical assumptions of international relations theory. *Review of International Political Economy* 1 (1):53–80. doi:10.1080/09692299408434268.

Al-Azmeh, A. 2003. Postmodern obscurantism and 'the Muslim question. *Journal for the Study of Religions and Ideologies* 2 (5):21–47.

Al-Azmeh, A., and E. Fokas, eds. 2007. *Islam in Europe: Diversity, identity and influence.* Cambridge: Cambridge University Press.

Allen, C. 2004. Justifying Islamophobia: A post-9/11 consideration of the European Union and British contexts. *American Journal of Islamic Social Sciences* 21 (3):1–25.

Anderson, B. 2006[1983]. *Imagined communities.* London: Verso.

Attalides, M. 1977. The Turkish Cypriots: Their relations to the Greek Cypriots in perspective. In *Cyprus reviewed*, ed. M. Attalides, 71–97. Nicosia: Jus Cypri Association.

Azar, E. 1985. Protracted international conflicts: Ten propositions. *International Interactions: Empirical and Theoretical Research in International Relations* 12 (1):59–70. doi:10.1080/03050628508434647.

Bahceli, T., and N. X. Rizopoulos. 1996/1997. The Cyprus impasse: What next? *World Policy Journal* 13 (4):27–39.

Bahcheli, T. 1972. Communal discord and the state of interested governments in Cyprus, 1955–70, Doctoral Thesis, University of London.

Bakhtin, M. 2004. Forms of time and of the chronotope in the novel. In *The dialogic imagination*, ed. M. Holquist, 84–258. Austin: University of Texas Press.

Bassin, M. 1987. Imperialism and the nation state in Friedrich Ratzel's political geography. *Progress in Human Geography* 11 (4):474. doi:10.1177/030913258701100401.

Basso, K. 1984. Stalking with stories: Names, places, and moral narratives among the Western Apache. *Cultural Anthropology* 3 (2):99–130. doi:10.1525/can.1988.3.2.02a00010.

Baudrillard, J. 1981. *Simulacres et simulation*. Paris: Galilée.

Bayraklı, E., and F. Hafez, eds. 2016. *European islamophobia report 2015*. Ankara: Seta.

Boedeltje, F., O. T. Kramsch, and H. van Houtum. 2007. The fallacious imperial geopolitics of EU enlargement: The case of Cyprus. *Tijdschrift Voor Economische En Sociale Geografie* 98 (1):130–35. doi:10.1111/j.1467-9663.2007.00381.x.

Bolukbasi, S. 1993. The Johnson letter revisited. *Middle Eastern Studies* 29 (3):505–25. doi:10.1080/00263209308700963.

Born, R., Dziewulski, M., and Messling, G. 2015. *The Sultan's world: The Ottoman orient in renaissance art*. Berlin: Hatje Cantz Verlag.

Borowiec, A. 2000. *Cyprus: A troubled island*. Westport, CT: Praeger.

Bottici, C. 2007. *A philosophy of political myth*. Cambridge: Cambridge University Press.

Bourne, A. K. 2003. European integration and conflict resolution in the Basque Country, Northern Ireland and Cyprus. *Perspectives on European Politics and Society* 4 (3):391–415. doi:10.1080/15705850308438870.

Boyd, J. M. 1966. Cyprus: Episode in peacekeeping. *International Organization* 20 (1):1–17. doi:10.1017/S0020818300002721.

Brambilla, E. 2009. Convivencia under Muslim rule: The island of Cyprus after the Ottoman Conquest (1571-1640). In *Routines of existence: Time, life and after life in society and religion*, ed. E. Brambilla and J. Carvalho, 121–38. Pisa: PLUS-Pisa University Press. http://www.cliohres.net/books4/books.php?book=3.

Branch, J. 2014. *The cartographic state: Maps, territory, and the origins of sovereignty*. Cambridge: Cambridge University Press.

Brotton, J. 2002. *The renaissance*. Bazaar. Oxford: Oxford University Press.

Bryant, R. 2003. Bandits and "bad characters": Law as anthropological practice in Cyprus, c. 1900. *Law and History Review* 21 (2):243–70. doi:10.2307/3595092.

Bueno-Lacy, R. 2011. The Unexpected Embrace of Europa: Conflict Resolution and the unintended consequences of the European Neighbourhood Policy. MSc dissertation, Radboud University Nijmegen, pp. 57–58. http://gpm.ruhosting.nl/mt/2011MASG07BuenaLaceyRodrigo.pdf.

Bueno-Lacy, R., and H. van Houtum. 2015. Lies, damned lies & maps: The cartopolitical invention of Europe. *Journal of Contemporary European Studies* 23 (4):477–99. doi:10.1080/14782804.2015.1056727.

Bulliet, R. W. 2006. *The case for Islamo-Christian civilization*. New York: Columbia University Press.

Buzanski, P. M. 1963. The interallied investigation of the Greek invasion of Smyrna, 1919. *Historian* 25 (3):325–43. doi:10.1111/hisn.1963.25.issue-3.

Byron, G. G. 1823. From Lord Byron in Greece (1823). http://www.rc.umd.edu/editions/mws/lastman/bylettrs.htm.

Çarkoğlu, A., and A. Sözen. 2004. The Turkish Cypriot general elections of December 2003: Setting the stage for resolving the Cyprus conflict? *South European Society and Politics* 9 (3):122–136. doi:10.1080/1360874042000271898.

Cassia, P. S. 1986. Religion, politics and ethnicity in Cyprus during the Turkocratia (1571–1878). *European Journal of Sociology* 27 (1):3–28. doi:10.1017/S0003975600004501.

Christou, G. 2002. The European Union and Cyprus: The power of attraction as a solution to the Cyprus issue. *Journal on Ethnopolitics and Minority Issues in Europe* 2:1–25.

Christou, M. 2006. A double imagination: Memory and education in Cyprus. *Journal of Modern Greek Studies* 24 (2):285–306. doi:10.1353/mgs.2006.0019.

Coleman, P. T. 2003. Characteristics of protracted, intractable conflict: Toward the development of a metaframework–I. *Peace and Conflict: Journal of Peace Psychology* 9 (1):1–37. doi:10.1207/S15327949PAC0901_01.

Collini, S., ed. 1992. *Interpretation and overinterpretation*. Cambridge: Cambridge University Press.

Constandinos, A. 2011. US-British policy on Cyprus, 1964-1974. *The Cyprus Review* 23 (1):18–19.

Constantinou, C. 2007. Aporias of identity: Bicommunalism, hybridity and the Cyprus problem. *Cooperation and Conflict* 42 (3):247–70. doi:10.1177/0010836707079931.

Craw, R. C. 1992. Reciprocal traces: From motherland to (m)otherlands. In *The body of the land*, ed. S. Rae, S. Griffiths, and D. Merritt, 15–20. New Zealand: Dunedin Public Art Gallery.

Critchley, S. 1999. *The ethics of deconstruction*. West Lafayette, IN: Purdue University Press.

Derrida, J. 1982. *Margins of philosophy*. Chicago: University of Chicago Press.

Deutsche Welle. 2004. Merkel calls for petition against Turkish membership. *Deutsche Welle*. http://www.dw.com/en/merkel-calls-for-petition-against-turkish-membership/a-1356052.

Dietzel, I., and V. N. Makrides. 2009. Ethno-religious coexistence and plurality in Cyprus under British Rule (1878–1960). *Social Compass* 56 (1):69–83. doi:10.1177/0037768608100343.

Dikomitis, L. 2005. Three readings of a border. *Anthropology Today* 21 (5):7–12. doi:10.1111/j.0268-540X.2005.00380.x.

Dimitrakis, P. 2008. British intelligence and the Cyprus insurgency, 1955–1959. *International Journal of Intelligence and Counterintelligence* 21 (2):375–94. doi:10.1080/08850600701854474.

Dimitras, P. E. 1985. Greece: A new danger. *Foreign Policy* 58:134–50. doi:10.2307/1148656.

Dunn, R. 2010. Big geography and world history. *Social Studies Review* 49 (1):14–18.

Eco, U. 1976. *A theory of semiotics*. Bloomington and London: Indiana University Press.

Elden, S. 2014. *The birth of territory*. Chicago: The University of Chicago Press.

Emilianides, A. C. 2014. The Cyprus question before the house of commons: 1954-1955. In *Great power politics in Cyprus: Foreign interventions and domestic perceptions*, ed. Kontos, M., N. Panayiotides, and H. Alexandrou. Newcastle: Cambridge Scholars Publishing.

Faustmann, F. 2004. Cyprus 1957-1963, from colonial conflict to constitutional crisis. *The Cyprus Review* 16 (1):154–59.

Finefrock, M. M. 1980. Ataturk, Lloyd George and the Megali idea: Cause and consequence of the Greek plan to seize Constantinople from the allies, June-August 1922. *The Journal of Modern History* 52 (1):D1047–D1066. doi:10.1086/242238.

Fisher, R. J. 2001. Cyprus: The failure of mediation and the escalation of an identity-based conflict to an adversarial impasse. *Journal of Peace Research* 38 (3):307–26. doi:10.1177/0022343301038003003.

Foucault, M. 1971. Nietzsche, la généalogie, l'histoire. In *Hommage à Jean Hyppolite*, ed. Bachelard, S., et al. Paris: Presses Universitaires de France.

Foucault, M. 1982. The subject and power. *Critical Inquiry* 8 (4):77–195. doi:10.1086/448181.

Foucault, M. 1986. Of other spaces. *Diacritics* 16 (1):22–27. doi:10.2307/464648.

French, D. 2015. *Fighting EOKA: The British counter-insurgency campaign on Cyprus, 1955-1959*. Oxford: Oxford University Press.

Fromkin, D. 2009. *A peace to end all peace: The fall of the Ottoman empire and the creation of the modern Middle East*. New York, NY: Henry Holt & Co.

Gellner, E. 1983. *Nations and nationalism*. Ithaca: Cornell University Press 1983.

Given, M. 2002. Maps, fields, and boundary cairns: Demarcation and resistance in colonial Cyprus. *International Journal of Historical Archaeology* 6 (1):1–22. doi:10.1023/A:1014862125523.

Goodwin, M., and T. Raines 2017. What do Europeans think about Muslim immigration? *Chatham House*. https://www.chathamhouse.org/expert/comment/what-do-europeans-think-about-muslim-immigration.

Goody, J. 2004. *Islam in Europe*. Cambridge: Polity Press.

Gregory, D. 1994. *Geographical imaginations*. London: Blackwell.

Gregory, D. 1995. Imaginative geographies. *Progress in Human Geography* 19 (4):447–85. doi:10.1177/030913259501900402.

Grivas, G. 1964. *The memoirs of General Grivas*. [edited and translated by Charles Foley]. London: Longmans, Green and Co. Ltd.

Grundy-Warr, C. 1994. Peacekeeping lessons from divided Cyprus. In *Eurasia. World boundaries*, ed. C. Grundy-Warr, Vol. 3. London: Routledge.

Gunther, R., and L. Diamond. 2003. Species of political parties a new typology. *Party Politics* 9 (2):167–99. doi:10.1177/13540688030092003.

Hadjioannou, X., S. Tsiplakou, and M. Kappler. 2011. Language policy and language planning in Cyprus. *Current Issues in Language Planning* 12 (4):503–69. doi:10.1080/14664208.2011.629113.

Harbottle, M. 1970. *The impartial soldier*. Oxford: Oxford University Press.

Hardt, M., and A. Negri. 2000. *Empire*. Cambridge, MA: Harvard University Press.

Helmreich, P. C. 1974. *From Paris to Sèvres*. Columbus: Ohio State University Press.

Hitchens, C. 1997. *Hostage to history: Cyprus from the Ottomans to Kissinger*. London: Verso 1997.

Hitchens, C. 2001. *The trial of Henry Kissinger*. London and New York: Verso.

Hobsbawm, E. J. 1987. *The age of empire*. New York, NY: Vintage Books.

Hobsbawm, E. J. 1990. *Nations and nationalism since 1780*. Cambridge: Cambridge University Press.

Hopkirk, P. 1990. *The great game*. London: John Murray.

Hymans, J. 2004. The changing color of money: European currency iconography and collective identity. *European Journal of International Relations* 10 (11):5–31. doi:10.1177/1354066104040567.

Idiz, S. 2010. Turkey's "French problem". *Institute Français des Relations Internationales* (Note franco-turque 3). http://www.ifri.org/sites/default/files/atoms/files/notefrancoturque3idiz1.pdf.

Johnson, L., and I. Inonu. 1966. President Johnson and Prime Minister Inonu: Correspondence between President Johnson and Prime Minister Inonu, June 1964, as released by the White House, January 15, 1966. *Middle East Journal* 20 (3):386–93.

Kaelberer, M. 2004. The Euro and European identity: Symbols, power and the politics of the monetary union. *Review of International Studies* 30:161–78. doi:10.1017/S0260210504005996.

Kaja, A. 2014. Islamisation of Turkey under the AKP rule: Empowering family, faith and charity. *South European Society and Politics* 20 (1):47–69.

Katsourides, Y. 2013. Determinants of Extreme right reappearance in Cyprus: The National Popular Front (ELAM), Golden Dawn's sister party. *South European Society and Politics* 18 (4):567–89. doi:10.1080/13608746.2013.798893.

Kennan, G. 1947. The sources of Soviet conduct. *Foreign Affairs* 25 (4):566–82. doi:10.2307/20030065.

Khaf, M. 1999. *Western representations of the Muslim woman: From termagant to odalisque.* Austin: University of Texas Press.

King, R., and S. Ladbury. 1982. The cultural reconstruction of political reality: Greek and Turkish Cyprus since 1974. *Anthropological Quarterly* 55 (1):1–16. doi:10.2307/3317371.

Kitromilides, P. M. 1977. From coexistence to confrontation: The dynamics of ethnic conflict in Cyprus. In *Cyprus reviewed*, ed. M. Attalides. Nicosia: Jus Crypti Association 1977.

Kitromilides, P. M. 1990. Greek irredentism in Asia minor and Cyprus. *Middle Eastern Studies* 26 (1):3–17. doi:10.1080/00263209008700801.

Kontos M., N. Panayiotides, and H. Alexandrou. eds., 2014. *Great power politics in Cyprus: Foreign interventions and domestic perceptions.* Newcastle: Cambridge Scholars Publishing.

Kristof, L. 1959. The nature of frontiers and boundaries. *Annals of the Association of American Geographers* 49 (3):269–82. doi:10.1111/j.1467-8306.1959.tb01613.x.

Kristof, L. 1960. The origins and evolution of geopolitics. *The Journal of Conflict Resolution* 4 (1):21–22. doi:10.1177/002200276000400103.

Kumar, K. 2000. Nation and empire: English and British national identity in comparative perspective. *Theory and Society* 29 (5):578–608. doi:10.1023/A:1026550830748.

Kumar, K. 2003. *The making of English national identity.* Cambridge: Cambridge University Press.

Kumar, K. 2017. *Visions of empire: How five imperial regimes shaped the world.* Princeton and Oxford: Princeton University Press.

Kyriakides, K. A. 2004. Legitimising the illegitimate? The origins and objectives of the Annan plan. In *The case against the Annan plan*, ed. V. Coufoudakis and K. A. Kyriakides. London: Lobby for Cyprus.

Lang, R. H. 1887. On archaic survivals in Cyprus. *The Journal of the Anthropological Institute of Great Britain and Ireland* 16:186–88. doi:10.2307/2841802.

Loizides, N. G. 2007. Ethnic nationalism and adaptation in Cyprus. *International Studies Perspectives* 8 (2):172–89. doi:10.1111/j.1528-3585.2007.00279.x.

Loizos, P. 1988. Intercommunal killing in Cyprus. *Man* 23 (4):639–53. doi:10.2307/2802597.

Markides, K. C. 1977. *The rise and fall of the Cyprus republic.* New Haven: Yale University Press.

Mikhail, E. H., ed. 1979. *Oscar Wilde: Interviews and recollections.* Vol. 2. London and Basingstoke: Macmillan.

Millas, H. 1991. History textbooks in Greece and Turkey. *History Workshop* 31:21–33. doi:10.1093/hwj/31.1.21.

Münkler, H. 2005. *Imperien.* Berlin: Rowohlt-Berlin Verlag GmbH.

Nevzat, A. 2005. *Nationalism amongst the Turks of Cyprus: The first wave.* Oulu: Oulu University Press.

Newson, D. D. 2001. *The imperial mantle. The United States, decolonization, and the third world.* Bloomington, IN: Indiana University Press.

Novo, A. 2012. Friend or foe? The Cyprus police force and the EOKA insurgency. *Small Wars & Insurgencies* 23 (3):414–31. doi:10.1080/09592318.2012.661609.

Nugent, N. 1997. Cyprus and the European Union: A particularly difficult membership application. *Mediterranean Politics* 2 (3):53–75. doi:10.1080/13629399708414630.

Ó Tuathail, G. 1996. *Critical geopolitics*. London: Routledge.

Özkırımlı, U., and S. A. Sofos. 2008. *Tormented by history: Nationalism in Greece and Turkey*. London: C. Hurst & Co.

Özbudun, E. 2014. AKP at the crossroads: Erdoğan's Majoritarian drift. *South European Society and Politics* 19 (2):155–67. doi:10.1080/13608746.2014.920571.

Papadakis, Y. 2008. Narrative, memory and history education in divided Cyprus: A comparison of schoolbooks on the "History of Cyprus". *History & Memory* 20 (2):128–48. doi:10.2979/his.2008.20.2.128.

Peckham, R. S. 2000. Map Mania: Nationalism and the politics of place in Greece, 1970-1922. *Political Geography* 19 (1):77–95. doi:10.1016/S0962-6298(99)00036-0.

Pedaliu, E. G. 2011. "A discordant note": NATO and the Greek Junta, 1967-1974. *Diplomacy & Statecraft* 22 (1):101–20. doi:10.1080/09592296.2011.549745.

Penn, V. 1938. Philhellenism in Europe, 1821-1828. *The Slavonic and East European Review* 16 (48):638–53.

Petropulos, J. A. 1976. The compulsory exchange of populations: Greek-Turkish peacemaking, 1922–1930. *Byzantine and Modern Greek Studies* 2 (1):135–60. doi:10.1179/030701376790206199.

Pollis, A. 1973. Intergroup conflict and British colonial policy: The case of Cyprus. *Comparative Politics* 5 (4):575–99. doi:10.2307/421397.

Pollis, A. 1979. Colonialism and neo-colonialism: Determinants of ethnic conflict in Cyprus. In *Small states in the modern world: The conditions of survival*, ed. P. Worsley and P. Kitromilides. Nicosia: Zavallis Press.

Pollis, A. 1996. The social construction of ethnicity and nationality: The case of Cyprus. *Nationalism and Ethnic Politics* 2 (1):67–90. doi:10.1080/13537119608428459.

Raento, A.,A. Hämäläinen, H. Ikonen, and N. Mikkonen. 2004. Striking stories: A political geography of Euro coinage. *Political Geography*. 23 (8):929–56. doi:10.1016/j.polgeo.2004.04.007.

Raquejo, T. 1986. The "Arab Cathedrals": Moorish architecture as seen by British travellers. *The Burlington Magazine* 128 (1001):555–63.

Renan, E. 1997[1882]. *Qu'est ce que c'est une nation?* Paris: Éditions Mille et une nuits.

Ridgeway, W. 1908. The origin of the Turkish crescent. *The Journal of the Royal Anthropological Institute of Great Britain and Ireland* 38:241–58. doi:10.2307/2843299.

Ross, I. 2012. *Oscar Wilde and ancient Greece*. New York, NY: Cambridge University Press.

Sahin, S. 2011. Open borders, closed minds: The discursive construction of national identity in Cyprus. *Media, Culture and Society* 33 (4):583–97. doi:10.1177/0163443711398694.

Said, E. 1978. *Orientalism*. New York: Vintage Books.

Schimmelfennig, F. 2009. Entrapped again: The way to EU membership negotiations with Turkey. *International Politics* 46 (4):413–31. doi:10.1057/ip.2009.5.

Schmitt, C. 1932. *Der begriff des politischen*. Berlin: Duncker und Humblot GmbH.

Scott, J. C. 1998. *Seeing like a state: how certain schemes to improve the human condition have failed*. London: Yale University Press.

Sertoglu, K., and I. Ozturk. 2003. Application of Cyprus to the European Union and the Cyprus problem. *Emerging Markets Finance and Tradex* 39 (6):54–70. doi:10.1080/1540496X.2003.11052557.

Smith, H. 2015. Divided Cyprus begins to build bridges. *The Guardian*. http://www.theguardian.com/world/2015/may/31/mustafa-ankinci-advocates-focus-future-for-splintered-cyprus.

Smith, H. 2018. "We're not Muslim enough" fear Turkish Cypriots as poll looms. *The Guardian*. https://www.theguardian.com/world/2018/jan/06/were-not-muslim-enough-fear-turkish-cypriots-as-poll-looms.

Spiteri, S. 2004. Verheugen feels 'cheated' by Greek Cypriot government. *Euobserver*. https://euobserver.com/enlargement/15270.

Spyrou, S. 2002. Images of "the Other": "The Turk" in Greek Cypriot children's imaginations. *Race, Ethnicity and Education* 5 (3):255–72. doi:10.1080/1361332022000004850.

Stefanidis, I. D. 1999. *Isle of discord*. London: C. Hurst & Co. Ltd.

Stouraiti, A., and A. Kazamias. 2010. The imaginary topographies of the Megali idea: National territory as Utopia. In *Spatial conceptions of the nation: Modernizing geographies in Greece and Turkey*, ed. N. Diamandouros, T. Dragonas, and C. Keyder. London & New York: I.B. Tauris Publishers.

Strandsbjerg, J. 2012. Cartopolitics, geopolitics and boundaries in the Arctic. *Geopolitics* 17 (4):818–42. doi:10.1080/14650045.2012.660581.

Sutton, C. 2017. *Britain's cold war in Cyprus and Hong Kong*. Switzerland: Palgrave Macmillan 2017.

Theophanous, A. 2004. *The Cyprus question and the EU – The challenge and the promise*. Nicosia: Intercollege Press.

Thompson, S., S. S. Karayanni, and M. Vassiliadou. 2004. Cyprus after history. *Interventions* 6 (2):282–99. doi:10.1080/1369801042000238373.

Tocci, N. 2007. *The EU and conflict resolution: Promoting peace in the backyard*. London and New York: Routledge.

Turner, F. J. 1920. *The frontier in American history*. New York: Henry Holt & Company.

Ugur, M. 2010. Open-ended membership prospect and commitment credibility: Explaining the deadlock in EU–Turkey accession negotiations. *Journal of Common Market Studies* 48 (4):967–91. doi:10.1111/j.1468-5965.2010.02082.x.

United Nations. 1954. Extracts relating to Article 2 (1)-(5) of the Charter of the United Nations: Supplement No. 1 (1954-1955), Vol. 1 (1954), p. 11. http://legal.un.org/repertory/art2/english/rep_suppl_vol1-art2_1-5_e.pdf.

US Department of State. 1974. Cyprus coup: Meeting with General Ioannides. https://wikileaks.org/plusd/cables/1974ATHENS04528_b.html.

van Houtum, H. 2012. Remapping borders. In *A companion to border studies*, ed. T. E. Wilson and H. Donnan, 405–17. Blackwell: London.

van Houtum, H., and R. Bueno-Lacy. 2016. Frontiers. In *International encyclopedia of geography: People, the earth, environment and technology*, ed. Richardson, D.,N. Castree, M. F. Goodchild, A. Kobayashi, W. Liu, and R. A. Marston. Hoboken, NJ: John Wiley & Sons Ltd

Van Straten, R. 1991. *An introduction to iconography*. London and New York: Taylor and Francis.

Varnava, A. 2005. Punch and the British occupation of Cyprus in 1878. *Byzantine and Modern Greek Studies* 29 (2):167–86. doi:10.1179/byz.2005.29.2.167.

Vaughan, A. T., and V. M. Vaughan. 1997. Before Othello: Elizabethan representations of sub-Saharan Africans. *The William and Mary Quarterly* 54 (1):19–44. doi:10.2307/2953311.

Vitkus, D. J. 1999. Early modern orientalism: Representations of Islam in sixteenth- and seventeenth-century Europe. In *Western views of Islam in medieval and early modern Europe*, ed. D. R. Blanks and M. Frassetto. New York: St: Martin's Press.

Von Kogelfranz, S. 1985. 'Genosse, wir wollten euch erledigen'. *Der Spiegel*. http://www.spiegel.de/spiegel/print/d-13512314.html

Vural, Y., and E. Özuyanık. 2008. Redefining identity in the Turkish-Cypriot school history textbooks: A step towards a united federal Cyprus. *South European Society and Politics* 13 (2):133–54. doi:10.1080/13608740802156521.

van Houtum, H., and T. van Naerssen. 2002. Bordering, ordering and othering. *Tijdschrift Voor Economische En Sociale Geografie* 93 (2):125–136. doi:10.1111/tesg.2002.93.issue-2.

Walker, A. M. 1984. Enosis in Cyprus: Dhali, a case study. *Middle East Journal* 38 (3):477–78.

Walters, W. 2002. Mapping Schengenland: Denaturalizing the border. *Environment and Planning D: Society and Space* 20 (5):561–80. doi:10.1068/d274t.

Webster, C., and D. J. Timothy. 2006. Travelling to the "other side": The occupied zone and Greek Cypriot views of crossing the Green Line. *Tourism Geographies* 8 (2):162–81. doi:10.1080/14616680600585513.

Wesseling, H. L. 1996. *Divide and rule: The partition of Africa, 1880-1914.* London: Praeger Publishers.

Wimmer, A., and N. Glick Schiller. 2002. Methodological nationalism and beyond: Nation-state building, migration and the social sciences. *Global Network* 2 (4):301–34. doi:10.1111/1471-0374.00043.

Wright, G. 2004. Greek Cypriot leaders reject Annan plan. *The Guardian.* https://www.theguardian.com/world/2004/apr/22/eu.cyprus.

Xydis, S. G. 1968. The UN general assembly as an instrument of Greek policy: Cyprus, 1954-58. *The Journal of Conflict Resolution* 12 (2):141–68. doi:10.1177/002200276801200201.

Yeşilada, B. 2009. Islam and the Turkish Cypriots. *Social Compass* 56 (1):49–59. doi:10.1177/0037768608100341.

Yilmaz, M. 2005. The Cyprus conflict and the Annan plan: Why one more failure? *Ege Acad. Rev* 5:29–35.

Zembylas, M., and H. Karahasan. 2006. The politics of memory and forgetting in pedagogical practices: Towards pedagogies of reconciliation and peace in divided Cyprus. *Cyprus Review-Nicosia-Intercollege* 18 (2):15–35.

EU's Cross-Border Cooperation and Conflict Transformation at Contested Borders in the European Neighbourhood: Lessons from the Turkish-Armenian Border

Gökten Doğangün and Yelda Karadağ

ABSTRACT

In the post-Cold War period, the European Union's neighbourhood policy towards its emerging eastern neighbours aims to surround the European Union (EU) with a ring of secure, stable and prosperous neighbouring countries. Advancing conflict transformation through cross-border cooperation initiatives constitutes a crucial part of the European neighbourhood policy. Cross-border interaction and cooperation are expected to lessen the heavy burden of sealed borders by decreasing isolation and indifference and promoting mutual interaction, dialogue and confidence-building between conflicting parties. However, there are several ethno-political contestations whose historical animosities cast a shadow on the effectiveness of the EU's neighbourhood and cross-border cooperation policies for conflict transformation. The Turkish-Armenian case testifies to the persistence of physical and mental borders that stem from competing historical memories, longstanding grievances and contesting national claims, as well as from regional dynamics. This article aims to assess the impact of the EU's neighbourhood policy and cross-border cooperation initiatives on conflict transformation on the Turkish-Armenian border. The EU's policies have remained partially relevant and effectual by initiating interaction and dialogue at the civil societal level. Advancing conflict transformation at the political level, however, would require the EU to develop a more comprehensive framework that considers the cross-cutting context of the competing historical memories and regional dynamics and shifts that currently undermine the impact of further transformative attempts.

Introduction

One of the most important characteristics of the post-Cold War period is the fundamental change in conceptualizations of sovereignty and territoriality that is identified as a symptom of a new 'post-Westphalian' international order. The dissolution of the Soviet Union and its attendant social, economic, cultural and geopolitical changes have influenced the understandings of state borders. These developments find correspondents in academic debate about major paradigmatic shifts in the understandings of border and territoriality (EUBORDERSCAPES 2016). Envisaging a 'borderless world' has become a topic of discussion within the academy (EUBORDERSCAPES 2016). Borders are no longer seen as fixed and stable phenomena associated with the territory and identity of the nation-state.[1] The changing understanding of borders opens up possibilities for questioning the rationales behind conflict-prone borders, which are constrained not only by physical limitations, but also by mental borders associated with historical memory, ethno-national prejudices and the fear and hatred of the 'other' ingrained in collective memory.[2]

The European integration project has been built upon a challenge to the traditional understanding of state sovereignty that is tightly coupled with securing and defending state borders. In this project, cross-border cooperation has become a 'trademark' of European integration (Scott 2012) and has been promoted as an endeavour that advances conflict amelioration and transformation and avoiding prevents regional conflicts. As McCall (2013) asserts, cross-border cooperation is integral to conflict amelioration and transformation because it aims to loosen the territorial borders of the state to promote the development of mutual relations and dialogue between both sides of the border.

The EU has assumed the role of stabilising and democratising the disoriented post–Cold War order as its political community has extended eastward towards the former Soviet Union (Scott 2005). The EU has envisaged a new common economic and social space, the so-called wider European area,[3] that includes the neighbouring countries of the East and the South for the purpose of stimulating mutual interdependence and regional cooperation rather than using security-oriented and coercive measures (Scott 2009). With this strategy, the EU has challenged the perception of borders as barriers and designed tools and incentives to promote borders as resources in achieving regional integration and cooperation in its newly emerging neighbourhood (Popescu 2008). The subsequent introduction of the European Neighbourhood Policy (ENP) aims at fostering stability and security through cross-border cooperation. Any form of cross-border cooperation across a variety of areas and local needs is assumed to build interdependence, dialogue and confidence between the conflicting sides, and thus, to ameliorate and transform conflicts stemming from border disputes.

In this article, we aim to assess the relevance and limitations of the EU's neighbourhood policy and cross-border cooperation endeavour for conflict transformation on the Turkish-Armenian border, which falls into the geographical scope of the European eastern neighbourhood. The land border has been closed for 24 years. The border was sealed not because of armed conflict between Turkey and Armenia, but through a political decision of the Turkish government following the Nagorno-Karabakh crisis between Armenia and Azerbaijan (see Çeviköz 2014).[4] The sealed border prevents any possibility of trade, commerce, mobility, dialogue or any other form of cross-border initiative between the border cities, although air traffic is allowed between Istanbul and Yerevan.[5]

In this study, we argue that the border conflict between these two countries has turned into a frozen situation within crosscutting contexts of competing historical memories, differing national representations and regional dynamics under the transformation of the political landscape in the post-Soviet period. In this context, the EU's neighbourhood policy and cross-border cooperation have only limited power to stimulate conflict transformation along the historically contested Turkish-Armenian border. The transformation of border conflict in the Turkish-Armenian case requires a long-term and multi-layered process, in which economic interests, cultural convergences, and the divergences of historical memory, national identity and territorial claims must be addressed from the point of view of regional cooperation and stability.

This study relies on empirical data gathered by semi-structured in-depth expert interviews, which are widely used as a legitimate method of obtaining data in qualitative social research (Bogner and Menz 2009). The interviews were conducted in the urban areas of Turkey (Ankara and Istanbul) and Armenia (Yerevan), where the experts are mostly based. In total, 44 expert interviews (12 in Ankara, 14 in Istanbul, 18 in Yerevan) were conducted between November 2014 and May 2015 in Ankara and Istanbul, and during two fieldwork trips to Yerevan in May 2014 and April 2015. Our sample consisted of political actors (mayors, members of parliament), senior state officers, academicians and representatives from non-governmental organisations, think tanks and professional organisations. In Turkey, nine interviews were conducted with leading figures from the Armenian community who are engaged in improving Turkish-Armenian relations. While selecting the interviewees, we aimed to reflect the position and viewpoints of those who have political, business or family ties to the border region; those who have strategic concerns, academic interest and/or project-driven engagement in transforming the border conflict in particular and Turkish-Armenian relations in general; and those who have experience of active involvement in the process of transforming the conflict between Turkey and Armenia. The interviews were designed to give insight into the (f)actors that limit border conflict transformation between Turkey and Armenia. The interviewees were asked to evaluate the concept of border, the relations and problems between Turkey and Armenia, the EU's role, the discourse and tools used in the border conflict transformation, the frozen conflict between Azerbaijan and Armenia and the impact of Azerbaijan and Russia as the regional parties involved in this border conflict – their domestic concerns, foreign policy orientations and bilateral relations with Turkey and Armenia. The interviews were conducted in Turkish in Ankara and Istanbul, and in English in Yerevan. The affiliations of the interviewees and the geographical locations of the interviews are identified, but names and other identifying information have been withheld for confidentiality reasons. There was no major problem either accessing the interviewees or obtaining desirable answers due to their engagement with the topic.

The article will begin by explaining the European neighbourhood policy and the efforts at cross-border cooperation in advancing conflict transformation in the eastern neighbourhood. In the second part, the contemporary relations between Turkey and Armenia will be briefly summarised to provide the historical backdrop of the border conflict. In the third part, we will present the findings of our field research under three sub-headings: contested historical memories, regional dimensions of the border conflict and the relevance and limitations of EU's neighbourhood policy and cross-border cooperation endeavour in the Turkish-Armenian case.

The EU's Cross-Border Cooperation and Conflict Transformation

European integration has emerged as a project that challenges the traditional understanding of borders as fixed and stable phenomena and their rigid association with the territory and identity of the nation-state (McCall 2013). The EU developed gradually out of a spatial vision of economic, political and social development that would occur through transcending state borders and promoting regional cross-border cooperation (Scott and Van Houtum 2009). As Scott (2015, 28) puts it, 'the European Union has attempted to appropriate the idea of "borderlands" as part of its drive to create new spatial contexts for social transformation, regional development and innovation'.

After the 2007 enlargement, the EU became immediate neighbours with the former Soviet countries in the east – Moldova, Ukraine and maritime border with Georgia. The political instability, economic crises and border disputes arising in these countries increased the EU's concerns about spillover of security threats in the region or threats towards the EU itself. Ensuring stability, predictability and synergy in its immediate neighbourhood became a priority, as the instability of any state border might have a damaging impact on the EU (Kharlamova 2015). To this end, the EU introduced the European Neighbourhood Policy (ENP) as a special partnership – an alternative to membership – with its eastern neighbours in 2003. The ENP aimed at extending 'stability, security, and well-being of all concerned' (ENP 2004) while transforming the EU's neighbours towards greater economic development, stability and better governance (Börzel 2011, Mayer and Schimmelfenning 2007). The ENP covers Moldova, Belarus and Ukraine as well as the three states of the South Caucasus – Armenia, Azerbaijan, and Georgia on the eastern borders, and Algeria, Egypt, Israel, Jordan, Lebanon, Libya, Morocco, Syria, Tunisia, and the Palestinian Authority in the Mediterranean. The Eastern Partnership Policy (EaP) was developed as a parallel policy in 2009 to bring a specific eastern dimension to the ENP.

Cross-border cooperation, as an integral component of the ENP, contributes to its overall objective of progress towards 'an area of shared prosperity and good neighbourliness' between the EU and its neighbours (European Commission Programming 2014–2020). The ENP aspires to strengthen the EU's contribution to the transformation and resolution of regional conflicts by fostering stability, security and prosperity in the eastern neighbourhood of the EU and developing 'integrated borderlands' instead of creating exclusionary borders (Gültekin-Punsmann 2010). Overcoming the exclusionary understanding of borders and prioritizing the practice of cross-border cooperation is among the main goals of the ENP (EUBORDERSCAPES 2016). As a former EU External Relations Commissioner Ferrero-Waldner stated in 2006, 'ENP can contribute to a more positive climate for conflict settlement' (German 2007, 360). Similarly, promoting multilateral cooperation and confidence-building in the areas of stability, economic integration, energy security and contacts among people is defined as the main goal of the EaP (Council of European Union 2009).

The ENP and EaP are not specifically formulated for conflict transformation, but the promotion of soft borders, cross-border cooperation and regional interdependence is conceived as a sustainable form of bottom-up pressure to induce the peaceful transformation of conflict at contested borders. The reconciliation between the conflicting parties is expected to rely on mechanisms that motivate the conflicting sides to be engaged with each other as humans-in-relationship (Lederach 1997). Accordingly, the EU's cross-border cooperation initiatives open up space for civil society organisations to initiate channels for cooperation, dialogue and collaboration and operate as intermediary actors between state and society.

Despite its positive impact in advancing engagement with conflict transformation at the civil societal level, the EU's neighbourhood policy and cross-border cooperation initiatives carry certain ambiguities and shortcomings in relation to conflict transformation. First, the ENP and the EaP do not promise EU membership, and thus cannot exert leverage on the associated countries. Although the associated countries perceive the EaP as a path towards further integration with the EU, the ENP is designed to prevent and contain possible conflicts without enlarging the EU any further (German 2007). In the absence of the prospect of accession, the political elites in the EU's eastern neighbourhood are unwilling to commit themselves to a difficult reform process of societal development and democratization.

Without an accession promise, such political efforts might cost the elites the loss of power (Popescu and Wilson 2009). Against this backdrop, the EU member states cannot develop a united stance to offer a coherent framework for conflict transformation in the frozen situations associated with contested borders, including South Ossetia.[6] Conversely, the EU member states privilege their own interests – particularly energy security and trade – and tend to establish bilateral relations on energy issues with the South Caucasus countries and Russia.[7]

Second, the European neighbourhood policy and cross-border cooperation initiatives do not provide a comprehensive regional framework that includes the other important players of the region – Russia and Turkey – in the ENP and EaP as associated partners. Russia has so far refused to be part of the ENP and EaP and insisted on keeping its relation with the EU on the 'separate basis of equal and mutually beneficial strategic partnership' (Haukkala 2008). Russia is concerned that the ENP and EaP may weaken its strategic position in the former territory of the Soviet Union. Turkey is not eligible to be a part of the ENP because of its candidacy status. Turkey has, however, expressed its wish to join the programme as a partner instead of a neighbour (Üstün 2010). Turkey's participation would be crucial in supporting the efforts for sub-regional integration and conflict resolution in the EU's eastern borderland, as the geographical coverage of the ENP and EaP overlaps with the neighbourhood of Turkey in the Black Sea and South Caucasus (Gültekin-Punsmann 2010). The EU has established its relations with the regional actors via different institutional frameworks, which prevents coherent and integrated cooperation possibilities while strengthening the demarcations in the region. Thus, the EU has not been able to efficiently use its vast experience to benefit from cross-border cooperation initiatives in the peaceful transformation of conflict situations in the eastern neighbourhood (Tocci 2007).

Finally, the EU's geopolitics of cooperation based on 'soft power' has failed to acknowledge the persistence of 'hard borders', as Bialasiewicz (2008) pointed out. In the South Caucasus, the focus area of the EaP, the questions of state territoriality and borders in the traditional sense of demarcating lines have yet to disappear. The post-Soviet transformation has rekindled nationalism and triggered ethno-territorial conflicts over borders (MacFarlane 1997; O'Loughlin, Kolossov, and Radvanyi 2007). The regional context of instability, insecurity and suspicion has reinforced nationalist discourses in the newly independent South Caucasus states. Borders associated with hard security concerns and historical memory gain importance in the nation-building process. Physical borders are still fixed and reinforce mental borders between 'us' and the 'other', which is identified as a threat, an enemy and a key driver of conflict. Contested borders become sacred spaces for a nation or ethnic community concerned with identity formation, represent

CROSS-BORDER COOPERATION 103

contesting ethno-national interpretations of the historical past, and carry longstanding grievances, hatred and fear (McCall 2013). Against this backdrop, the protection or defence of borders becomes a political matter of great significance and a national security concern.

Before presenting the empirical findings from our field research, we will provide a brief historical background of the relations between Turkey and Armenia and their relevance to the border.

The Cross-Cutting Context of the Border Conflict between Turkey and Armenia

With the dissolution of the Soviet Union, Turkey became a neighbour of the new state of Armenia, alongside Georgia and Azerbaijan on the eastern border. Turkey recognised Armenia's independence in 1991, and diplomatic dialogue was immediately initiated to develop bilateral relations and open the border between Turkey and Armenia. However, the result was not good neighbourly relations, but a frozen conflict in the Turkish-Armenian borderland. Just a year later, Turkey suspended all diplomatic relations with Armenia due to the issue of 'genocide' and the territorial claims of Armenia on eastern Turkey.[8] The tension between Turkey and Armenia escalated with the rise of conflict in Nagorno-Karabakh. In 1993, Turkey closed its border following Armenia's occupation of Azerbaijani territory (Özbay 2011).

The closed border became one of the key issues when the Turkish Justice and Development Party (*Adalet ve Kalkinma Partisi*, AKP) government defined the normalisation of relations with Armenia as a strategic priority and assumed a proactive role in the historically impeded process of conflict resolution (Terzi 2010). Turkey's EU accession process, which had been prioritized by the earlier AKP governments, required a reconsideration of the sealed border between Turkey and Armenia. The EU did not require Turkey and Armenia to open the border. Rather, Turkey, as a candidate country, was encouraged to establish good diplomatic and neighbourly relations with Armenia for the sake of regional stability and peaceful conflict resolution (European Parliament Resolution 2006). In a similar vein, Armenia, as a member of the ENP, was urged to promote regional cooperation and development through the exchange of people and goods with Turkey (EU-Armenia ENP Action Plan 2006).

For the purpose of normalising relations with Armenia, the Ministry of Culture and Tourism of Turkey started the restoration of Akdamar (Aghtamar) Church in 2005.[9] In 2008, President Serzh Sargsyan invited President Abdullah Gül Yerevan to watch the 2010 World Cup qualifying match between Turkey and Armenia, in a gesture later called 'football diplomacy'. In 2009, the rapprochement process took a step further. Under the mediatorship of Switzerland, the parties agreed on a road map for the normalisation of relations, the development of good neighbourly relations and the promotion of peace, security and stability in the whole region (Joint Statement of the Ministries of Foreign Affairs 2009). Accordingly, the Zurich Protocols, which aimed at establishing diplomatic ties, opening the border and starting a dialogue on the historical past, were signed in 2009 with the participation of representatives from Switzerland, the United States, France, Russia and the EU (Avetisian and Musayelyan 2010). However, the Protocols encountered criticism from within and outside Turkey and Armenia.[10] Subsequently, the Turkish and Armenian political elites showed reluctance and did not step forward to ratify the Protocols in their respective parliaments. In February 2015, President Sargsyan declared the withdrawal of the Protocols from parliament. Although the agreement was not annulled, the normalisation process was halted with no clear prospect of advancement. In this process, however, the EU's visibility and involvement in initiating or sustaining the rapprochement process remained limited.

Persistence of Historical Memory in the Formation of Mental Borders

Our research showed that the border conflict between Turkey and Armenia is related to not only the geopolitical border but also the mental borders between these communities. Based on our interviews, we found that the mental borders are founded on two fundamental historical and socio-political occurrences: the existence/dissolution of the Soviet Union and the 1915 tragedy. The existence/persistence of the mental borders, which reinforce suspicion and/or enmity towards the other side, overshadows the difficulties of the (closed) physical border in the Turkish-Armenian case. The assassination of Hrant Dink, who was a Turkish journalist of Armenian descent and tried to contribute peace-building between Turkey and Armenia, however, was a significant turning point for raising awareness about the mental borders involved in the Turkish-Armenian dispute.

Depending on the historical context, the physical border between Turkey and Armenia has contained varied meanings, symbols and abstractions. Many interviewees in Turkey underlined that until the dissolution of the Soviet Union, Turkey viewed 'its eastern border' (Doğu Kapı/Akuryan)[11] from a security perspective and as a monolithic unity representing the Soviet neighbourhood. The security dimension attributed to the Turkish-Armenian border emphasizes 'the other', which mostly corresponds to a threat or enemy, as indicated by the interviewees in both Turkey and Armenia. One interviewee that we conducted with an interview in İstanbul in May 2015 stated, 'The border was perceived as "a gate to communism" or "communist threat" so that any violation could be interpreted as a threat to national sovereignty'. Others made similar remarks. Apparently, the border

CROSS-BORDER COOPERATION

demarcated 'the "us" and the "here" being located inside the border while the "other" and "there" is everything beyond the border', conceived as a frontline between NATO and the Soviet Union (Newman 2006). An expert in Armenia stated:

> It was the Soviet-NATO border, a big border between Soviet Union and the foreign states. And on that border, there were some fortifications that were prepared just for world war, and they also affected people's perceptions of that border. And the border with Iran was not so fortified, but it was closed anyway, but [it was] like any of the Soviet borders.

The dissolution of the Soviet Union changed the Soviet/NATO border to the Turkish-Armenian border, and its conceptualization and representation changed from a narrative of security and 'othering' based on communism to another narrative shaped by competing historical memories.

The physical and mental borders re-produce and re-construct themselves through the collective memories of both societies. Collective memory and collective consciousness are the component parts of historical memory, which represents the past shared by a group or community (Kansteiner 2002). Historical memory also refers to how we remember and perceive the past and to how all of these processes and components contribute to building cultural and/or national identity as a social phenomenon. Our research confirmed that the perception of material and abstract understandings of borders is part of the larger framework of collective memory, which is co-constitutes by the contested representation of national histories of Turkish and Armenian society. We found that those competing collective memories, which are determined by the century-long history of tragedies, mutual accusations and prejudices on both sides, are the root cause of the Turkish-Armenian border conflict.

Against this backdrop, the border becomes a significant part of the 'national issue'. For Armenia, it is closely associated with the 1915 tragedy, while for Turkey it addresses Armenia's 'genocide claim' and its claim to the eastern territory of Turkey. The 'genocide' issue is of the utmost importance for both sides, as it raises questions of territoriality in their historical memory regarding the border. For Turkey, the 1915 events evoke issues of morality, financial reparation and territorial compensation, while both the diasporic Armenian community and Armenia claim that a significant part of Eastern Turkey should be returned to Armenia. Therefore, the Turkish refusal to recognize the 'genocide' is not only determined by the moral repercussions of doing so, but is also closely linked to the territorial question, as repeatedly stated by several interviewees in Turkey (see also Cornell 2005). The recognition of the 'genocide' would lead to a perception that Turkey should accept Armenia's right to territory in Eastern Turkey, including (bordering) cities such as Kars, Iğdır, Ardahan, that are claimed to be part of 'Western Armenia'. A director of a research centre that was interviewed in Yerevan in April 2015 stated:

They were living here, telling their children this is not our land, you go to Muş, Diyarbakır, and then you will see what our land is there. Then the ownership of that place is very difficult to establish here, you always think this, your place is behind that border, it is difficult to be responsible to be here and now, thinking that one day you will go and live in the land of your ancestors.

In Armenian collective identity, the 1915 tragedy is a unifying phenomenon that consolidates Armenian historical memory with reference to 'a lost homeland'. Armenian collective memory and national identity are deeply rooted in the 1915 tragedy, which is embedded in Armenians' historical memory and strengthens a national identity that informs their ideas about where they have come from, who they are and how they should act in the present and future (Gillis 1994). All of the interviewees in Armenia mentioned the 1915 events, which constitute an incontestable element of Armenian national identity and statehood.

In contrast, Turkey's perception of national identity is not determined by the same element. The 1915 events never resonated in the same way in Turkey as they did in Armenia. In Turkish politics and mainstream media outlets, the 1915 tragedy is presented with an emphasis on Armenia's territorial claims.[12] These claims over Eastern Anatolia invoke nationalist sentiments and provide the Turkish political elites with convenient grounds for escalating nationalist discourses. However, Armenia's unequivocal refusal to recognize the Turkish-Armenian border has precluded discussions of the 1915 tragic events from a moral perspective.[13] It has, instead, paved the way for Turkish nationalism to fiercely assert the indispensability of Turkish territorial integrity, with the categorical rejection of the 1915 events as a subject of discussion. This reciprocal triggering of nationalist discourses has long diminished the chance of conflict transformation. A senior state official, who was interviewed in İstanbul in May 2015, underscored that the major source of the Turkish-Armenian conflict lies in 'the nationalist discourses' exacerbated by the political elites of both sides. S/he also added that 'the conflict has mainly been used as a domestic policy tool with a "nationalist rhetoric", which has deepened the political deadlock between the two sides'.

The assassination of Hrant Dink in 2007 had a tremendous impact on the perception of Armenians and Armenia in Turkey, as all interviewees in Turkey stated. Dink, a Turkish journalist of Armenian descent, was a well-known figure who worked for peace between Turkey and Armenia. After Dink's assassination, public opinion in Turkey began reconsidering the prejudices emanating from the past. The data obtained in our field research indicate that the unexpected loss of Dink brought a certain 'awareness' about 'rediscovering the shared past' and the 1915 events to Turkish society. Dink's murder was related to the encounter between his efforts at reconciliation and deeply rooted ultra-nationalist sentiments that prove the persistence of mental borders (prejudices, hatred, longstanding grievances) in Turkish society. Almost all of the interviewees in Turkey mentioned that after Dink's murder, the conflict between Armenia and Turkey, the 1915 tragedy, and minority problems rose to the surface and started to raise questions. The interviewees also underlined that Dink's assassination paved the way for the emergence of reactions like the apology campaign and public protests attended by thousands of people. Most importantly, it made the century-old conflict visible. Public debate on the matter focused on normalizing bilateral relations, opening the border and discovering the two countries' shared past.

Regional Dimensions of the Border Conflict

All of the interviewees on both sides were asked about the regional dimension of conflict transformation between Turkey and Armenia. Invariably, the interviewees involved in politics, from the bureaucracy, civil society and academia, stated that the border cannot be opened at the bilateral initiative of Turkey and Armenia, and that the resolution is inextricably linked to the Nagorno-Karabakh conflict. The alliances between Turkey and Azerbaijan and between Russia and Armenia respectively mean that Azerbaijan and Russia are involved parties in conflict transformation.

All of the interviewees from Turkey defined Russia as the most important player in the region. The evolution of Russia's relations with the South Caucasus countries is related to its foreign and security policies. Particularly during Putin's rule, Russia has challenged the hegemonic influence of the West in the international order. Russia has staked a claim to equal status in international affairs and is regaining an influential role in the areas around it, including in the South Caucasus (Averre 2007). Here Russia aggressively seeks to maintain its influence by either using threats and coercion or offering economic benefits and security guarantees (Flenley 2008; Gretskiy, Treshchenkova, and Golubev 2014). As a policy analyst from Ankara stated, 'Russia has always been a hard power in the region. It is more powerful than any country and always displays its power to all. [Russia] never lets any other country in its backyard'. According to a representative from a think tank based in Istanbul, 'Russia doesn't want the Turkish-Armenian border to be opened. As long as the border remains closed, Russia will preserve its leverage in Armenia'. An Azerbaijani journalist, who was interviewed in Ankara in May 2015, stated, 'I do not believe that Russia aspires to opening the border [between Turkey and Armenia] after resolving this conflict'. The director of an international NGO based in Yerevan, who was interviewed in May 2014, similarly said that 'for Russia, the more problematic the region, the easier it is to manage'.

In our research, the regional political-military and economic arrangements that Russia has offered Armenia are listed as the main reasons for the 'strategic partnership' between Armenia and Russia. The majority of the interviewees from Yerevan addressed the political, economic and security needs of Armenia under the conditions of post-Soviet instability and insecurity. Russia was pointed out as the only country that offers Armenia political support, economic benefits and military protection. From the Armenian point of view, only Russia promotes Armenia's territorial claims in the Nagorno-Karabakh region. Thus, Russia's presence is seen as essential for military protection and stability, as the Western powers remained silent during and after the escalation of the conflict. Besides, Russia has dominated the Armenian economy with its increasing investments in the telecommunication industry, the energy sector, the financial system and the railway system. Russia encouraged Armenia's participation in the Eurasian Economic Union (EEU) and the Collective Security Treaty Organisation (CSTO). An interviewee from Yerevan remarked that Russia serves as the main pillar of the Armenian security system. The Armenian borders with Turkey and Iran are jointly protected by Armenian and Russian border guards, and they cooperate in air defence. The lease on Russian military bases, including one in Gymri close to the Turkish border, was recently extended to up to 2044.

While evaluating bilateral relations with Russia, the Armenian interviewees tended to compare these relations with Armenia's bilateral relations with the EU. From their point of view, the EU policy lacks a security framework, which is very important for Armenia, and the EU does not have an interest in and/or the power to open up the border with Turkey or resolve the frozen conflict with Azerbaijan. 'European politics, they [the EU actors] never discussed with us our security problems and I think that they must understand that main problem for Armenian society is security. We can be hungry, we can have many problems in our society, but the main problem in our subconscious is our security problem, of course because of the Genocide', said a university professor from Yerevan in May 2014. A former public officer from Yerevan, who was interviewed in April 2015, described the relationship between Armenia and Russia versus relationship with the EU in this way: 'Russia [invests in] the spheres of business/economic and military security, which are more [urgently] needed in Armenia. Armenia needs a security guarantee and the only place to get it is from Russia. Religious freedom, sexual freedom [or other liberal values that the EU promotes] are not the most important topics for this country'. A project director at a non-profit organisation from Yerevan addressed the role of Russia versus that of the EU in the region as a whole as follows:

We understand that there are two external positions, or powers. And in order to stay above water, we need to balance between these two superpowers. In this respect, EU membership can be shaped in the consciousness of the Armenian people only when there is no need to balance, which is a quite hard thing to do, because as we saw in Ukraine, Russia is very aggressive when it comes to losing power in its previously, let's say, controlled territories.

On the Turkish side, the close relations with Azerbaijan are often mentioned as a considerable factor in any further steps to be taken towards conflict transformation with Armenia (see also Hill, Kirişci, and Moffatt 2015). Kinship ties constitute the backbone of the close relations between Turkey and Azerbaijan, especially in political discourse. 'One nation, two states' is a motto frequently invoked by the ruling elites and the public to define the cultural and kinship ties between Azerbaijan and Turkey, as one of the former Turkish ambassadors, who was interviewed in İstanbul in May 2015, emphasized. 'The prevailing attitude in Turkish public opinion, the media and political parties has always been pro-Azerbaijani, especially when there is a confrontation between Armenia and Azerbaijan', a representative of the civil societal organisation stated.

As one policy analyst from Ankara, who was engaged with various EU-funded projects between Turkey and Armenia, explained, economic collaboration between Azerbaijan and Turkey entails paying attention to Azerbaijan's reaction to further steps towards reconciliation with Armenia. He went on to say that Azerbaijan relies on Turkey for its oil market and transportation to Europe, in addition to diplomatic support in Nagorno-Karabakh. In return, Turkey's foreign trade with and foreign direct investment in Azerbaijan have been steadily increasing. In 2015, the volume of bilateral trade exceeded 3.5 billion USD, and more than 600,000 tourists from Azerbaijan visited Turkey in 2015. Turkish contracting firms have successfully completed 347 projects (with a total value of 11 billion USD) in Azerbaijan so far.[14] Azerbaijan's national oil company has made a heavy investment in petro-chemical facilities.[15] Turkey largely depends on Azeri oil and derives inalienable strategic benefits from the Trans-Anatolian gas pipeline (TANAP), the Baku-Tbilisi-Ceyhan oil pipeline (BTC), the Baku-Tbilisi-Erzurum natural gas pipeline (BTE) and the Kars-Tbilisi-Baku railway (KTB). Under these conditions, as one of the former ambassadors of Turkey among the interviewees stated, 'Turkey cannot make the decision on its own to open the border with Armenia. Azerbaijan is an important factor. As long as Turkey prioritizes its relations with Azerbaijan, there will be no further move towards opening the border'.

In fact, Azerbaijan showed itself as an important player in the transformation of conflict during the rapprochement process between Turkey and Armenia. In the early 1990s, the Turkish government supported Azerbaijan in the Nagorno-Karabakh conflict and closed the border with Armenia as a reaction to its occupation of the Azerbaijani regions surrounding Nagorno-Karabakh (Çeviköz 2014). During the process of rapprochement, officials and politicians from Azerbaijan pointed out the decades-long solidarity and collaboration between the two countries on several state-level occasions (Aydın 2009). The Turkish government reaffirmed its solidarity with Azerbaijan and stated that Turkey would not ratify the Zurich Protocols without progress towards resolving the Nagorno-Karabakh conflict (Hürriyet 2009a; Türenç 2009). Before signing the Protocols, Turkey asserted that conflict resolution in Nagorno-Karabakh was a *sine qua non* for Turkey to open the border and establish diplomatic relations with Armenia (Ergan 2009; Hürriyet 2009b). The majority of the interviewees mentioned that the Protocols led to discomfort in Turkish-Azerbaijani relations. As one policy analyst from a think tank in Ankara explained, Azeri diplomats and officials visited Turkey in search of support in the media, public opinion and the border region for securing the withdrawal of Armenian troops from the occupied territories as a precondition for opening the border.

Our research indicated that under these circumstances, opening the border with Armenia does not appeal to Turkey, as doing so would jeopardize its economic cooperation with Azerbaijan. Most of the policy analysts and state officers touched upon the volume of imports and exports between Turkey and Azerbaijan and stated that the Armenian market remains unattractive for Turkish traders and investors. However, a Turkish member of parliament from the border city underlined the need to evaluate the economic pros and cons of opening the border from a regional perspective. S/he stated, 'the closed border prevents the development of the border region as a hub of regional communication, transportation and networking for reaching neighbouring markets'. He insisted that the adoption of a regional perspective would display the economic potential of opening the border for the entire region, thereby invigorating pressure from below for peaceful conflict transformation among Turkey, Armenia and Azerbaijan. In a similar vein, several representatives from civil societal organisations and business associations in Ankara and Istanbul drew attention to the Turkish-Armenian border as the most efficient route, in terms of physical distance and transportation costs, connecting Europe to the Caucasus, Central Asia, Iran and Russia. They underlined the need to approach the conflict transformation between Turkey and Armenia from a regional perspective and to convince all parties of the socio-economic advantages of an open border.

All of these factors have created a *status quo* from which not only the parties involved but also third parties have benefited for various reasons. Some Turkish respondents regretfully stated that conflict resolution in the region is inextricably linked to a shift in the *status quo*, which might happen as a result of a possible controlled conflict between Armenia and Azerbaijan. Similarly, most interviewees from both the Turkish and Armenian sides agreed that the *status quo*, mostly linked to Nagorno-Karabakh, not only constrains the foreign policy choices of Armenia and Azerbaijan but also eliminates any possibility of conflict transformation or regional cooperation among Armenia, Azerbaijan and Turkey.

EU Cross-Border Initiatives on the Turkish-Armenian Border: relevant or Limited?

All of the interviewees were asked to evaluate the role of the EU in conflict transformation on the Turkish-Armenian border. The findings show that the EU is perceived as a soft power that promotes peace-building from below through cross-border cooperation in conflict transformation. However, the EU's neighbourhood policy was criticised for its ineffectiveness at conferring benefits at the civil societal level that would promote the development of further economic, social and political initiatives for conflict transformation. The EU's neighbourhood policy and cross-border cooperation initiatives do not offer instruments to challenge contested borders, which turn into frozen situations under the impact of historical memories and regional (f)actors. We concluded that to initiate and sustain the peaceful transformation of conflict on the Turkish-Armenian border, caution should be exercised not to overemphasise the significance of the cross-border movement and cooperation.

The overwhelming majority of the interviewees from Ankara, Istanbul and Yerevan admitted that the EU has had a positive impact on initiating dialogue at the civil societal level. During the rapprochement process between Armenia and Turkey, the EU and several European states such as Germany, France and Sweden supported and funded various mutual initiatives, projects and civil society activities for peace-building. These efforts carry potential for building up 'common ground', rediscovering 'cultural heritage' and overcoming prejudices between the Turkish and Armenian communities. An expert from a think tank based in İstanbul, who was interviewed in May 2015, evaluated the progress achieved via the EU-led initiatives as follows:

> Civil society in Turkey has covered a lot of ground. Cultural tourism, journalist exchanges and civil society exchanges have been conducted. There are many institutions, both in Armenia and Turkey. CIVILNET, The Civilitas, CHREST, Open Society, Friedrich Ebert Stiftung, the German Marshall Fund (…) An Armenian fellow can come to a civil societal organisation in İstanbul or Kars, for instance. There are still some difficulties, but civil society has made meaningful progress.

A representative of a civil societal organisation based in Yerevan put it as follows:

EU has contributed significantly in terms of dialogue between the societies. Right now we are implementing a project, the Armenia-Turkey project – four organisations from Armenia and four from Turkey are implementing various activities in the spheres of civil society, media, youth etc., so in that respect, in terms of fostering dialogue in civil society, the EU is quite active and is making a good contribution.

One of the most prominent programmes funded by the EU, titled "Support to the Armenia-Turkey Normalisation Process" under the Instrument for Stability, was cited by many interviewees from Turkey for its positive impact. The programme consortium consists of eight civil society organisations from Turkey and Armenia.[16] This initiative aims to develop ties and build confidence between the Turkish and Armenian communities to eliminate mutual prejudices, and most importantly, to overcome hindrances to the official negotiation process. Many Turkish interviewees mentioned that it also provides grants to other civil society organisations, initiatives and individuals from Armenia and Turkey for projects that contribute to opening up the dialogue process between the Turkish and Armenian societies. An interviewee from one of these organisations based in Istanbul made the following comment in May 2015:

> The main objective of our foundation was to initiate a dialogue between the Turkish and Armenian societies with activities in art and culture because there is a lack of connection between the Armenian and Turkish societies. We think we can develop a connection between the two societies with art and culture… The first idea was to bring filmmakers together and to make movies together, but the real aim is to motivate people to work together.

Most respondents from both sides admit that the EU's cross-border cooperation efforts initiate opportunities for developing deeper understanding, building confidence and opening dialogue at the civil societal level between Turkey and Armenia. As discussed above, our research showed that strong physical and historical borders are closely intertwined with mental borders, such as fear of the 'other', the association of the other side of the border with threats and enmity, longstanding prejudices and historical grievances emanating from the 'other side'. Such mental borders often result from a lack of meaningful cross-border communication and a lack of knowledge about the other side of the border (Kolosov and Scott 2013). It is significant, then, that the focus of cross-border cooperation initiatives on raising awareness of the other side through inter-cultural dialogue, literature, art and cultural activities, and the positive impact of these initiatives on conflict amelioration, were acknowledged by almost all Turkish and Armenian interviewees. An expert from a civil society organisation that we interviewed in Yerevan in May 2014 shared this experience with one of these activities:

We first gathered in Muş, and then we went to a place in Armenia, where people had migrated from Muş. For instance, we visited several villages where the people had never met any people from Turkey in their lives. We spent time with an old person and started to listen to his memories, where his family came from, what happened to them. And he stressed his prejudice toward the Turkish people who could invade their village if they wanted to. However, when we showed him a girl among our group and said she was Turkish too, then, he said such a nice girl, [she] is not responsible for what happened. He thinks this way because he had never encountered a Turkish person [before]. For this reason, meetings and gatherings are very important for building dialogue opportunities.

However, we were informed that despite its rising visibility at the civil societal level, the EU's outreach has remained limited in its ability to raise awareness about and promote interconnection with the 'other' in public opinion. As a manager of an EU-funded project that was interviewed in İstanbul in May 2015 remarked, 'There is increasing cultural interaction between the two countries. Many activities are taking place but these interactions are limited to a specific milieu. They do not spread out among the people. They are more prevalent among the intellectual milieu'. As s/he explained, the beneficiaries of the EU-funded projects and programmes are mostly from the academic, intellectual, educated and urban middle class. Similarly, some of the interviewees from Yerevan confirmed the limited sphere of influence of the EU policies' influence. One said, for example, that 'the ENP is still not very widely known and mostly people who either work in the government or NGOs would know about it; the majority have very little awareness [of it]'.

The security dimension of the EU's neighbourhood policy and cross-border cooperation endeavour, which is highly related to border disputes not only between Turkey and Armenia but also between Azerbaijan and Armenia, was questioned particularly by the Armenian interviewees. Despite its success in building up dialogue through civil society organisations, the question of whether the EU wants to be an assertive leader in conflict transformation was brought up in most interviews conducted in both Turkey and Armenia. The EU was generally perceived as being reluctant to take a proactive role in overcoming the on-going political problems and/or transforming the *status quo* in the region. An interviewee from Yerevan stated, 'The EU's policy towards the region has failed. What it offers is capacity building, strengthening civil society, human rights, soft power'. The Azerbaijani journalist stated:

> The EU and ENP could have an impact in conflict resolution only if the EU played a more active role, particularly in the Karabakh conflict. But it is not a priority for the EU now. The way conflict resolution is promoted is also important. Promoting dialogue engagement at the civil societal level is an effective method, but we cannot obtain concrete outcomes if the governments are not included in the processes.

The majority of the interviewees from both Turkey and Armenia criticised the EU for failing to play a decisive role and/or follow a consistent and coherent policy in major occurrences related to the border conflicts intertwining Armenia, Azerbaijan and Turkey, such as the ratification of the Protocols and the Nagorno-Karabakh conflict. In the Zurich Protocols, the bilateral talks between Turkey and Armenia did not take place under an EU initiative. While the EU had a minor role, the process was led by the United States, Russia, France and Germany. In addition, the EU also fell short of exercising assertive leadership when the issues of ratifying the Protocols, opening the border and establishing diplomatic relations came to inhibit the continuation of the rapprochement process between the two countries.

All of the interviewees agreed that the EU has emerged as a barely visible and relatively ineffective power in the resolution of the frozen conflict with Azerbaijan, particularly on the Armenian side. It was often mentioned that the EU did not present a united response to the Nagorno-Karabakh war due to the differing security concerns of its member states and to the bilateral relations that individual EU member states had established with Azerbaijan, particularly on energy security and trade. A director of a research centre stated, 'The negotiations between Azerbaijan and Armenia [were held] in the Minsk group and the co-chair of the Minsk group is France, which is one of the leaders of the EU countries. So we can speak about a certain impact of the EU, but I don't think it is connected with regulations or new definitions of borders'. Many of the Armenian interviewees drew attention to Armenia's hard security concerns associated with the contested borders and the EU's lack of the necessary attention to these concerns. A programme manager from a non-profit organisation said, 'If you are talking about the general public, the main problem with both the Russia-led union and the EU is that people do not feel the impact of the EU activities on their lives directly'. The presence of Russia is justified by Armenia's security concerns, as the following comment by an academician from Yerevan shows:

> The most important thing in the EU is the value system. We were very disappointed when due to pressure from Russia, our President refused a year ago to sign the Association Agreement with EU and made a 'U' turn (...), but of course for very important security reasons (...) [the EU] never discussed with us our security problems and I think that they should understand that the main problem for Armenian society is security.

On the Armenian side, some public officers criticised the EU's lack of interest in the situation with Turkey. An interviewee stated, 'Europe is kind of far [away] and it is not really supportive on many very important issues like security, the Karabakh issue or the Armenia-Turkish part. It [the EU] is getting out [of the Nagorno-Karabakh conflict]'. Another interviewee added, '[The EU] didn't play much of a role in Armenia-Turkey relations. The border is still closed. It would be good if it had some kind of influence, but obviously it is not in the scope of the EU's interests'. A senior public official remarked, 'The Armenian-Turkish border [was not mentioned] in the last six to seven reports. It was replaced by the cost of ratifying the Protocols. In our opinion, the Turkish-Armenian border should be treated separately [whether] the Protocols are ratified or not'. As an academician stated, 'The European neighbourhood, I believe, [will be] eventually [realised]; whenever these conflicts are solved, it will be because of some kind of integration project, it will [happen] one day if the EU decides to take it seriously'. An expert from a think tank in Yerevan summarised the repercussions of the EU's lack of interest in border disputes on regional balance as follows:

> Turkey is a member of EU Customs Union and its border with Armenia is closed. We want to see [from the EU] at least efforts to open the borders (...) Russia tries to be in good trade relations with Turkey and Armenia became a member of the Eurasia Customs Union. Then, Armenia tries to raise this issue with Moscow.

In a similar vein, almost all of the Turkish interviewees complained that the EU did not manage to use accession talks with Turkey and the association agreement with Armenia as leverage to force and/or encourage the parties involved into conflict transformation through a European path. They addressed the declining support for European integration 'because of being tired of waiting at the gate of Europe for more than 50 years', as a Turkish policy analyst summarised it. Yet a vague roadmap to special partnership, the reluctance of the EU to offer a functioning conditionality mechanism and the uncertainty of the accession talks with Turkey impede the likelihood of advancing conflict transformation and regional cooperation.

Against this backdrop, the structural limitations of the European neighbourhood policy were frequently mentioned as a factor that damages the credibility of the EU as an actor in overcoming the border conflict between Turkey and Armenia. As Scott and Van Houtum put it, the asymmetry between enlargement fatigue and the need to spread democracy, prosperity and security in its external borders constitutes the major obstacle of the ENP. The most recent obstacle is the emergence of securitisation within the EU due to rising Islamophobia, nationalist populism, the threat of illegal migration and the fear of loss of control over borders (Scott and Van Houtum 2009). Our research confirmed these findings and pointed out the result of the EU's self-withdrawal: the prevailing feeling of othering and exclusion in both Turkey and Armenia.

Conclusion

With the end of the Cold War, a drastic shift took place in the perception of borders: from territorial lines of demarcation, they became signifiers of interdependence and interconnectedness between nation-states beyond territoriality. Parallel to these shifts, the EU's foreign policy initiatives towards its emerging neighbours are built upon regional integration and cross-border cooperation. Regional cross-border cooperation is expected to open sealed borders and challenge mental borders by creating the grounds for interdependence, mutual dialogue and confidence-building, thereby leading to contribute conflict transformation and peace-building from below. Indeed, the EU's approach to conflict transformation relies on fostering cooperation across a variety of areas and local needs to build confidence and trust between the conflicting sides.

The EU has attempted to exercise these policies and tools for the transformation of the border between Turkey and Armenia. However, the Turkish-Armenian border remains physically, mentally and historically contested. The Turkish-Armenian conflict is overburdened by the historical past and cultural prejudices. Despite promising efforts in the recent decade, competing historical memories and a lack of mutual recognition of borders hinder the improvement of bilateral relations on the basis of mutual trust, respect and cooperation. Moreover, the conflict between Turkey and Armenia has turned into a regional conflict under post-Soviet conditions. After the dissolution of the Soviet Union, the South Caucasus became a region fragmented by divisive ethno-national politics and contested borders. Due to kinship ties and economic relations, Turkey supported Azerbaijan against Armenia in the Nagorno-Karabakh conflict. On the other side, Russia has intensified its political, economic and military relations with Armenia and did not play a contributing role in the Nagorno-Karabakh conflict resolution. With the involvement of Russia and Azerbaijan, this conflict is becoming more complicated and multi-layered.

Under these circumstances, the EU's neighbourhood and cross-border cooperation efforts have had a limited impact on conflict transformation at the Turkish-Armenia border. The proposal of strategic partnership as a replacement for EU membership was identified as reducing the leverage and credibility of the EU as an assertive actor in the eastern neighbourhood. Particularly in conflict transformation, the EU's neighbourhood policy has remained incoherent, contradictory and indifferent. According to the analysis of our findings in the field research, the EU's policies and instruments regarding the eastern neighbourhood remain ineffectual. Hence, the EU's neighbourhood and cross-border cooperation initiatives have not led to a transformative change in the overly politicised conceptualisation of the border, which is based on contested historical memories, longstanding grievances and national claims and is trapped in regional dynamics, alliances and shifts.

The EU's neighbourhood and cross-border initiatives based on exerting 'soft power' aim to stimulate mutual dialogue, confidence-building and

CROSS-BORDER COOPERATION 117

capacity-building and to strengthen civil society. It should be admitted that the EU-funded initiatives support mutual interaction at the civil societal level and lead to a gradual change in mental borders. The initiatives taken by civil society organisations provide a neutral zone in which participants from both sides can face the prejudices derived from a century's worth of problems, lack of interaction and mutual accusations. In addition, empowering civil societal actors to initiate a bottom-up dialogue process could lead to sustainable reconciliation among people, even though state-level negotiations may be easily stalled by changing discourses or policy orientations.

Notes

1. For the 'constructivist turn' in conceptualising bordering as something continually 'being made', see Van Houtum and Van Naerssen (2002); Newman (2011); Scott (2011); Bechev and Nicolaidis (2010).
2. For further analyses about collective memory, see, Assmann (2006), Funkenstein (1989), Halbwachs (1992), Narvaez (2006), Sontag (2003).
3. The 'wider Europe' initiative indicates "a far-reaching association of the EU's eastern and southern neighbours that offers "everything but institutions" as alternative to membership (Prodi 2002). The ENP was developed to substitute "the golden carrot" of membership, which has been considered the crucial factor for the success of the EU's enlargement policy. See Börzel and Lebanidze (2015), Börzel and van Hüllen (2014), Lavenex (2004), Prodi (2002).
4. The Nagorno-Karabakh conflict is a territorial and ethnic conflict between Armenia and Azerbaijan over the disputed region of Nagorno-Karabakh and its seven surrounding districts. The conflict turned into an armed conflict between these two countries between 1988 and 1994 when a ceasefire was proclaimed. Since then, the region has been a *de facto* independent country in the South Caucasus but internationally recognized as the territory of Azerbaijan.
5. Yerevan, the capital city of Armenia, is only 40 km away from the border, while the distance between Ankara, the capital city of Turkey, and the border is almost 1000 km. There are small villages with low population density on both sides of the border.
6. In the Russo-Georgian war, Italy and Bulgaria, mostly for energy concerns, accused Georgia of aggression against South Ossetia, whereas Poland condemned Moscow. See Popescu and Wilson (2009), Wisniewski (2013, 10–11).
7. While France and Greece traditionally have had closer links with Armenia, Germany has stronger historical and economic ties to Azerbaijan. Russia, Germany, and France are often considered friends, and therefore, Germany and France might refrain from intervening or counteracting against Russia in its closer neighbourhood whereas the UK is more sceptical about developing bilateral relations. See Van Hoof (2012, 294–295).
8. There is a deep controversy between Turkey and Armenia to call the 1915 events that took place on the eve of First World War in the Ottoman Empire as genocide or not. For the official positions of the Turkish and Armenian states, see http://www.mfa.gov. tr/data/DISPOLITIKA/the-events-of-1915-and-the-turkish_armenian-controversy-over-history-br.pdf and https://www.mfa.am/en/genocide.

9. Akdamar (Aghtamar) Church has survived as the most important example reflecting the culture and art of the Armenian Kingdom of Vaspurakan, which ruled over the region of Van between 908 and 1021 AD as a vassal of the Abbasids, and became the centre of the Armenian Catholicosate for a period of time and one of the most sublime examples of Armenian religious architecture. Van remains within the borders of the Turkish Republic since 1923.
10. The Turkish and English of Protocols are available at: http://www.mfa.gov.tr/site_media/html/zurih-protokolleri-en.pdf, http://www.mfa.gov.tr/data/DISPOLITIKA/türkiye-ermenistan-turkce.pdf.
11. The name of the border, Doğu Kapı/Akuryan, was defined by the Kars Treaty in 1921.
12. The concept of Greater Armenia is an Armenian ethno-nationalist-irredentist concept referring to areas within the traditional Armenian homeland that are currently or have historically been mostly populated by Armenians throughout the 20th century, including Eastern Turkey, Nagorno-Karabakh, Nakhichevan of Azerbaijan and the Javakheti region of Georgia.
13. In January 1991, Soviet Armenia refused to issue a declaration to the effect that it recognized the existing borders between Turkey and Armenia.
14. For economic relations between Turkey and Azerbaijan, see http://www.mfa.gov.tr/economic-relations-between-turkey-and-azerbaijan.en.mfa.
15. SOCAR Turkey Energy is the most important representative of the ever-stronger economic collaboration between Turkey and Azerbaijan. The State Oil Company of Azerbaijan has been carrying out its activities in Turkey under the name SOCAR Turkey Energy since 2011. SOCAR Turkey Energy owned a 51% stake in PETKIM, the leading petrochemical company of Turkey, by 2011. See http://www.petkim.com.tr/Sayfa/2/820/INVESTING-IN-PETKIM.aspx.
16. The Civilitas Foundation (CF), the Eurasia Partnership Foundation (EPF), the Public Journalism Club (PJC) and the Regional Studies Centre (RSC) from Armenia; Anadolu Kültür, the Economic Policy Research Foundation of Turkey (TEPAV), the Helsinki Citizens' Assembly (hCa), and the Hrant Dink Foundation from Turkey.

Acknowledgements

This research was carried out as a part of EUBORDERSCAPES Project with the collaboration of Centre for Black Sea and Central Asia at Middle East Technical University from Turkey and Centre for Advanced Study from Bulgaria. Our special thanks is to our colleague Vanya Ivanovna for her contribution in the field research in Armenia.

References

Assmann, A. 2006. Memory, individual and collective. In *The oxford handbook of contextual political analysis*, ed. R. E. Goodin and C. Tilly, 210–24. Oxford: Oxford University Press.

Averre, D. 2007. Sovereign democracy and Russia's relations with the European Union. *Demokratizatsiya* 15 (2):173–90. doi:10.3200/DEMO.15.2.173-190.

Avetisian, T., and S. Musayelyan. 2010. One year on, Turkey-Armenia rapprochement stalled. Accessed September 15, 2017. http://www.rferl.org/content/One_Year_On_TurkeyArmenia_Rapprochement_Stalled/2186246.html.

Aydın, M. 2009. Azerbaycan, Türkiye-Ermenistan Anlaşmasının Neresinde? [Where does Azerbaijan stand in the agreement between Turkey and Armenia?] Accessed September 10, 2017. http://www.tepav.org.tr/tr/yayin/s/262

Bechev, D., and K. Nicolaidis. 2010. Introduction: Frontiers, memory, and conflict in the mediterranean. In *Mediterranean frontiers: Borders, conflict and memory in a transnational world*, ed. D. Bechev and K. Nicolaidis, 1–12. London: Tauris Academic Studies.

Bialasiewicz, L. 2008. The uncertain state(s) of Europe? *European Urban and Regional Studies* 15 (1):71–82. doi:10.1177/0969776407081279.

Bogner, A., and W. Menz. 2009. The theory-generating expert interview: Epistemological interest, forms of knowledge, interaction. In *Interviewing experts*, ed. A. Bogner, B. Littig, and W. Menz, 43–80. Hampshire: Palgrave MacMillan.

Börzel, T. A. 2011. When Europe hits beyond its borders: Europeanization and the near abroad. *Comparative European Politics* 9 (4/6):394–413. doi:10.1057/cep.2011.8.

Börzel, T. A., and B. Lebanidze. 2015. European neighbourhood policy at the crossroads: Evaluating the past to shape the future. MAXCAP Working Paper Series, No. 12, Berlin.

Börzel, T. A., and V. van Hüllen. 2014. One voice, one message, but conflicting goals. Cohesiveness and consistency in the european neighbourhood policy. *Journal of European Public Policy* 21 (7):1033–49. doi:10.1080/13501763.2014.912147.

Çeviköz, Ü. 2014. Turkish-Armenian relations need a new game-changer. Accessed September 10, 2017. http://www.hurriyetdailynews.com/Default.aspx?pageID=238&nID=74245&NewsCatID=396

Cornell, S. E. 2005. *Small nations and great powers: A study of ethnopolitical conflict in the Caucasus*. UK: Taylor & Francis.

Council of the European Union. 2009. Joint declaration of the Prague EaP summit. Accessed October 15, 2017. http://www.europarl.europa.eu/meetdocs/2009_2014/documents/depa/dv/200/200909/20090930_04en.pdf

Ergan, U. 2009. Karabağ krizi çıktı. [The crisis on Karabagh took place]. Accessed September 17, 2017. http://www.hurriyet.com.tr/karabag-krizi-cikti-12665246

EU-Armenia ENP Action Plan. 2006. Accessed September 20, 2017. http://eeas.europa.eu/enp/pdf/pdf/action_plans/armenia_enp_ap_final_en.pdf.

EUBORDERSCAPES. 2016. Project final report Bordering, political landscapes and social arenas: Potentials and challenges of evolving border concepts in a post-cold war world. Accessed September 10, 2017. www.euborderscapes.eu.

European Commission. 2014. Programming on cross-border cooperation (2014-2020). Accessed October 21, 2017. https://ec.europa.eu/neighbourhood-enlargement/neighbour hood/cross-border-cooperation_en

European Neighbourhood Policy. 2004. Strategy paper. Communication from the commission. Commission of the communities. Brussels, 12. 5.2004. COM 373 Final. Accessed November 1, 2018. https://ec.europa.eu/neighbourhood-enlargement/sites/near/files/2004_communica tion_from_the_commission_-_european_neighbourhood_policy_-_strategy_paper.pdf

European Parliament. 2006. Resolution on Turkey's accession progress. Accessed September 20, 2017. http://www.europarl.europa.eu/sides/getDoc.do?pubRef=-//EP//TEXT+REPORT +A6-2006-0269+0+DOC+XML+V0//EN

Flenley, P. 2008. Russia and the EU: The clash of new neighbourhoods. *Journal of Contemporary European Studies* 16 (2):189–202. doi:10.1080/14782800802309805.

Funkenstein, A. 1989. Collective memory and historical consciousness. *History & Memory* 1 (1):5–26.

German, T. C. 2007. Visibly invisible: EU engagement in conflict resolution in the South Caucasus. *European Security* 16 (3–4):359–60. doi:10.1080/09662830701751141.

Gillis, J. 1994. Memory and identity: The history of a relationship. In *Commemorations*, ed. J. Gillis, 3–40. Princeton: Princeton University Press.

Gretskiy, I., E. Treshchenkova, and K. Golubev. 2014. Russia's perceptions and misperceptions of the EU eastern partnership. *Communist and Post-Communist Studies* 47:375–83. doi:10.1016/2Fj.postcomstud.2014.10.006.

Gültekin-Punsmann, B. 2010. Linking Turkey's EU accession process and the ENP regional initiative: Necessary cross-border cooperation with South Caucasus. In *Neighbourhood challenge: European union and its neighbours*, ed. B. Balamir-Coskun and B. Demirtas-Coskun, 379–96. Boca Raton: Universal Publishers.

Halbwachs, M. 1992. *On collective memory*, ed. and trans. Lewis A. Coser. Chicago and London: Chicago University Press.

Haukkala, H. 2008. The Russian challenge to EU normative power: The case of European neighbourhoood policy. *The International Spectator* 43 (2):35–47. doi:10.1080/03932720802057117.

Hill, F., K. Kirişci, and A. Moffatt. 2015. Armenia and Turkey: From normalization to reconciliation. *Turkish Policy Quarterly* 13 (4):127–38.

Hürriyet. 2009a. Protokolün Meclis'e sunumu 21 Ekim'de. [Introducing the protocol to the parliament will be on the 21st of october]. Accessed September 15, 2017. http://www.hurriyet.com.tr/protokolun-meclis-e-sunumu-21-ekim-de-12676339

Hürriyet. 2009b. Türkiye - Ermenistan yakınlaşması dönüm noktasında. [Turkish-Armenian Rapproachment is at the Crossroads]. Accessed September 17, 2017.

Joint Statement of the Ministries of Foreign Affairs of the Republic of Turkey, the Republic of Armenia and the Swiss Federal Department of Foreign Affairs. 2009. Accessed September 18, 2017. http://www.mfa.gov.tr/no_-56_-22-april-2009_-press-release-regarding-the-turkish-armenian-relations.en.mfa.

Kansteiner, W. 2002. Finding meaning in memory: A methodological critique of collective memory studies. *History and Theory* 41 (2):179–97. doi:10.1111/0018-2656.00198.

Kharlamova, G. 2015. The European Union and the Eastern partnership: Convergence of economies. *Procedia Economics and Finance* 27:29–41. doi:10.1016/S2212-5671(15)00968-5.

Lavenex, S. 2004. EU external governance in 'wider Europe'. *Journal of European Public Policy* 11 (4):680–700. doi:10.1080/1350176042000248098.

Lederach, J. P. 1997. *Building peace: Sustainable reconciliation in divided societies.* Washington: United States Institute of Peace.

MacFarlane, S. N. 1997. Democratization, nationalism and regional security in the Southern Caucasus. *Government and Opposition* 32 (3):399–420. doi:10.1111/j.1477-7053.1997.tb00777.x.

Mayer, S., and F. Schimmelfenning. 2007. Shared values: Democracy and human rights. In *Governing Europe's neighbourhood partners of periphery?* ed. K. Weber, M. Smith, and M. Baun, 39–57. Manchester: Manchester University Press.

McCall, C. 2013. European union cross-border cooperation and conflict amelioration. *Space and Polity* 17 (2):197–216. doi:10.1080/13562576.2013.817512.

Narvaez, R. F. 2006. Embodiment, collective memory and time. *Body & Society* 12 (3):51–73. doi:10.1177/1357034X06067156.

Newman, D. 2006. Borders and bordering: Towards an interdisciplinary dialogue. *European Journal of Social Theory* 9 (2):171–86. doi:10.1177/1368431006063331.

Newman, D. 2011. Contemporary research agendas in border studies: An overview. In *Ashgate research companion to border studies*, ed. D. Wastl-Water, 33–47. Aldershot: Ashgate Publishing.

CROSS-BORDER COOPERATION 121

O'Loughlin, J., V. Kolossov, and J. Radvanyi. 2007. The Caucasus in a time of conflict, demographic transition, and economic change. *Eurasian Geography and Economics* 48 (2):135–56. doi:10.2747/1538-7216.48.2.135.

Özbay, F. 2011. Türkiye Ermenistan İlişkileri. Accessed September 21, 2017. http://www.bilgesam.org/Images/Dokumanlar/0-96-201403263turkiye-ermenistan-iliskileri.pdf.

Popescu, G. 2008. The conflict logics of cross-border reterritorialization: Geopolitics of Euroregions in Eastern Europe. *Political Geography* 27 (4):418–38. doi:10.1016/j.polgeo.2008.03.002.

Popescu, N., and A. Wilson. 2009. *The limits of enlargement-lite: European and Russian power in the troubled neighbourhood.* London: ECFR. June.

Prodi, R. 2002. A wider Europe - A proximity policy as the key to stability. Speech at the Sixth ECSA-World Conference, Brussels, Belgium, December 5–6. doi:10.1044/1059-0889(2002/er01)

Scott, J. W. 2005. The EU and 'Wider Europe': Toward an alternative geopolitics of regional cooperation? *Geopolitics* 10 (3):429–54. doi:10.1080/14650040591003471.

Scott, J. W. 2009. Bordering and ordering the European neighbourhood: A critical perspective on EU territoriality and geopolitics. *TRAMES* 13 (63/58) (3):232–47. doi:10.3176/tr.2009.3.03.

Scott, J. W. 2011. Borders, border studies and EU enlargement. In *Ashgate research companion to border studies*, ed. D. Wastl-Water, 123–42. Aldershot: Ashgate Publishing.

Scott, J. W. 2012. European politics of borders, border symbolism and cross-border cooperation. In *The blackwell companion to border studies*, ed. H. Donnnan and T. M. Wilson, 83–99. Oxford: Wiley- Blackwell.

Scott, J. W. 2015. Bordering, border politics and cross-border cooperation in Europe. In *Neighbourhood policy and the construction of the European external borders*, ed. F. Celata and R. Coletti, 27–36. Switzerland: Springer International Publishing. doi:10.1007/978-3-319-18452-4_2.

Scott, J. W., and H. Van Houtum. 2009. Reflections on EU territoriality and the "bordering" of Europe. *Political Geography* 28 (5):271–73. doi:10.1016/j.polgeo.2009.04.002.

Scott, J. W., and V. Kolosov. 2013. EUBORDERSCAPES working paper 4: Selected conceptual issues in border studies. Accessed September 10, 2017. http://www.euborderscapes.eu/fileadmin/user_upload/Working_Papers/EUBORDERSCAPES_Working_Paper_4_Kolosov_and_Scott.pdf.

Sontag, S. 2003. *Regarding the pain of others.* New York: Farrar, Straus and Giroux.

Terzi, Ö. 2010. *The influence of the European union on Turkish foreign policy.* Farnham and Burlington: Ashgate.

Tocci, N. 2007. *The EU and Conflict Resolution. Promoting peace in the backyard.* London and New York: Routledge.

Türenç, T. 2009. O Zürih gecesindeki Charles Aznavour [Charles Aznavour in that Zurich Night]. Accessed September 15, 2017. http://www.hurriyet.com.tr/o-zurih-gecesindeki-charles-aznavour-12668396

Üstün, Ç. 2010. EU and Turkish neighbourhood policies: Common goals. *Caucasian Review of International Affairs* 4 (4):342–53. Autumn.

Van Hoof, L. 2012. Why the EU is failing in its Neighbourhood: The case of Armenia. *European Foreign Affairs Review* 17 (2):285–302.

Van Houtum, H., and T. Van Naerssen. 2002. Bordering, ordering, and othering. *Journal of Economic and Social Geography* 93 (2):125–36. doi:10.1111/1467-9663.00189.

Wisniewski, P. D. 2013. *The Eastern partnership-it is high time to start a real 'partnership'.* Moscow: Carnegie Moscow Centre.

On (In)Definite Topography: National Identity and European and Regional Imaginaries in the Post-1989 Croatian Literary Narratives

Ivana Trkulja

ABSTRACT

The present article enquiries into the formation of Croatian national identity and regional bordering processes traced in the post-1989s Croatian literary narratives. During the 1990s self-identification debates mainly reflected perception of Croatian national belonging as distinct from the Balkans and European oriented. From 2000 until 2013 when Croatia received full European Union membership, the articulation of 'national' was altered and correlated with new socio-geographic imaginaries linking Croatia with 'Mitteleuropa', the Mediterranean and the post-Yugoslav space. The changes in articulation of Croatian national identity can be seen in the changing rhetoric of literary narratives where the legacy of prominent Croatian and former Yugoslav writer Miroslav Krleža is a transversal element. The aim of this article is to explicate the relevance of Croatian literary narratives for the geopolitical research of national identity and bordering processes referring to the macro-regional level.

Introduction

The comprehensive nation-building process during the 1990s in Croatia was a contentious process where the future of proper national belonging was re-oriented towards 'Europe' turning away from its Balkan neighbourhood. The related national identity debates were consequential to broader socio-political transformations connected with the fall of the Berlin Wall in 1989, the disintegration of the Yugoslav federation in the early 1990s and the Croatian national independence in 1991. These international and regional historical landmarks were further overshadowed by the ferocious Balkan conflicts in the 1990s followed by the challenging European integration process and eventual Croatian membership in 2013. The intensity of these events and the complete transformation of the regional socio-political tissue have indisputably affected the perception of borders and bordering processes in Croatia and the entire Balkans. They have also attracted the attention of

CROSS-BORDER COOPERATION

scholars from the fields of nationalism, conflict, area studies, orientalism and Europeanisation (Bakić-Hayden 2006; Ivan Čolović 2009; Vlaisavljević 2006).

As a contribution to these enquires, the present work examines how regional literary sources discuss and represent bordering processes in the post-1990 Croatian national context. It analyses literary texts, main literary currents, use of rhetoric and interaction of authors with a wider intellectual setting in the region. The main linking figure in this context is eminent Croatian and former Yugoslav writer Miroslav Krleža (1893–1981). The present work first outlines the historical context and the foundations of national identity pursuit as seen through the legacy and reception of Krleža's work. The article then focuses on the 1990s articulation of the 'national' and perception of regional borders in Croatian literary narratives through the work of Stanko Lasić a Croatian and former Yugoslav literary critic and prominent 'Krležologist'. Lasić's work is explored in connection with the altering rhetoric of national borders perceived in his public engagement, literary writings and relations with the other 'Krležologists'. Finally, the article analyses articulation of the Croatian national identity in the post-2000 literary narratives using macro-regional perspective with a reference to 'Mitteleuropa', the Mediterranean and the post-Yugoslav space.

Historical Preface – from Kostanjevac to 'Ljubljana's Report'

Following Croatian independence from the former Yugoslav federation in 1991, pursuit of national identity and the future of national belonging was firmly placed in the realm of 'Europe' departing from its Yugoslav and Balkan heritage. The national self-identification process has been widely debated in the literary narratives revealing both new aspects and thematic continuity with the period before national independence. The particular focus on literary sources is justified through the important consideration that a national identity has not been publicly discussed in Yugoslav times either in the political space or in the respective national institutions. As a consequence, the important issues connected with 'national projects' in the Balkan region were examined in other venues, where the changing rhetoric about national identity issues and bordering process are remarkably captured in the regional narratives (Mandić in Palavestra 1989, 65–66). In fact, transformations in the literary narratives mirror the actual change of 'national projects' confines. Hence, the presence of politically engaged literature provides a valuable source towards understanding of Croatian national identity dynamics and its contemporary contextualisation. At times, especially in the 1990s, the actors from literary circles not only mirrored the national socio-political context in their literary writings but also openly favoured certain political options causing a significant influence of the literary narratives in the public intellectual space. Ultimately these processes added an active dimension to the Croatian literary works demonstrating continuity with pre-1990s public debates and its importance for geopolitical research (Lasić 1992).

The metaphor of '(in)definite topography' advanced through the literary work of Miroslav Krleža captures exceptionally well the main themes related to Croatian national identity building process.[1] The thematic and spatial framework of this symbolic topography was introduced by Krleža in his renowned novel *Povratak Filipa Latinovicza* [The Return of Filip Latinovicz] (1932). In the first lines of this novel, its main character Filip Latinovicz arrives to the 'Kaptol station' of his hometown Kostanjevac after a long stay abroad (Krleža 1954, 9). Krleža sets his novel in the imaginary town of Kostanjevac that resembled a faithful description of Zagreb's old city, if only for the fact that Kaptol's station has never existed there. Filip Latinovicz's identity search, as a principal theme of Krleža's book, has been widely analysed in literary context. Yet, the 'Kaptol station' in Kostanjevac – an inexistent place of Filip's arrival – was never itself considered over the seven decades since the book was published (Mandić 2012, 21). It was only in the more recent discussions of Croatian intellectuals on the process of national identity building that this element in Krleža's work was rediscovered.[2] In the context of this peculiar failure of Filip's return, Igor Mandić (b.1939) renowned Croatian and Yugoslav literary critic made a reference to the collection of essays by the intellectual and cultural theorist Boris Buden (b.1958) entitled *Kaptolski kolodvor* [The Kaptol Station] (2002). In his work, Buden states that 'Kaptol station':

> '[…] is more than Krleža's literary fiction. The Kaptol's station is the name for an utopia of return, for the fiction of national homeland as the final destination of all journeys. Who once has left the realm of the national culture and in political sense the universe of national democracy, presently has nowhere to return. That is the actual message of Krleža's novel: do not step out at the Kaptol's stations! Do not repeat Filip's mistake, traumas of rejection, frustration, self-destruction, that have created the whole constellation of literary characters, in which as in one's own cult victims, the national culture ultimately sadistically relishes' (Buden in Mandić 2012, 24).

In this short reflection, Buden emphasises the 1990s Croatian and overall regional drama of national self-identification processes. Furthermore, Mandić a decade later recalls Buden's work and urges towards the necessity of revisionism and social commitment as it has been present also in Krleža's politically engaged literary opus. The significance of Krleža's work in the present context comprises following three elements: his remarkably versatile literary authorship, undeniable public authority and legacy in Croatian and Balkan context. Throughout seven decades of Krleža's literary and public engagement, he manifested exceptional capacity to maintain both ideological independence and close ties with the changing political authorities (Krleža

1932). The significant landmark in the post-World War II context was Krleža's speech at the Congress known as *Ljubljanski referat* [The Ljubljana's Report] that have discussed historical interpretation of literary and artistic elements of the new Yugoslav socialist culture referring to its uniqueness and authenticity. Arguably, it is following this speech that Krleža has emerged as the moral authority, maintaining his literary and public significance.[3] The author's dilemmas expressed in his public engagement, literary and political writings, regardless of critics and opponents, have become essential in many ways for the future generations of Croatian and Yugoslav authors. The 'Krležianity' moved beyond a mere intellectual current becoming a critical approach and factor of social mobilisation that used Krleža's polemic figure as a medium for the articulation of institutional and public critique (Matvejević 1982, 7). The acknowledgement of Krleža's legacy remains an essential element in understanding the changes in perceptions of regional bordering and qualifies as a transversal theme within the present work.

The Articulation of 'National' in the 1990s

The perception of the 'national' remains remarkably articulated in the Croatian cultural and literary narratives during the 1990s. The key themes unavoidably reflect the challenging period following the dissolution of the Yugoslav federation and the establishment of the sovereign Croatian state. The Croatian narratives from this period closely reflect aspirations of the 'national project' and confirms the country's European orientation moving away from the regional context of the Balkans. In the present section, these themes are discussed by focusing on the authorship of Stanko Lasić (1927–2017) – a Croatian and Yugoslav literary historian, critic, international scholar and one of the most authoritative 'Krležologists'. Lasić substantially dealt with Krleža's principal themes related to the scrutiny of national and ideological questions in the former Yugoslav context. His lasting enquiry has resulted in a six-volume philosophical study of literary history entitled *Krležologija ili povijest kritičke misli o Miroslavu Krleži* [Krležology or The History of Critical Thinking about Miroslav Krleža] published in 1989 and 1993 respectively.[4] Lasić's comprehensive work focused on Krleža's life and work, often depicting key Croatian politico-literary debates in the former-Yugoslav and wider European contexts (Visković in Radaković-Vinchierutti 1993, 40–41). During the 1990s Lasić reconfirms his conceptual affinity with the 'Krležianity', remaining engaged in the national identity building process both as a scholar and a public intellectual.

Among the selected works of Lasić from these times, we analyse *Tri eseja o Evropi* [The Three Essays about Europe] published in 1992 significant for their emphasis on the main conceptual framework for articulating the 'national' during the period of 1990–1992. Then, we examine an article

Zastave kao Krležina filozofija povijesti [The Flags as Krleža's Philosophy of History] published in 1993 (with a reprint in 1997), that takes further the national identity theme while evoking Krleža's literary opus. Finally, we look into the public debate known as the *'Bulgarian question' of Croatian culture* in 1997 involving a number of prominent 'Krležologists' and discussing the contentious relationship between Croatia and Serbia at the time. The selected works and discussions analyse the socio-political anxieties of the 1990s where Krleža's inheritance remains largely preserved in terms of the thematic concerns and argumentation mechanisms.

A Dance at the Élysée Palace

Tri eseja o Evropi [The Three Essays about Europe] volume of collected works encompasses Stanko Lasić's speeches at the Assemblies of Croatian European Movement (CEM) in 1990, 1991 and 1992. Lasić's speeches at the CEM's Assemblies offer an understanding of changing 'rhetoric' in the context of Croatian political and cultural narratives underlining the significance of the national commitment towards the European integration process and parting with its Balkan heritage. The selected works are easy to contextualise in the changing political context of the early 1990s leading to the Croatian national independence. Nonetheless, what is less immediately recognisable is the continuous use of literary instruments referring to Krleža's opus and conceptual framework. The focus on *'consciousness'*, and in particular its national and dialogic nature, is one of the recurring concepts of Lasić's scholarship. It is from here that, the author discusses challenging questions regarding the relations between Croatian and Serbian people in the 1990s, in particular whether the latter were willing to be part of Croatian nation-state (Lasić 1992, 23–24). Lasić has underlined the tragic nature of both nations departing from their impossible desire to achieve territorial unity, which is particularly evident for the Serbian people given its dispersed nature (Lasić 1992, 25). The reference towards 'dispersed nature' of Serbian people is based on their historical migrations resulting in a multinational state structure within the region. The other significant reference is the notion of *'contradiction'* analysed as a part of 'contradictory nature of Europe' – also a recurring concept in Lasić's works. The reference to contraction indicates the application of Krleža's thematic and methodological frame. By using this term Krleža articulated a particular understanding of Europe and its relation with the region.

During the first speech entitled *Pristup* [The Accession] in 1990, Lasić evoked his old memories about the lasting challenges of Croatian integration process in European context while at the same time confirming its belonging within the European family.[5] Even though at that time Croatia was still part of the federal Yugoslav state, Lasić foresaw a challenging path towards becoming a European Community member and stressed his belief in the necessity to comprehend Europe's contradictory nature and its persisting internal power confrontations (Lasić 1992, 7). Lasić emphasised that joining the European Community would not be an invitation for a *'dance at the Élysée Palace'* and it would mean instead a participation in the lasting power struggles among the European nations (Lasić 1992, 8). Considering the proximity of 1989, the dissolution of socialism and the overall transformation of the political system, Lasić accentuated the emerging importance of the nation-state and national identity building process. In particular, he referred to the national struggle of the Central and Eastern European countries for recognition of their historical and ethnic territories that was also a relevant direction for the Croatian nation-state building (Lasić 1992, 11–12).

The second speech entitled *Hrvatska danas* [Croatia Today] from 1991 is situated in the aftermath of the federal Yugoslav state disintegration and after the beginning of the warfare between Croatia and its neighbours. Lasić pointed out again the particular role of the European Movement in internationalisation or rather 'Europeanisation' of the 'Croatian question' (Lasić 1992, 13). He emphasised the importance of CEM and its capacity to act as an agent of change focusing on intellectual and moral matters in a wider European context, cultivating an approach of the truth and ethical consciousness often compromised in the 1990s (Lasić 1992, 26–27). Croatian national sovereignty was already in place when Lasić again referred to the conceptual framework of 'Krležianity' emphasising the relation with Europe and the necessity to recognise its internal contradictions (Lasić 1992, 16–18). Lasić focused on Croatian statehood in terms of the realisation of the national unity in the Balkan context. He argued that an evolution of Croatian national consciousness into a 'dialogic consciousness' would enable a dialogue with its own individuality and affirmation of its national being (Lasić 1992, 20–21).

The third selected speech was *Evropa danas* [Europe Today] given after the first year of warfare in Croatia in 1992. It aimed at contextualisation of European role at the time in regional affairs. Lasić discusses the question of responsibility both in the European and Croatian contexts, disclosing his hopes that the Croatian people would preserve their 'consciousness disquiet' grounding their spirit in dialogue, self-dialogue and toleration (Lasić 1992, 29–30, 32, 35). Lasić mentions the patience of Croatian people while waiting for the response of Europe, which ultimately came as the recognition of the new nation-state (Lasić 1992, 35, 41).

The Flags

The changing 'regional rhetoric' of Croatian literary narratives is further contextualised within Lasić's article 'The Flags as Krleža's Philosophy of History' (Visković in Radaković-Vinchierutti 1993, 40-41, 1997a). The article is related to Krleža's novel *Zastave* [The Flags] (1967)[6] that discusses the challenges related to the process of emerging national consciousness after the Balkan wars (1912–1913) and until the World War I period. *The Flags* are one of the central works in Krleža's literary opus that reflect the key themes surrounding the processes of national identity building and respective ideological frameworks. Lasić's article is based on his book *Struktura Krležinih 'Zastava'* [The Structure of Krleža's 'The Flags'] (1974) conceived as a literary study that emphasised a new phase in Krleža's writing at the time (Lasić 1974, 56). Indeed, Lasić reintroduced Krleža's work related to the theme of national building, using him as a medium for articulation of contentious national issues and in order to discuss his own dilemmas in the 1990s. In this manner, Lasić further affirms the continuity of Krleža's authority and the legacy of his intellectual heritage.

In the 1990s Lasić conceived his enquiry related to the Croatian national pursuit in the context of Krleža's philosophy of history. Krleža's approach in this context was founded upon the connection between the categories of affirmation and negation, meaning that everything contains also its opposite. In this way, all historical subjects were destined to perceive themselves in the 'Other' while struggling between the desire to climb the power ladder or to return towards a lost totality (Lasić 1997a, 24). In Krleža's philosophy of history, 'Europe' is considered as a symbolic civilisationial 'centre' that is surrounded initially by two metaphoric imaginaries of 'periphery' and further a 'devastation' (Lasić 1997a, 23–24). Krleža argued that significant historical decisions are taken by the centre that had knowledge and power to generate culture and new sublime structures (Lasić 1997a, 26). The centre separated itself from the periphery by the wall, allowing it to move closer while the 'periphery' waited for its promised recognition and possibility to enter in the 'centre', granted only when it becomes convenient to the 'centre' (Lasić 1997a, 26). In Krleža's work the periphery is visualised as an imitation of the 'centre' driven by two dominant objectives: first, an aspiration to become part of the 'centre' and secondly, an attempt to prevent 'devastation' to enter into the 'periphery' as another competitor seeking recognition from the 'center' (Lasić 1997a, 26). Following this philosophical vision, Krleža manifested his dissatisfaction with a role Croatia and the Balkans seeking ways in which they could leave the 'periphery' and become part of the 'center'.

Another significant component in Krleža's philosophy of history, which aimed at resolving contradiction between 'Self' and 'Other' was the nation (Lasić 1997a, 29). Krleža's politico-philosophical work was mainly directed towards an understanding of the national question among the Balkan states. Serbia in this regard was perceived as a nation-state, while Croatia was subjected to Hungarian rule perceiving itself as a 'subject', and perceived by others as an 'object' (Lasić 1997a, 30). Lasić refers in his article to *The Flags* which covered the period from 1912 to 1922, described as 'ten bloody years' and characterised by imperialistic conquering and Serbian state expansionism (Lasić 1997a, 31). In order to overcome the numerous contradictions accumulated among the Balkan nations together with domination of the mythical past, Krleža promoted instead the creativity of the scientific, cultural, artistic and 'spiritual' conquest, opposing authoritarian discipline and lack of freedom (Lasić 1997a, 31). It remains thought-provoking that following the publication of *The Flags* and its success in 1960s, Krleža's was asked about his view concerning the 'Europeanisation' of Yugoslav literature at the time. He responded that in the Yugoslav literary history there were no 'non-European' periods, hence he did not understand why it had to be 'Europeanised' at all (Krleža 1966, 9).

The European 'Book'

The legacy and use of Krleža's thematic and analytic instruments in the articulation of the 'national' during the 1990s emerges also in Croatian cultural debates of the time. Following the publication of *Romani krize* [The Crisis Novels] in 1996 by Igor Mandić, a Croatian and former Yugoslav literary critic, there was an open public discussion over issues of post-conflict relations with Serbia and the persisting Croatian dilemma regarding its relations with 'Europe'. Mandić's book, even though of purely literary nature, included both Croatian and Serbian novels from the 1980s (Mandić 1996). As it was not feasible to publish it in the Croatian context at the time, ultimately the book was published in Belgrade. Its stormy public reception in Croatia was followed by an engaging public correspondence between Mandić and Lasić in the cultural journal *Vijenac* during 1997. Their correspondence discussed the historical relation between the Croatian and Serbian literature where Lasić metaphorically defined 1990s Serbian literary production as '*Bulgarian literature*", hence distinguishing it from the Croatian literature and placing it outside the sphere of his interests (Lasić 1997b, 15). On the other hand, Mandić argued differently by underlining the necessity to recognise the presence of a shared common past (Mandić 1997, 16). This correspondence resulted in a larger public confrontation known under the metaphor of the 'Bulgarian question' of Croatian culture, whereby the wider public and intellectuals granted their support to Lasić, marginalising Mandić's view.

This additional layer of the debate tackled more specifically perceptions of Europe in the 1990s and was discussed in two other letters written in late 1997 by Stanko Lasić to the well-known Croatian 'Krležologists' Vlaho Bogišić (b. 1960), and once again to Igor Mandić (Lasić 2004, 478–491, 493–496). The letters indicated an additional tonality related to the 'Bulgarian question' debate in which Lasić called for re-contextualisation of his own arguments in order to understand truly his opinions. Lasić acknowledged that his initial judgements were a consequence of the 1990s war with Serbia. Perhaps, even more importantly, he stated, the discussion was founded in his lasting obsession with the so-called European 'Book'. He thus alluded to the notion of European cultural totality, and his persisting dilemma related to Croatian belonging to it (Lasić 2004, 495). Hence, Lasić concluded that in context of 'European' literature, Croatian, Serbian and other regional literatures, all remain distanced and metaphorically 'Bulgarian literatures' (Lasić 2004, 495). Lasić continued to find extremely difficult to accept that Croatia was on the sidelines of this European cultural totality (Lasić 2004, 495).

The debate was also discussed by Boris Buden in a critical magazine *Arkzin* opposing the war and widespread articulation of the 'national' in the 1990s Croatia. As a response to the 'Bulgarian question' debate the magazine challenged the expressed viewpoints and instituted an ironic literary prize 'Bulgarica', which in 1996 was awarded to David Albahari as the first author from Serbia published in Croatia at the time. Further to this, in his collected volume *Barikade* [The Barricades] published in 1996/7 and 1998 respectively, Buden reflected upon an articulation of that 'national' that focused on an existing connection between intellectuals and the 'national project' in Croatia. In his essay, *Mudri predsjednikov savjetnik Miroslav Krleža* [The President's Wise Counsellor Miroslav Krleža] Buden quoted Stanko Lasić who envisaged the role of a 'counsellor' for Miroslav Krleža to the Croatian president Franjo Tuđman in order to realise the Croatian statehood with fewer victims (Visković in Buden 1996/7, 42–43). Buden indicated that existing discrepancies in the Croatian intellectual milieu during the 1990s remained indifferent towards severe social misconducts, while at the same time becoming wholeheartedly involved when discussing the national matters (Visković in Buden 1996/7, 41). Buden argued that Lasić's statement was beyond an immediate political contextualisation and it should have been considered more broadly through the reflection about the role of Krleža and the whole Croatian intellectual heritage (Visković in Buden 1996/7, 44–45).

Revisiting Narrative Trends in the Post-2000

In the previous sections, the transformation of the regional rhetoric of the bordering processes was closely associated with the pursuit of the national project during the 1990s. In the post-2000 period national self-identification processes as represented in literary production, become associated with new imaginaries allowing space for novel themes and reinterpretation of the past legacies.[7] During this period, Croatia once again parts from its regional neighbourhood while revisiting an affiliation of its cultural heritage in the context of Mitteleuropean and, respectively, Mediterranean cultural traditions. It is noteworthy that the actual origins of these processes in the Croatian cultural narratives have existed in different forms prior to 1989 and national independence in 1991. What remains significant in our context is the ability of post-2000 narratives to re-consider these trajectories related to identity search, and to offer an alternative response to the predominantly national rhetoric of the 1990s.[8] Furthermore, albeit with a rather distinct geographical focus on Central Europe and the Mediterranean, these accounts mirror each other in a number of ways. Both interpretations represent new theoretical frameworks that introduce the national identity search into space beyond the strict national boundaries as a part of 'cross-cultural space', 'geopolitical totality' and moving 'beyond geography'. The related authors analyse the multiplicity of regional identity layers and apply new theoretical frameworks, such as post-modernism and post-colonialism, while neverthe-less maintaining 'Krležianity' as one of the central explorative matrixes. These two accounts are complemented through more recent revisionist assessments of a younger generation of regional authors that discuss the borders of national identity building in the context of so-called 'post-Yugoslav space' providing a third response to the altering 'regional rhetoric' and bordering practices in the post-2000 period.

Literature as History

One of the significant aspects related to the post-2000 Croatian literary narratives is its further departure from the Balkans and its relations with the Mitteleuropean cultural tradition. In this respect, the work of Nikola Petković (b.1962) is particularly valuable as the author adopts new theoretical framework and attempts to re-conceptualise the unified cultural past of Central Europe including also Croatian cultural heritage. Petković proposes an approach that links literature with the study of history and borders and draws on the corrective functions of literature and its ability to capture individual accounts; thus indicating the true history (Petković 2003a, 7–8). For this purpose, the author employs theoretical frameworks associated with post-modernism and post-colonialism arguing that the term 'colonialism' and 'post-colonialism' are seldom discussed in the history of ideas, cultural studies and literature in the Central Europe (Petković 2003a, 7). Reference to the post-colonial theoretical context is important also for further under-standing of scholarship that since 1990s has introduced notions of 'Orientalism' and, respectively, 'Balkanism' when studying identity issues in the regional context.[9] Following the disintegration of the Yugoslav federation and the emergence of new sovereign states, identity building processes, both in the context of 'post-conflict' and of European integration, were discussed in an emerging body of literature connected with the frameworks of 'Orientalism' and, respectively, 'Balkanism'. These concepts mediated through post-colonial theoretical models aimed at addressing the multiplicity of regional identity layers and integrating research on the Balkans in a wider framework of international studies. Petković's post-colonial framework, dis-tinct from the well-established scholarship evolving from the 'orientalist' tradition, actually moves away from the Balkans and more importantly, uses Miroslav Krleža's opus in its conceptual framework.[10]

In order to understand more recent historical dynamics in Central Europe, Petković has underlined the importance of the emerging sub-discipline of 'literature as history' (Petković 2003a, 7). The author focuses on the 'geocultural reality' of Central Europe, recognising its peculiar post-1989 transformations together with its unique historical tradition (Petković 2003b, 13–14). The spatiality of his project envisages Central Europe along the notion of Benedict Anderson's imagined communities with no precise geography or dominant culture and as a 'cross-cultural space' (Petković 2003b, 7–8) What remains significant for the present work is that the author ultimately extends the boundaries of Mitteleuropean cultural tradition by also including in its framework 'voices from the margins'. Together with the Italian author Claudio Magris, Miroslav Krleža now becomes the representative of these marginalised voices of Central Europe (Petković 2003b, 18). While Magris refers to the 'geopolitical totality of Mitteleuropa' following political and cultural narratives of the Danubian basin, Krleža's enquiry is directed towards the 'culturally colonised reality' of Southern Central Europe that eventually combines viewpoints from these two different types of margins: Danubian and South Central European (Petković 2003b, 17–18). The author argues further that the 'Central European culture continues to impose itself as an 'imagined community' on the identities and the lives of its intellectuals and authors, even when it has no official existence' in the geopolitical making of a region which is perpetually postcolonial (Petković 2003b, 9–10).

The legacy of Krleža's literary framework is also manifested in Petković's identity enquiry that down-scales the narrative from the national to the individual level and provides an intersection between often disputed national and personal identities. The strong inclination of Petković's work towards inclusion of social reality from an inter-generational and individual perspective further demonstrates the deployment of Krleža's thematic structures (Petković 2010, 240).

'Ploughing of the Sea': Mediterranean Response[11]

In Petković's work *Kaptolski kolodvor Predraga Matvejevića* [Predrag Matvejević's Kaptol Station] (2013) the author takes the themes discussed above even further and examines emerging identity forms in the works of Predrag Matvejević's (1932–2017). Petković discusses Matvejević's work in the context of the extraterritorial nature of literature and addresses topics such as departing, de-territorialisation, and living in-between asylum and exile (Petković 2013, 88–89). Matvejević's authorship, renowned for his insightful cultural history of the Mediterranean, here offers a bridge between the Mitteleuropean and the Mediterranean narratives. Moreover, his literary writings once again reflect the cultural pattern and legacy of Miroslav Krleža.

CROSS-BORDER COOPERATION

Predrag Matvejević, important Croatian and former Yugoslav intellectual, literary critic, writer and 'Krležologists', has extended the spatiality of the Balkans towards the Mediterranean Sea in his famous book *Mediteranski brevijar* [Mediterranean Breviary] (1987) translated and reprinted in numerous editions from 1990s onwards. Matvejević has described the Mediterranean as the founding place of Europe that is located beyond geography with undefined borders both in space and time (Matvejević 1996, 18). In his Breviary, the author recalls Miroslav Krleža's vision about the south-Slavs as a third component between Orient and Occident discussing their presence in the Mediterranean (Matvejević 1987, 137–138). Matvejević indicated that Krleža was neither passionate about the sea, nor about the Mediterraneans. Instead, Matvejević perceives Krleža more as a writer belonging to Mitteleuropa, even though Krleža himself would have disagreed (Matvejević 1987, 138). This complex interplay between maritime and continental enquiries brings the two regional narratives of Mitteleuropa and Mediterranean closer and indicates additional dimensions in Croatian narratives with respect to the Balkans and Europe. In fact, Claudio Magris (b.1939) wrote an introduction to Matvejević's book representing him as an important voice of the Mitteleuropa who wrote a remarkable book about the Mediterranean (Magris in Matvejević 1987, 1).

The other significant work of Matvejević in this context is his *Razgovori s Miroslavom Krleža* [The Conversations with Miroslav Krleža] (1969), that, among other themes, touches upon the so-called 'Central-European' complex developed by Krleža who identified such categorisations as 'phantoms' resulting out of literary fiction and nostalgias (Matvejević 1969, 95–97). Hence, the revival of a Mitteleuropean narratives carries out an inherent duality. It responds to the Croatian national narratives by situating them within a larger Central European heritage, and thus it introduces a novel spatiality, methodological apparatus and collocation of the national self. However, rather than actually originating from established and grounded cultural premises, the narratives and the very need towards its explorations are arguably a product of a specific historical time. The comprehensive direction of the Mediterranean narratives is not only perceived through its close relation with the Central European imaginary, but it is also integrated into long-standing accounts related to the Adriatic Sea.[12] The Adriatic narratives, nonetheless, traces different thematic directions and has enquired more specifically into the notion of 'liminality'[13] in the context of neighbouring countries such as Croatia and Italy.[14]

The focus of Croatian post-2000 literary narratives on the Mediterranean region reconfirms its moving away from the Balkan cultural heritage. Even if the narratives have more profound origins and they are not entirely grounded in the post-2000 period, it appears as an alternative response to the articulation of national rhetoric in the 1990s. Reframing Croatian

The Revival of 'Our' Space

The 1990s dominant national imaginary has evolved in a way that contextualises the post-2000 Croatian cultural heritage within described Mitteleuropean and Mediterranean tradition. In the more recent literary and cultural narratives there is nonetheless also a re-emergence of regional cross-border initiatives in the so-called 'post-Yugoslav space'. This is conceptualised as a third alternative response in the context of the changing 'regional rhetoric'. Here narratives expend and continuously readjust the boundaries of the region. The primary significance of this third approach is its capacity to revive those themes that were discussed in the federal Yugoslav context since 1980s and also debated among the 'Krležologists'. They encompass issues such as active citizenship, nationalism, post-conflict perceptions of Eastern neighbours, regional relations with Europe and the European integration process. These discussions are captured in critical scholarship and literary works that belong to a younger generation of regional authors who commonly define the space where these themes are discussed as the 'post-Yugoslav space'.

Questions related to a former Yugoslav identity and its new embodiments are examined in the works of authors from the region born from the mid-1960s onwards. Their work reflects a multiplicity of identities as it is interwoven in the lives of people from the region, including author's own families backgrounds, the languages they use in their writings, differing native and workplaces. Vladimir Arsenijević (b.1965) argued that these multiple identities were tolerated and integrated in the former-Yugoslav context, following the breakup of federal state. This sensitive and subjective question for many, including himself, has been resolved in being the '(post)Yugoslav writer' (Arsenijević 2009, 172). For instance, he defines his language of use as an eastern idiom of the language called Croatian, Bosnian, Montenegrin, or Serbian that is accessible for readership throughout the 'BIHCGHRSR-space'[15] (Arsenijević 2009, 172). Arsenijević has also presented the post-Yugoslav literary style and its rhetorical devices as an author's ability to bypass chauvinist and nationalist agendas and embrace more open worldviews (Arsenijević 2009, 166). He argued that regional authorship has moved from an academic postmodernist 'discourse' and has started to use a new language style that expresses more directly their political opinions (Arsenijević 2009, 166). The notion of 'space', irrespective of how it is named or by which borders it is confined, Arsenijević argues, remains exactly what it was before all the wars in the 1990s, namely 'Our' space (Arsenijević

2009, 172). Neither the arrival of new borders, national flags, coats of arms or anthems, could succeed in changing this spatial reality where, regardless of the dramatic experiences lived by the inhabitants of the Western Balkans, Arsenijević argues, a persisting sense of proximity remains simultaneously a curse and a blessing (2009, 172–173). It is precisely this sense of proximity that remains the foundation of: a post-Yugoslav literature, but also music and film, the post-Yugoslav subcultures and alternative streams, as well as the post-Yugoslav 'trash'; all of this emerges from this – *Our* – post-Yugoslav space (Arsenijević 2009, 173).

The existence of this peculiar space and proximity among its inhabitants has also provided the foundation for regional academic and cultural projects where the trans-national dimension dominates over the national. For instance, in more recent scholarship such as the work of Katarina Luketić (b.1969), it is possible to find a critical re-assessment related to the 'national project' in the context of regional socio-political agenda (Luketić in Čolović 2009, 90). Luketić calls for a transformation of political concepts such as 'the national' and 'the ethical' in Croatia into the notion of active citizenship, hence transforming the understanding of national identity as a primary element of Croatian independent statehood. Luketić's enquiry was a part of a collected volume published on the occasion of the twentieth anniversary of the fall of the Berlin Wall. It was conceived as a regional response following two decades of the existence of a unified European political space. In contrast to the post-1989 transformations in the rest of the Eastern European context where the old socialist system was transformed with an open call towards democracy, the former Yugoslav case appeared as rather different resulting in the domination of national politics and the ethnicisation of society, violence and warfare of the 1990s (Luketić in Čolović 2009, 79). Following the elections in the 1990s, in Serbia 'nationalism' that became the state ideology and in Croatia the heritage of so-called 'national silence',[16] both have influenced revival of the national self-identification processes in the respective countries (Luketić in Čolović 2009, 85–86).

In this context, it is significant that a number of *Arkzin* issues, a critical anti-war magazine from 1990s, were republished in the late 2013 with the implication that the contentious socio-political debates about the use of the Latin and the Cyrillic alphabets in Croatia signalled a return to 1990s. Miljenko Jergović (b.1970) wrote on the occasion of the twenty-fifth anniversary of Miroslav Krleža's passing away, stating that Krleža was no longer remembered by society and his writings remained deeply unread regardless of his importance for the Croatian literature, comparable to the role of Goethe in German or Njegoš in Montenegrin literatures (2010, 299).[17] Jergović argued that in contemporary Croatia, Krleža is not widely read because his fierce critique of society during his times could equally be applicable to the contemporary times, particularly in relation to contentious national identity issues embedded into questions of language and religion (Jergović 2010, 300).

Concluding Notes

The understanding of the 'regional rhetoric' in Croatian narratives and respective bordering processes remains inseparable from the understanding of changing national and regional socio-political trends. The work has illustrated the significance of lasting search among the Balkan nations towards embodiment of their national being. In the Croatian context, this is manifested through the pursuit of the national project, relations with its neighbours and relations with Europe. The article focused particularly on the formation of Croatian national identity described in literary text, and its main currents and protagonists in the social realm. The work argued that the articulation of the national and perception of borders in the literary narratives had faithfully resembled the transformation of national identity, where the literary sphere acted as an alternative space for public discussions about the national identity dilemmas. The narratives moved beyond its literary frame becoming not only a direct reflection of regional socio-political realities but shaping this in its turn. Hence, qualifying in the context of existing disciplinary and theoretical frameworks associated with identity enquiries in the Balkans. The selected literary sources showed that the post-independence period of the 1990s was characterised by a reclusive understanding of the national identity that was gradually transformed only in the post-2000 period. The dilemmas connected with the national identity pursuit were further explored as a part of post-2000 literary narratives that has outstandingly mirrored an altering 'regional rhetoric' and new bordering processes associating the Croatian national identity with Mitteleuropean, Mediterranean and post-Yugoslav space. The post-2000 literary narratives proposed an alternative response to the predominantly national rhetoric of the 1990s and introduced the critical identity examination of younger generation of regional authors.

In the context of Croatia, the literary narratives confirm the historically intriguing relationship between national, regional and European influences. These correlated processes have been substantially examined in the literary works of prominent Croatian and Yugoslav writer Miroslav Krleža. The critical articulation of 'national' has been one of the primary concerns behind Krleža's opus that inspired successive generations of future 'Krležologists' to take further his deliberative heritage. The themes derived from 'Krležianity' analysing the national issues and identity building processes are also of contemporary interest as a part of understanding of changing border perceptions in the Balkans. Indeed, 2013 introduced a significant new landmark in

CROSS-BORDER COOPERATION

the context of regional border perception following Croatian membership in the European Union. Miljenko Jergović acknowledged this new topographic dimension by suggesting that, rather than as an event that could bring direct economic benefit, this occasion should be understood as producing an 'order-ness' where the destinies of Croatia and its eastern neighbourhood would finally be interrelated with the destinies of Paris, Prague, Berlin and other European cities (Jergović 2011).

Acknowledgments

The present research is associated with the FP7 project 'Bordering, Political Landscapes and Social Arenas: Potentials and Challenges of Evolving Border Concepts in a post-Cold War World (Euborderscapes)' coordinated by the University of Eastern Finland (UEF) in partnership with the Queen's University Belfast and the Centre for Advanced Study Sofia (CAS). The author expresses gratitude to editors, reviewers and project teams for their generous support, and to Milena Komarova and anonymous reviewer for their editorial work.

Funding

This work was supported by the Seventh Framework Programme.

Notes

1. The notion of '(in)definite topography' was developed from Igor Mandić's term 'inaccurate topography' used in reference to Miroslav Krleža's novel *Povratak Filipa Latinovicza* [The Return of Filip Latinovicz] (1932) (Mandić 2012, 20–21).
2. For further information on this discussion please see (Buden 2002; Mandić 2012; Petković 2013).
3. The Krleža's speech at the Congress of Yugoslav writers in Ljubljana during 1952 ended so-called 'dispute on literary left' (1928–2952). For further information please see (Krleža 1952, 206; Lasić 1970; Boškov 1987, 446; Visković 2012).
4. For further reference on 'Teleology' please see Lasić (2013).
5. Extract from Lasić's essay: 'During the spring of 1970s, when I have travelled to Prague and I was to encounter Brezhnev's troupes that have shattered the Prague's spring, I had remained for some days in Vienna. As it was my habit during those mornings, I went out to the street at dawn. Vienna was still sleeping. I was roaming around and slowly went into the direction of the Cathedral. I was walking in the middle of the street, there was no traffic and street lights were still on. The early birds broke the morning silence and then suddenly there were sharp voices. Someone was speaking Croatian, shouting, mumbling, weeping, cursing, threatening and calling. I was turning all around and there was nobody. I needed some time to grasp that these voices were coming from the below of me. At the underground level of ten to fifteen meters in the water until the waist, half-naked, bloody and dirty, with yellow helmets on their heads, and with the muscles as gorillas, shouting as tribal savages, swallowing mud and underground gases – my people were working. I was looking at these canals, in these holes, for a long time. Ten minutes, perhaps the whole eternity. I turned around,

walking sharply to the hotel, packed my luggage and disappeared from Vienna.' (Lasić 1992, 5–6, author's translation).

6. The term 'Zastave', specifically related to M. Krleža's novel, in the present work is translated as 'The Flags' where in literary translations the term 'The Banners' would be more accurate.

7. It is noteworthy that bordering process is not only spatial but has also been reflected in transformation of the national language itself. During the Yugoslav times, the language was codified as Serbo-Croatian that after the national independence has changed into Croatian and, respectively, other national languages in the neighbouring countries. For more information about evolution of this issue please see document and debates related to *Deklaracija o nazivu i položaju hrvatskog književnog jezika* [Declaration on the Name and Position of Standard Croatian (1967)].

8. To some extent, Lasić's perceptions related to the existence of Mitteleuropean space are discussed in his book review of Dor (1996), reviewed by Lasić originally in French (1999). Dor (1923–2005) as a contemporary Austrian author born in Budapest and raised in Serbia claimed an existence of spiritual totality of Mitteleuropa located from Florence to Prague, from Istria to Vojvodina, from Venice to Đerdap, from Dubrovnik to Budapest. He used a novelistic rather than critical scientific way of presenting the Central European imaginary relating his argument mainly to the work of Claudio Magris. Part of these imaginaries include also the Balkans where Dor avoids nationalist arguments, bypasses nations and rather includes the cities and provinces. As a consequence, his references towards Belgrade and Serbia in the 1990s are challenged by Lasić who perceived him as a dreamer (Lasić 2004, 353–355).

9. It is significant to note that notion of 'Balkanism' has been perceived distinctively from 'Orientalism' in regional scholarship and has been further interpreted differently as it has originated from distinct scholarly traditions. For further reference please see (Bjelić and Savić 2003; Buden 2002; Luketić 2013; Todorova 2010).

10. Milica Bakić-Hayden that has worked on Balkan identity issues since 1990s and developed a recognised well-known concept of 'nesting orientalism'. She noted that long prior to the publication of Maria Todorova's book Imagining the Balkans (Todorova 1997), her professor Roland Inden had been working on the book Imagining India in 1990 (Bloomington: Indiana University Press). Bakić-Hayden perceives Inden's work as a model for epistemic critique of the orientalist literature on India expanding also the framework of Edward Said's analysis. She further notes that precisely Inden's seminars have inspired her to apply the 'orientalist' model in the 1990s Yugoslav context. Furthermore, the strong presence of a post-colonial theoretical framework in the regional intellectual dimension indicates need for an additional research correlating the post-colonialism with the use of post-modernism and post-socialism. Please see: (Bakić-Hayden 2006, 10,15; Vlaisavljević 2006; Sarkanjac 2009).

11. The Ploughing of the Sea' is a symbolic concept that belongs to Simón Bolivar. Please see further: Palavestra (2001).

12. For thematic publications on an Adriatic narratives please see (Cocco and Minardi 2007, Ivetic 2014; Marin 2007; Matvejević 2005; Tomizza 2007).

13. Aljoša Pužar has developed his writings in Croatian context starting from the theme related to 'our' borderlands and different minority aspects referring to Croatian city of Rijeka (Fiume) that has lived its authentic and disputed history of belonging to present-day Croatia, Hungary and Italy (Pužar 2007, 6–8).

14. The work of Sanja Roić's is dedicated to the understanding of cultural and literary rapport between Croatia and Italy focusing on the individuals from the so-called 'margins' or 'border'. Some literary authors in her research are presented as belonging

CROSS-BORDER COOPERATION

139

to the eastern Adriatic yet actually they belong to both cultures; some have spent significant time in the Croatian context while others went in the opposite direction having travelled to Italy. Roić enquires into the language used by these writers introducing the notion of 'foreigner in the homeland' (Roić 2006, 7–8).

15. The author uses a reference 'BIHCGHRSR-space' that indicates acronyms of the following countries: Bosnia and Herzegovina (BIH), Montenegro/ Crna Gora (CG), Croatia/Hrvatska (HR) and Serbia (SR).

16. The notion of 'Croatian silence' ('hrvatska šutnja') is a reference towards an attitude of Croatian socialist authorities during the Yugoslav federation towards issues of a national relevance as for instance the status of the Croatian language (Croatian Spring 1968). In the 1990s arguably this attitude dating back to 1960s has influenced a greater acceptance of the nationalism on the state level (Luketić in Čolović 2009, 85).

17. Rather than in the Croatian literature, there is a more recent revival of Krleža's work in the theatre plays. During 'Dubrovnik Summer Festival' in 2018, Slovenian director Sebastijan Horvat produced a theatre play '*Michelangelo*' offering more contemporary reading of Krleža. Already previously based on Krleža's work, Horvat directed in 2014 '*Hrvatski bog Mars*' (Croatian God Mars) in Zagreb's Gavella Drama Theatre, and in 2015 '*Hrvatska rapsodija*' (Croatian Rhapsody) re-named into '*Nad grobom glupe Europe*' (At the Grave of Stupid Europe) in Croatian National Theatre Ivan Zajc in Rijeka (Pavić 2018, 55).

18. Arguably Jergović refers to Krleža's critical attitude and dual identity being equally 'Croatian' and a 'former Yugoslav' (2010, 300).

References

Arsenijević, V. 2009. *Jugolaboratorija* [Yugolaborotory]. Beograd: Biblioteka XX vek.

Bakić-Hayden, M. 2006. *Varijacije na temu 'Balkan'* [Variations on the Theme of 'Balkans']. Beograd: Institut za filozofiju i društvenu teoriju I.P."Filip Višnjić".

Bjelić, D., and O. Savić, eds. 2003. *Balkan kao metafora: Između globalizacije i fragmentacije* [Balkan as Metaphor: Between Globalisation and Fragmentation]. Beograd: Biblioteca Collectenea, Beogradski krug.

Boškov, Ž., ed. 1987. *Leksikon pisaca Jugoslavije* [The Encyclopaedia of Yugoslav Writers], 446. Beograd: Matica Srpska.

Buden, B. 2002. *Kaptolski kolodvor. Politički eseji* [The Kaptol's Station. Political Esseys]. Beograd: Centar za savremenu umetnost.

Cocco, E., and E. Minardi, ed. 2007. *Immaginare l'Adriatico: Contributi alla riscoperta sociale di uno spazio di frontiera* [Immagining Adriatic: Contributions Towards the Social Rediscovery of Border Spaces]. Milano: Franco Angeli.

Čolović, I. ed. 2009. *Zid je mrtav, živeli zidovi! Pad Berlinskog zida i raspad Jugoslavije* [The Wall is Dead, Long Live the Walls! The Fall of the Berlin Wall and Breakup of Yugoslavia]. Beograd: Biblioteka XX vek.

Dor, M. 1996. *Mitteleuropa, Mythos oder Wirklichkeit* [Mitteleuropa. Myth and Reality]. Salzburg: Otto Müller Verlag.

Ivetic, E. 2014. *Un confine nel Mediterraneo: L'Adriatico orientale tra Italia e Slavia (1300–1900)* [A Boundary in Mediterranean: Oriental Adriatic Between Italy and Slavia (1300–1900)]. Roma: Viella.

Jergović, M. 2010. *Zagrebačke kronike* [Zagreb's Chronicle]. Beograd: Biblioteka XX vek.

Jergović, M. 2011. *Hrvatska u EU: Ne može biti da to nije dobro* [Croatia in the EU: It Could Not Be Other than Good]. Accessed December 10, 2018. http://www.politika.rs/rubrike/Pogledi-sa-strane/Hrvatska-u-EU-ne-moze-biti-da-to-nije-dobro.lt.html.

Krleža, M. 1932. *Moj obračun sa njima* [My Settling of the Scores With Them]. Zagreb: Self-published.

Krleža, M. 1952. Govor na kongresu književnika u Ljubljani [The Speech at Congress of Yugoslav Writers in Ljubljana]. *Republika* 8-2 (10–11):206, 239, 242.

Krleža, M. 1954. *Povratak Filipa Latinovicza* [The Return of Filip Latinovicz]. Zagreb: Zora.

Krleža, M. 1966. Njegoševo ime daje nagradi i književni i politički značaj [The Njegoš's Name Provides Literary and Political Significance to the Award]. *Pobjeda* 2551:9.

Krleža, M. 1967. *Zastave* [The Flags]. Zagreb: Zora.

Lasić, S. 1970. *Sukob na književnoj ljevici 1928–1952* [The Dispute of the Literary Left 1928–1952]. Zagreb: Liber.

Lasić, S. 1974. *Struktura Krležinih 'Zastava'* [The Structure of Krleža's 'The Flags']. Zagreb: Liber.

Lasić, S. 1992. *Tri eseja o Evropi* [The Three Essays About Europe]. Zagreb: Hrvatsko vijeće Europskog pokreta.

Lasić, S. 1997a. Zastave kao Krležina filozofija povijesti [The Flags as Krleža's Philosophy of History]. *Lettre Internationale* 7 (19–20):23–34.

Lasić, S. 1997b. Moral tjeskobe (Pismo Igoru Mandiću) [The Morality of Anxiety (Letter to Igor Mandić)]. *Vijenac* V (93–94):14–15.

Lasić, S. 2004. *Članci, razgovori, pisma* [The Articles, Conversations, Letters]. Zagreb: Gordogan.

Lasić, S. 2013. In *Hrvatski bibliografski leksikon* [Encyclopaedia of Croatian Biography], ed. T. Macan, 564–65. Zagreb: Leksikografski zavod Miroslav Krleža.

Luketić, K. 2009. Prošlost je naša budućnost [The Past is our Future]. In *Zid je mrtav, živeli zidovi! Pad Berlinskog zida i raspad Jugoslavije* [The Wall is Dead, Long Live the Walls! The Fall of the Berlin Wall and Breakup of Yugoslavia], ed. I. Čolović, 76–106. Beograd: Biblioteka XX vek.

Luketić, K. 2013. *Balkan: Od geografije do fantazije* [The Balkans: From Geography to Fantasy]. Zagreb: Algoritam.

Mandić, I. 1989. Romani krize [The Crisis Novels]. In *Novija srpska književnost i kritika ideologije* [The Recent Serbian Literature and Ideology Critique], ed. P. Palavestra, 65–66. Beograd, Niš: SANU.

Mandić, I. 1996. *Romani krize* [The Crisis Novels]. Beograd: Prosveta.

Mandić, I. 1997. Vježbanje skromnosti (Pismo Stanku Lasiću) [The Exercising of Modesty (Letter to Stanko Lasić)]. *Vijenac* V (93–94):16–17.

Mandić, I. 2012. Povratak krležijanstvu (?!) Dobar dan krležoljupcima i onima koji se takvima prave [The Return to Krležianity (?!) Greetings to Krleža's Admirers and Those Pretending to Be]. *Književna republika (Zagreb)* 10-7 (9):20–24.

Marin, B. 2007. *Le due rive: Reportages adriatici in prosa e in versi* [Two Shores: Adriatic Reportages in Prose and Verses]. Reggio Emilia: Diabasis.

Matvejević, P. 1969. *Razgovori s Miroslavom Krležom* [The Conversations with Miroslav Krleža]. Zagreb: Napried.

Matvejević, P. 1982. *Razgovori s Miroslavom Krležom* [The Conversations with Miroslav Krleža]. Zagreb: Spektar.

Matvejević, P. 1987. *Breviario Mediterraneo* [Mediterranean Breviary]. Milano: Garzanti.

Matvejević, P. 1996. *Mediterraneo Un nuovo breviario* [Mediterranean A New Breviary]. Milano: Garzanti.

Matvejević, P. 2005. Introduzione. In *Un mare: Orizzonte adriatico* [A Sea: Adriatic Horizon], ed. F. Fiori. Reggio Emilia: Diabasis.

Palavestra, P. 2001. *Orali smo more* [We ploughed the Sea]. Beograd: NIN.

CROSS-BORDER COOPERATION

Pavić, S. 2018. Michelangelo na Lokrumu je kazališni događaj ljeta [Michelangelo on Lokrum is the theatre event of the summer]. *Jutarnji list* 21 (7):55.

Petković, N. 2003a. *Srednja Europa: Zbilja-mit-utopija. Postmodernizam, postkolonijalizam, postkomunizam i odsutnost autentičnosti* [A Central Europe: Reality-Myth-Utopia. Postmodernism, Postcolonialism, Postcommunism and the Absence of Authenticity]. Rijeka: Adamić.

Petković, N. 2003b. *A central europe of our own – Postmodernism, postcolonialism, postcommunism and the absence of authenticity.* Rijeka: Adamić.

Petković, N. 2010. *Identitet i granica: Hibridnost i jezik, kultura i građanstvo 21. stoljeća* [Identity and Border: Hybridism and Language, Culture and Citizenship of 21st century]. Zagreb: Naklada Jesenski i Turk.

Petković, N. 2013. Kaptolski kolodvor Predraga Matvejevića' [Predrag Matvejević's Kaptol Station]. *Književna republika (Zagreb)* 4–6 (4–5):87–92.

Pužar, A. 2007. *Granice Granice: Studije i ogledi* [Borders of the Border: Enquiries and Essays]. Pula: Nova Istra.

Roić, S. 2006. *Stranci: Portreti s margine, granice i periferije* [The Foreigners: Portraits from the Margins, Borders and Periphery]. Zagreb: Hrvatska sveučilišna naklada.

Sarkanjac, B. 2009. *Po svoe: Makedonski katahrezis ili Kako da se zboruva za Makedonija* [Our way: The Macedonian Catachresis or How it Should be Spoken About Macedonia]. Skopje: Makavej.

Todorova, M. 1997. *Imagining the Balkans.* Oxford: Oxford University Press.

Todorova, M. 2010. *Balgaria, Balkanite, svetat: Idei, procesi, sabitia* [Bulgaria, Balkans, and the World: Ideas, Processes, Events]. Sofia: Prosveta.

Tomizza, F. 2007. *Adriatico e altre rotte: Viaggi e reportage* [Adriatic and Other Routes: Travels and Reportages]. Reggio Emilia: Diabasis.

Visković, V. 1993. In *Republika (Zagreb, 1945): 'Lasić, za i protiv' Razgovor o Krležologiji I-VI. Stanka Lasića održan u prostorijama DHK, 19.X.1993* ['Lasić, for and against' A Discussion about Krležology I-VI held in the premises of DHK, 19.X.1993], ed. V. Radaković-Vinchierutti, vols. 49–50/1–3, 40–60. Zagreb: Republika.

Visković, V. 1996/7. In *Barikade II* [The Barricades II], ed. B. Buden. Zagreb: Biblioteka Bastard.

Visković, V. 2012. *Krležijana. Encikopedija Miroslava Krleže'* [Krležijana. Miroslav Krleža's Encyclopaedia]. Zagreb: Leksikografski zavod Miroslav Krleža. Accessed December 11, 2018. http://krlezijana.lzmk.hr/clanak.aspx?id=1781.

Vlaisavljević, U. 2006. *Etnopolitika i građanstvo* [Ethnopolitics and Citizenship]. Mostar: Dijalog.

Re-Thinking Border Politics at the Sarajevo Film Festival: Alternative Imaginaries of Conflict Transformation and Cross-Border Encounters

Maria-Adriana Deiana ⓘ

ABSTRACT
EU peacebuilding efforts in Bosnia-Herzegovina have largely contributed to further cement stark geopolitical imaginaries that, on the one hand, crystallise belonging along exclusionary and fixed notions of ethnonational identity and, on the other, reify civilisational differences between the EU and the post-Yugoslav space. The kaleidoscopic lens of the borderscape opens opportunities to move beyond this impasse by highlighting alternative narratives and sites of border politics that are often overlooked in institutionalised approaches. At the interface between aesthetics, cultural politics and post-conflict transformations, the Sarajevo Film Festival provides a privileged vantage point to explore border negotiations and harness opportunities for conflict transformation through the medium of cinema.

Introduction

On my last day at the 2015 Sarajevo Film Festival (SFF), I attended the screening of *One Day in Sarajevo* (2015), a documentary film/project which earned Bosnian director Jasmila Žbanić the festival's Human Rights Award. Composed by fragments filmed in Sarajevo on 28 June 2014, the piece is set on the 100th anniversary of the assassination of Franz Ferdinand which sparked the beginning of the First World War. The film depicts how the celebrations held in the city attracted a large and incongruent entourage made of tourists, EU officials and funders, fans of historic re-enactments, defenders and detractors of Gavrilo Princip, anti-EU and anti-capitalist protesters, and of course local Sarajevans. Alongside the frenzy of the celebrations are scenes of ordinary life: a traditional wedding, the large shopping centres recently mushroomed in the city's precarious economy, a local memorial service at Princip's tomb, a father returning to Sarajevo for the summer with his two children. Continuously switching between multiple perspectives, the film is thought-provoking and

CROSS-BORDER COOPERATION   143

demanding in its visualisation of complex intersections and tensions between local everyday experiences, national(ist) and transnational imaginaries converging into the city. Through shifting points of views and ambivalent perspectives, the anniversary celebrations become a catalyst for action and memory that raises questions about Sarajevo's contested history, its symbolic status as site of warfare, as well as on Bosnia-Herzegovina's (BiH's) unresolved status in Europe. A certain dissensual energy imbues the film that unsettles conventional geopolitical imagination by stubbornly re-inserting Sarajevo's life post-conflict into the map and history of Europe. *One Day in Sarajevo* works to momentarily lift the *cage* of isolation and international marginalisation, projecting Bosnia's neglected everyday experiences and unfulfilled promises of peace at the centre stage in the complex and ambiguous European imaginary the film 'scapes'.

The presentation of Žbanić's film at the SFF, alongside a panel titled 'Take down the Fences', made its aesthetic enactment and geopolitical re-orientation even more poignant. From a vernacular site of cultural resistance born out of the conflict and the city's siege, the SFF has now entered the international festival circuit as a specialised event for the promotion of cinema and cultural co-operation from/in Central and South-East Europe. This reconfiguration has seen a shift from its initial emphasis on international cinema for a local audience to an outward-looking regional and international platform.[1] Albeit temporarily, the Festival has become an annual occasion in which Sarajevo garners international spotlight not exclusively as site of (post)warfare but also as the home to the art of cinema devoted to artistic reflections on the war, cultural co-operation within and beyond the post-Yugoslav space, and the promotion of regional talents. Situated at the interface between aesthetics, cultural politics and post-conflict transformation, the festival offers a privileged vantage point to observe the negotiation of shifting cultural and geopolitical imaginaries mediated through cinema.[2]

I contend that the festival can be conceived as a site of border politics. More specifically, I deploy the notion of borderscape which captures the continuously (un)making of borders as occurring at multiple levels, from geopolitics and institutions to everyday life and cultural practices.[3] Through this multidimensional framework the Film Festival, as a film showcase and social/cultural encounter, can be seen as an interesting site to explore key border-making processes in post-Dayton Bosnia, alongside and in productive tension with dominant imaginaries and socio-spatial processes at stake internally to Bosnia, in the wider post-Yugoslav region, and in the construction of 'borderlands of Europeanisation'.[4] Given the post-Dayton Peace Agreement history, border imaginaries and politics are inevitably intertwined with tensions around the contested legacy of conflict and the three ethnonationalist identities, on the one hand, and various attempts to stay attached to a post-Yugoslav/regional sense of belonging on the other. Since the EU's presence as major international actor for the region, bordering practices are also infused with the promises of peace(building) through Europeanisation enacted both through the prospect of EU integration and through programmes of cross-border co-operation. In this context, the SFF becomes an interesting, yet overlooked, milieu to critically reflect on the geopolitics of European peacebuilding, and push the boundaries of current EU approaches to borders and conflict transformation.

My analysis focuses on interviews and documents related to the EU's approach to cross-border co-operation and peacebuilding in the region, as well as to the Festival and cinematic production in BiH since the conflict. I also draw upon an ethnographic field trip at the 21st SFF conducted in August 2015. Combining observations, film viewing, interviews and informal conversations, I discuss the festival's heuristic potential to examine borderscape negotiations and opportunities for conflict transformation through the medium of cinema. In what follows I start by situating the paper within the critical research on cross-border co-operation as a contested instrument of EU border politics and peacebuilding. Here I contend that the notion of borderscape offers a fruitful analytical perspective to overcome limitations in current practices and discourses. Practising its multiperspectival view, I unearth the complexities at stake in the post-Dayton border landscape sustained and kept alive by legacies of conflict and international intervention, and the promises of peace through Europeanisation. Returning to the SFF, I outline three dimensions that potentially offer avenues for moving beyond entrenched borderscape contentions: the re-imagining of key border themes – conflict, national identities/regionalism and Europeanisation – in the promotion of regional co-operation and cultural exchanges; the exhibition of war-themed films that visualise complex everyday negotiations of the post-Dayton borderscape, and the creation of spaces for discussion where local, regional and international festival-goers make sense of these experiences.

Cross-Border Co-operation as Conflict Transformation: Limitations and Tensions at the EU External Frontier

Born out of post-Cold War transformations cross-border co-operation has increasingly assumed a paradigmatic status as an EU instrument for rapprochement and development whereby borders can become resources for economic and cultural exchange.[5] In this process previously divided border regions can be brought together through various policies that aim at the creation of a more cohesive European space.[6] In this sense, it is argued, cross-border co-operation has a conflict amelioration potential because it might open opportunities for intercultural dialogue and intercommunal relationships across conflictual and contested borders and borderlands.[7] Yet, although the promotion of EU-sponsored territorial co-operation and cross-border governance has been intensive in theory and rhetoric, in practice its success and diffusion has been much more ambivalent and uneven.[8] As the existing literature testifies, despite rhetorical statements, transcending borders is a much more complex and multi-layered socio-spatial process than envisioned in institutionalised EU practices and policies of cross-border co-operation, particularly when border imaginaries are entangled in the legacies of protracted conflict and competing senses of belonging.[9]

Ambivalences about Europeanisation and cross-border co-operation as forces for border conflict transformation are further amplified at EU external boundaries. Here, cross-border co-operation increasingly emerges as double-edged instrument of EU border politics. By consolidating an idea of political community, it also reiterates geographical and cultural historical differentiation between the present member states, prospective members and those considered unsuitable.[10] Not only has cross-border co-operation at EU external frontiers become underfunded, technocratic and mundane, but in the ensuing context of enlargement fatigue and security concerns, is devoid of the transformative value it might had originally assumed in the heyday of European integration.[11] From the perspective of post-Yugoslav candidate countries such as BiH, EU geopolitics of co-operation and peacebuilding emerges as a technocratic exercise that essentially privilege security and stability at the peril of conflict transformation. All rhetoric to the contrary, it also reinforces sharp civilisational differences between the EU core and prospective members.

Relying on the commonplace that increasing political, technocratic and economic co-operation necessary for the accession process will eventually have a *spillover* effect into conflict transformation, EU peacebuilding practices and discourse in post-Dayton BiH are emblematic of the tensions undercutting the transformative potential of cross-border co-operation. At the institutional level, the need to address the necessary reforms to join the EU family has been a constant mantra in EU engagement with the local nationalist elites who have dominated political life since Dayton Peace Agreement. [12] While the peace settlement was arguably instrumental to put an end to the war, its complex and contested governance system has mutated into an apparatus that is dysfunctional, unresponsive and removed from everyday politics.[13] The overarching principle of ethnic proportionality has essentially entrenched the politics of ethnic conflict in institutions and political life, offering lucrative opportunities for ethnonationalist elites. In this context, EU efforts to push for *progress* have largely resulted in a protracted Kafkaesque scenario whereby many of the parties that should negotiate reforms are indeed the very political elites benefiting from the Dayton status quo.[14]

At the local level, the logic of peace through Europeanisation has been promoted through both capacity-building programmes aimed at sustaining civil society and funding for cross-border co-operation. The latter specifically targets programmes across ethnically divided areas within BiH and for the border regions respectively between BiH, Croatia, Serbia and Montenegro (see Figure 1).[15] Following the *spillover logic*, the expected impact in all programmes is 'both-accession driven and political' and includes the 'promotion of reconciliation in the region'.[16] Yet, available data provided by the EU shows that rather than conflict amelioration and reconciliation, economic priorities have consistently received the bulk of cross-border co-operation funding.[17] The latest programme for 2014–2020 confirms this tendency with an increasing focus on economic co-operation, while reconciliation has essentially fallen off the agenda.[18]

This paper contends that the deterministic Europeanisation assumption, implying that increasing forms of political and economic co-operation will necessarily have a spillover effect on reconciliation, fails to capture the trans-formation of border and conflict contentions as an ongoing, tortuous and often ambivalent process.[19] Crucially, it pays insufficient attention to the multifaceted everyday borderscape negotiations that experiencing and surviving conflict produce.[20] Rather than enabling the acknowledgement of these experiences and creating opportunities to move beyond the dysfunctional post-agreement politics, EU interventions in BiH have largely contributed to further cement the eternal status quo favouring nationalist elites in the name of stability at the expenses of local demands for transformation, for instance as seen in the 2014 waves of citizens' protests.[21] As Aida Hozic writes in relation to the temporal and political implications of Bosnia's *post-conflict moment*: 'Left to its own devices as political project, Bosnia and Herzegovina floats in the European netherland, clobbered by EU demands to reform itself while straitjacketed by the Dayton Peace Agreement.'[22] The result has been protracted political impasse and unfulfilled EU commitments to take Bosnia's post-conflict and post-agreement *everyday* challenges seriously.

To make sense of this site of impasse I propose an alternative approach that captures precisely the multi-sited and multidimensional negotiation of borders as an ongoing and complex endeavour and identifies opportunities where dominant border conflict narratives might be challenged and re-imagined.[23] Deploying the borderscape lens, I zoom in into the complexities at stake in border making practices in post-Dayton Bosnia emerging from intersections and tensions between conflict, nationalist imaginaries and alternative sense of belonging, and the post-conflict and post-agreement governance.

Weaving through the Post-Dayton Borderscape: The Legacy of Conflict and Post-Conflict Border-Making

The notion of borderscape emerges from recent moves in critical border studies to conceptualise the increasing complexity of borders in global politics, their radical redistribution, (de)construction and negotiation at the hands of multiple actors with diverse effects and in multiple spaces beyond the lines at the edge of nation states.[24] The term identifies a complex border landscape displaying 'cultural and political complexities, contested discourses and meanings, struggle over inclusion and exclusion, involvement of multiple actors'.[25] Understood in its broadest sense, it captures the relations and contentions between border, identities, representations and imaginaries, as well as the concrete sociopolitical, spatial and cultural configurations produced by various practices of border-making constitutive of a complex border landscape.[26] It entails investigating borders through a kaleidoscopic view which, Chiara Brambilla writes, 'is able to grasp the 'variations' of borders in space and time, transversally to different social, cultural, economic, legal, and historical settings criss-crossed by negotiations between a variety of different actors, and not only the State.'[27]

Through this perspective, I view the problem/space post-Dayton BiH as made and continuously kept alive by a large ensemble of border-making policies and practices, as well as imaginations and discursive strategies, emerged from and informed by a number of historical conditions and bordering processes. Significant here are the spatial, political and cultural boundaries of a-place-that-once-was Yugoslavia, the internationally drawn and highly contested external and internal boundaries of the *Bosnian State*, the contested relationship with neighbouring Serbia and Croatia, and crucially *Europe's* external frontier (see Figure 1). These overlapping and entangled trajectories intimately shape contemporary figurations of/in the post-Dayton *borderscape*.

The framing of post-conflict governance operates at different levels determining both discursive and material bordering. Driven by post-1989 Western interventionism it has seen a crystallisation of ethnonational politics and an entrenchment of political, symbolic and cultural bordering along *dominant ethnonational* fault lines.[28] Materially and institutionally, this is most visible in a key component of the Dayton Peace Agreement which involved the re-drawing of BiH's borders as a sovereign state and the creation of the internationally supervised Brčko district, two separate entities, the Republika Srpska and the Croat-Bosniak Federation, made up of ten cantons, as a result of wartime ethnic cleansing and population shifts.[29]

Dominant ethnonationalist discourses mobilise socio-spatial identities and imaginaries that both mirror and add complexity to the contested borders of the state. This is epitomised in challenges to the legitimacy of BiH's sovereignty from political elites in the Republika Srpska, such as the recent decision to hold a controversial referendum deemed anti-constitutional by BiH's supreme court.[30] In the Federation, border controversies are often met with occasional demands for the creation of a third Croatian entity and in the staunch defence of the state from the Bosniak nationalist parties.[31]

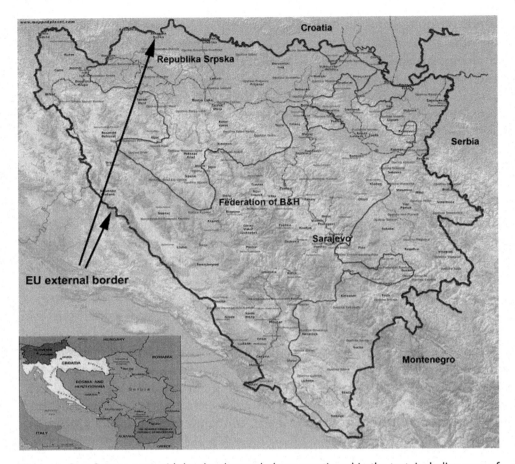

Figure 1. Post-Dayton map with key borders and places mentioned in the text, including map of the former Yugoslavia (map: Gordon Kavanagh, source of original: BiH map is based upon the free geodata of OpenStreetMap: Geodata © OpenStreetMap, CC-BY-SA and is liable to the OpenStreetMap licence, http://www.mappedplanet.com/karten/c24/image3.png, former Yugoslavia's map: Courtesy of the University of Texas Libraries, The University of Texas at Austin, https://www.lib.utexas.edu/maps/europe/fm_yugoslavia_pol96.jpg).

Dayton's complex border imaginary is also imbued with attachments to a regional/post-Yugoslav belonging that continuously trouble official and imagined contours of the SFRY successor states.[32] These senses of belonging – excessive to the dominant paradigm of ethnonational identity – are officially forced out of political representation and relegated to category of 'the Others' in a constitution that prioritises the Constituent People as Bosniaks, Croats and Serbs. Reflecting on the political conditions that led to widespread citizens' protests in 2014, Selma Tobudić illustrates how the implications of post-conflict/post-Dayton border-making governance reach far beyond institutions infusing everyday life with dominant tropes about identity, place and belonging:

CROSS-BORDER COOPERATION

In every aspect of life, what one is and can be, including how one is to remember, is encompassed and encapsulated within an ethnic identity. In this country 'being' has come to be thought of only within the parameters of belonging to either/or one of three 'nationalities.' These 'nationalities' are then (un)represented by the major avatar-like political parties. The imposed and imposing regimes of remembering have proved to be crucial, particularly since they serve as a tool to overwrite any other remembering out of the general code of belonging. This enactment of 'belonging' confines it to a clearly delineated and patriarchal collective. It is this patriarchal collective which has repetitively ensured, for the past twenty years, the (re) production and (re) mobilization of the electorate, enabling the continuity of the positioning of political elites in power more or less unchanged.[33]

Mirrored in the redrawing of BiH's borders, the respective nationalist geo-political aspirations are sustained by Dayton's governance. Here ethnic representation and vetoes embedded in the power-sharing institutional apparatus not only restrict the possibilities for reform and change, but also overwrite alternative narratives and belonging.

Mobilising the promises and logic of Europeanisation, EU interventions add further complexities to bordering practices and negotiations in post-Dayton BiH. In their continued support for the status quo, EU efforts implicitly reproduce deterministic notions of borders, as defined exclusively within ethnonationalist parameters. Technocratic EU programmes of cross-border co-operation privilege simplistic notions of border crossings along the edges of Yugoslav successor states or BiH entities (see Figure 1). Furthermore, *the road into EU* has a productive force that is imbued with sharp civilisational differences. The 'Peace through EU governance' agenda and its attendant framing of cross-border co-operation are intrinsically linked to the making of a European space and hence should be understood as disparate technologies of discursive and material b/ordering.[34] At work here is a dominant geopolitical imaginary that upholds Europe as the ultimate political project and space of democracy while detaining Bosnia to its backward and regressive periphery on the grounds that Bosnian society and its democratic structures are not enough functional, not professional, not European *yet*.[35]

Infusing the everyday, the elusive *road into Europe* imaginary yields criticism, resistance and apathy among the ordinary citizens.[36] Yet this imaginary also inevitably sustains aspirations to normality and investments in the promise of progress, inclusion and prosperity that a 'Europe to come' might hold for outliving BiH's isolation and perpetual impasse.[37] Albeit situated in the interior part of BiH, these complex contentions and experiences are refracted through Sarajevo, as capital of the contested Bosnian state, symbolic site of warfare, as well as epicentre of civic and artistic reflections on the conflict such as those hosted at the SFF.

Re-Thinking Border Politics through Cinema(tic) Encounters: The Making of the Sarajevo City of Film

Situated at the interface of cultural politics, cinematic production and imagination, and post-conflict border transformations, the SFF offers an exclusive vantage point, to explore the negotiations of socio-spatial identities (local, national, regional, European) beyond institutionalised practices that privilege top-down interventions and dominant notions of borders at the outer edges of nation state.[38] Discussing the relationship between aesthetics and the Norwegian-Russian border, Johan Schimanski writes, 'The borderscape concept is a way of thinking about the border and the bordering process not only on the border, but also beyond the line of the border, beyond the border as a place, beyond the landscape through which the border runs, and beyond borderlands with their territorial contiguities to the border.'[39] This diffused understanding places greater emphasis on the creative and aesthetic dimension that border negotiations and imaginations inevitably entail.[40] The relationship between aesthetics and social/geopolitical imaginaries is indeed crucial to the conceptualisation of the borderscape as an assemblage of material, symbolic and discursive signification of borders[41] Aesthetic languages produce the border as they 'scape' its material and symbolic universe in ways that mirror, alter and possibly subvert existing imaginaries.[42] In their productive and dissensual energy, that is, in their potential of articulating alternative border imaginaries, aesthetic interventions are thus inherently political.[43] In their transnational circulation, digital diffusion and often international production, films are particularly poignant cultural artefacts for the study of bordering and borders as they are performed, narrated, visualised and crossed.[44]

Zooming into the SFF, thus, both as a film showcase and social/cultural encounter revolving around cinema, offers interesting opportunities to observe how shifting border-making processes at stake in the post-Dayton borderscape are refracted, mediated and potentially transformed through cinema. Cinema here understood in its broadest to encompass cinematic narratives, film industries and cultural institutions. I consider three key aspects that are relevant to understand the complexities of socio-spatial relations at stake and harness possibilities for transformative cross-border encounters: the mobilisation of multiple socio-spatial and cultural narratives underpinning the SFF's creative vision, aesthetic enactment of borderscape experiences in selected films and the emergence of spaces for the articulation of 'border stories from below' hosted by the Festival.

Useful here is Chris Rumford's insight into the vernacular and transformative mobilisation of borders wherein ordinary people, including cultural actors, are able to capitalise on specific border histories and identities as gateways for regional and international connectivity, rather than simplistic nationalist (re)bordering.[45] Drawing on this insight I illustrate how key border themes of local conflict narratives, national identity/regionalism and Europeanisation become resources that emphasise the Film Festival's uniqueness and offer opportunities to negotiate its positioning, and that of attendant films it promotes, internationally. At the SFF the emphasis on local conflict imaginaries, the promotion of national cinema and regional film production become intricately entangled with claims to a European cosmopolitan identity in ways that complicate existing cartographies and imaginaries of the region viewed exclusively through the lens of dominant ethnonationalist contentions and relegated to 'one big Oriental periphery of Europe'.[46] Here local, national, regional and South-East European borders do not lose their significance, but in the making of the Festival's profile and encounters these socio-spatial imaginaries interweave in composite and often contradictory ways. Multiple border histories converging into the city are invoked and re-imagined as a gateway to the world of transnational cinema, and the opportunities this offers for minor cinematographies, such as those from the SEE region, to travel across borders.[47] Paying attention to the festival multifarious borderwork reveals opportunities to, even momentarily, move beyond entrenched border narratives and might highlight alternative, less technocratic, routes for conflict transformation.

As discussed in earlier sections, conflict experiences and narratives of identity are fraught with antagonisms between the three (dominant) ethnonationalist communities whose geopolitical aspirations are mirrored in the complex administrative system of post-Dayton governance and its material demarcation. Significant here is how these narratives emerge at the festival in ways that trouble the neat categories of this division, attempting to negotiate and project a more fluid identity for the Festival. The emphasis on the socio-spatial imaginary produced by the conflict emerges through screenings in locations that have assumed iconic status during the siege, and in the selection of local films and public discussions that encourage reflection and debate on the region's recent history. The online presentation and vision of the festival also continuously highlight its roots in wartime cultural resistance. The trope of 'Made in War',[48] as a unique feature of the SFF, thus implicitly evokes existing border contentions that focus on the Yugoslav conflict, while at the same time mobilising its wartime inception to produce the festival's *civic and cosmopolitan* identity.

The festival denotes a clearly defined national focus exemplified in a dedicated programme for BiH films, which account for least 50 per cent of the regional selection. Identifying media and political pressures that might have led the organisers to fulfil the Festival's *patriotic* duty as a promoter of national (i.e. nationalist Bosniak) culture, Kristine Kotecki points out that the increasing focus on national cinema compromises and complicates SFF's self-portrayal as a regional, cosmopolitan event.[49] In this respect, however, the

SFF is not unique. Rather, a national/cosmopolitan tension is inescapable to the phenomenon of film festivals, wherein ideas about universal cinematic communication, transnational film diffusion and production rub against the continued reliance on national frameworks for selecting and classifying films.[50] In a way, the national turn at the festival could be seen as an example of (re)bordering that mirrors nationalist territorial logics and existing borderscape contentions.[51] Analysing the Festival's multiple cultural narratives, Kotecki suggests that the category 'national' camouflages that filmmakers represented at the Festival have been mostly based in the Federation, which is also the entity that figures among the sponsors unlike Republika Srpska.[52] While this might situate the festival in proximity to ethnonational disputes, the possibilities of a narrow ethnonationalist identification are less significant than the networking and economic potential offered by its well-established narrative as symbol of 'the cosmopolitan spirit of the city'.[53] It is notable that, at the 2015 edition, the BiH programme featured *Bosnian* films produced across the ethnonationally defined entities, regional co-productions, as well as films by Bosnian directors not-longer based within (contested) state borders. This suggests SFF's self-portrayal as an attempt to project a more fluid *Bosnian and Herzegovinian* identity alongside its emphasis on regional co-operation.

A defining feature of SFF's international profile, the promotion of transnational regional co-operation involves the institution of a regional film competition programme, the composition of a regional forum and the creation of Cinelink, the flagship co-production programme offering funding, networking and developing opportunities for regional cinematographers. From Cinelink promotional material to the festival's online presence, the narration of SFF's regional identity complicates deterministic cartographies of the region and dominant border contentions. An interview with long-standing organiser and SFF programmer Elma Tataragić describes the Festival's regional reconfiguration as resulting from ongoing negotiations of identity and cultural memory in the aftermath of war, as well as the more practical pursuit of economic interests. As she explains, the political and cultural impetus of promoting regional cinema underscore an attempt at countering 'the falling apart of the country' in the breakup of Yugoslavia.[54] With the loss of available funds for cinema and culture resulting from both post-conflict and post-socialist transformations, regional co-operation has also assumed an increasingly economic dimension which is crucial for the sustainability of SEE *peripheral* cinemas. The significance of such a regional re-orientation for a potential critical re-imagining of belonging should not be understated given SEE's history and the entrenchment of nationalist politics outlined earlier.[55]

Not only are the boundaries of the *SEE region* the Festival represents shifting from an initial focus on the former Yugoslavia, to encompass post-communist and post-soviet countries, as well as Greece and Turkey, but the socio-spatial imaginaries invoked illustrate a complex historicity that exceeds dominant ethnonationalist framing of the region. For example, an interview featured in the 2015 Cinelink brochure evokes a complex historical narrative. Here regional documentary practices are captured as engaging with 'new identities, new realities, starting from the newly formed states, new established regimes, new faces of Europe' and 'the transition to liberal capitalism, searching for identity and overcoming the trauma of war and of the Communist regime'.[56] These openings to a wider regional scenario are revealing as they could intensify the possibilities for cultural exchange and contacts within and beyond the immediate post-Yugoslav space. Drawing together Yugoslav, Balkan and post-socialist identities with the new political realities and claims to *Europeannes*, cultural politics and artistic production with marketing strategies, the regional socio-spatial imaginary (re)produced at the festival complicates deterministic cartographies of the region that mask and dissolve its complex history. To the contrary, the festival's vernacular signification of borders relies precisely in foregrounding the complexities of socio-spatial relations in the post-Dayton borderscape and its deep entanglement in post-socialist and post-conflict border transformations of South-East Europe to challenge its continuous political and economic marginalisation. In doing so, South-East Europe's contentious history becomes a resource for regional cultural exchanges and contacts, as well as international connectivity.

Through its new trajectory as a regional platform for cinema, the SFF has gained a place in the international film festival circuit, developing a growing network of funders and partners, as diverse as the Berlinale, the British Council, the Council of Europe, as well as Creative Europe, which also provides funds for film production. Reflecting investments in the promises of a 'Europe to come' discussed in earlier sections, themes consistent with the logic of Europeanisation emerge in the festival's creative vision: not only its neo-liberal promotion of economic and cultural co-operation, but also in the inclusion of events that focus on themes increasingly associated with European values, such as human rights and civil society activism. The implications of such efforts to 'Europeanise the Balkans' are ambivalent as they resonate with the mantra of transition to neo-liberal Europe, and implicitly invoke its attendant geopolitical imaginary that detains Bosnia and the region to its backward and regressive periphery.[57] Yet, precisely because of the history of marginalisation and post-Cold War transformations that access to European networks of production, distribution and consumption becomes so important at the Festival: these are the networks through which local stories and imaginaries might travel and remain in circulation internationally. Despite this uneven cultural terrain, it would be misleading to read the Festival simply as a problematic vehicle for Europeanisation.

Rather, I view these efforts as part of moves in the region that, as Dina Iordanova suggested, are beginning to 'capitalise on the togetherness that is bestowed on them and try to turn the undistinguished qualification of 'being Balkan' from liability into an asset'.[58] In a process that resonates with Rumford's discussion of vernacular borderwork, the complex histories of local, national and regional borders are not erased.[59] Rather, they are reinvented and mobilised by SFF organisers and participants as instruments of regional connectivity that potentially allow local/national/regional films, as well as the imaginaries their foster to 'jump' across the EU external border and the world beyond. In the process, the divisive tropes of nationalist identity as all-encompassing framework of belonging might be even momentarily reconsidered in relation to a more dynamic sense of regional mutuality.

As a film showcase dedicated to the promotion of cinema from/about BIH and the SEE region broadly defined, the SFF regularly hosts cinematic narratives that engage creatively and critically on the region's history and contemporary lived experiences. The exhibition of film on the war, its aftermath, as well as post-conflict and post-socialist border contentions entails a transformative potential, whereby socio-spatial imaginaries and cultural identities at stake in the conflict might be rearticulated but also challenged. Films and documentaries presented at the 2015 Festival's edition thematise various aspects of the conflict reflecting an unescapable emphasis on the divisions brought up by the war and the unresolved legacy of nationalism. In this respect, the films' deep entanglement with war narratives might also continue to feed in the trope of Balkanization by continuously reproducing the imaginary of violent and conflict ridden Balkans that conforms to the expectations of Western markets and public.[60] Yet, local conflict films are also powerful vehicles for creative self-expression and signification that enact complex experiences and engage multiple senses.[61] In this sense, they might allow for new affective connections and challenge given assumptions about the conflict, by fostering new attitudes towards one's own identity and culture and those of others.

Several war-themed films presented at the 2015 festival share an underlying concern with complex everyday negotiations of identity ushered in by the conflict. In a similar vein to Žbanić's *One Day in Sarajevo*, other cinematic narratives confront the audience with dramas, hopes and failures that undergoing and surviving conflict engenders across the region and beyond.[62] The transformative potential of these films lies in enacting *small stories* of border conflict, that is, those multifaceted negotiations and deeply personal war/post-war experiences often foreclosed in competing projects of collective of nation(list) belonging. Dalibor Matanić's *High Sun* delves into three love stories tainted by ethnic divisions across Serbian/Croatian communities. In a co-production between BiH, Serbia and Croatia, Mladen Mitrović's *Chasing a Dream* narrates the director's quest to get school friends and former actors re-united in Sarajevo decades after having been displaced because of the war. Vladimir Tomic's *Flotel Europa* offers autobiographical accounts of a group of Bosnian refugees resuming everyday life in an improbable home, a giant boat harboured in Copenhagen, while divisive echoes of the siege reverberate. Documentaries such as Marija Ristic and Nemanja Babić's *The Unidentified* and Samir Mehanović's *The Fog of Srebrenica* engage with unresolved contentions of transitional justice in the region. Overall films of this kind offer imaginative interventions where local ordinary people's experiences take centre stage and viewers, including those from the region, bear witness to their longings for hope and redemption, as well as to the divisions and conflict still fracturing their communities in the everyday. Screenings at the festival are often followed by a Q&A discussion where the audience can share impressions and discuss the films with directors and crew members.

This Festival's participatory approach opens even momentarily a space for dialogue, encounters and discussion for attendees, film industries' participants and other accredited guests, international, local and from the region. Among these events, poignant is the Docu Corner organised in co-operation with the regional organisation *Youth Initiative for Human Rights*.[63] Involving students, aspiring film directors and young activists from the region, as well as any interested accredited guests, this event revolves around a series of discussions, talks and Q&A with directors of the documentaries included in the SFF programme. The functioning of these spaces is ambivalent. For example, it raises questions about the festival's ability to attract a specific 'privileged' audience who might be already inclined to engage in dialogue and cultural exchange. Furthermore, initiatives such as the Docu Corner resonate with top-down EU interventions that aim at fostering human right and developing civil society, bringing into question how participants/ organisers negotiate international norms in their activities. While untangling these dynamics would require further research, here I suggest that zooming into the micro-politics of encounters offers a glimpse into exchanges that might enable acknowledgement of reciprocal experiences of grief and critical reflections on the legacy of war.[64] In the 2015 edition, for instance, Q&A discussion revolved around questions that are integral to the divisive and contentious politics of memory around the conflict, such as the legacy of the Srebrenica genocide and other unresolved war crimes in the region, but also the place of Sarajevo in European geopolitics and history, and its identity as a cosmopolitan city.[65]

Responses to the films and to the discussions were often emotional which attests to the complex ramifications of conflict and violence for the communities affected even after generations. In my observations, participants commented that those difficult conversations felt 'healthy', in contrast with the politicisation of any aspect of everyday life, from memory to language, to culture.[66] Attendees at the post-screening Q&As expressed an interest to learn more about issues affecting communities perceived as 'other', even if it meant acknowledging atrocities committed in their own name. Reflecting on the quest for outliving the legacy of grief and trauma after conflict, Emma Hutchinson and Roland Bleiker write that 'embracing concrete practices that refuse the habitual, reflex-like push to memorialise (and gloss over) the traumas of war, and instead enable the potentially alternative expression, acknowledgment and acceptance of the profound and frequently reciprocal emotional impact of violence and suffering, is [...] key'.[67] I view cinematic interventions, cultural exchanges and spaces for discussion promoted at the festival as privileged, yet interesting, *laboratories* of border crossings where glimpses of a critical politics of grief might emerge and alternative conflict transformation imaginaries could thrive.

Conclusions

With its focus on state-building, capacity-building and economic co-operation, EU peacebuilding efforts in BiH pay insufficient attention to the multifaceted everyday borderscape negotiations that experiencing and surviving conflict produce. Rather than enabling the acknowledgement of these embodied and emotional experiences and creating opportunities to move beyond the dysfunctional post-agreement politics, EU interventions in BiH have largely contributed to further cement stark geopolitical imaginaries. In this landscape belonging remains delineated along exclusionary and fixed notions of ethnonational politics, while civilisational differences between the EU and the post-Yugoslav space are (re)produced. The logic of Peace through EU governance and cross-border co-operation essentially works to constitute the post-Dayton borderscape as a liminal space: unable to move post-conflict, not either quite in Europe.[68]

The kaleidoscopic lens of the borderscape opens opportunities to move beyond this impasse by highlighting alternative narratives and sites of border politics that are often overlooked in institutionalised and technocratic approaches. Situated at the interface between aesthetics, cultural politics and post-conflict transformations, the SFF provides a privileged vantage point to explore border negotiations through the medium of cinema. Focusing on the promotion of regional co-operation and cultural exchanges, the exhibition of war-themed films and the creation of spaces for discussion, I have attempted to outline the SFF's heuristic potential to engender critical reflections on the legacy of war and imaginative practices of conflict transformation. My research suggests that the festival produces a unique, albeit temporary and privileged, site where to experience and sense everyday border negotiations through cinema's aesthetic and creative energy, and where film-lovers[69] come together and make sense of these experiences. Although a short article cannot provide a full picture of the complex and ambivalent dynamics shaping the making and un-making of borders and cross-border encounters at the festival, I suggest that paying attention to the SFF as an interesting laboratory of border crossings and aesthetic engagements might enrich our imaginaries and practices of conflict transformation.

Acknowledgements

I wish to thank Giulia Carabelli, Milena Komarova and Cathal McCall for their feedback on an earlier draft and Gordon Kavanagh for technical support. I also wish to thank the editorial team and the three anonymous reviewers for their insightful comments and productive suggestions. I am indebted to Elma Tataragić and the Youth Initiative for Human Rights activists I met in Sarajevo and Prishtina for their contribution. Any mistakes I have made are my own.

Funding

Research for this paper was made possible by the EUBORDERSCAPES project (FP7-SSH-2011-1-290775), financed by the European Commission.

Notes

1. Kristine Kotecki, 'Europeanizing the Balkans at the Sarajevo Film Festival', *Journal of Narrative Theory* 44/3 (2014) pp. 344–66.
2. For an overview of relevant literature on film festivals as complex and multifaceted events, see, for example, Kenneth Turan, *Sundance to Sarajevo: Film Festivals and the World They Made* (Oakland: University of California Press 2003); Dina Iordanova, *The Film Festival Reader*, 2013; Marijke de Valck, *Film Festivals: From European Geopolitics to Global Cinephilia* (Amsterdam: Amsterdam University Press 2010); Owen Evans, 'Border Exchanges: The Role of the European Film Festival', *Journal of Contemporary European Studies* 15/1 (2007) pp. 23–33; Aida Vallejo and Marìa-Paz Peirano, *Film Festivals and Anthropology* (Cambridge: Cambridge Scholars Publisher 2017).
3. Chiara Brambilla, 'Exploring the Critical Potential of the Borderscapes Concept', *Geopolitics* 20/1 (2015) pp. 14–34; Chiara Brambilla et al., *Borderscaping: Imaginations and Practices of Border Making* (Farham: Ashgate 2015).
4. Marta Zorko, 'The Construction of Socio-Spatial Identities alongside the Schengen Border: Bordering and Border-Crossing Processes in the Croatian–Slovenian Borderlands', in Chiara Brambilla et al. (eds.), *Borderscaping: Imaginations and Practices of Border Making* (2015) p. 99.
5. James W. Scott, 'Bordering, Border Politics and Cross-Border Cooperation in Europe', in *Neighbourhood Policy and the Construction of the European External Borders* (New York: Springer 2015) pp. 27–44.
6. Ibid.
7. Cathal McCall, *The European Union and Peacebuilding: The Cross-Border Dimension* (New York: Palgrave/McMillan 2014).
8. Scott (note 5).
9. Ibid.; Gabriel Popescu, 'The Conflicting Logics of Cross-Border Reterritorialization: Geopolitics of Euroregions in Eastern Europe', *Political Geography* 27/4 (2008) pp.

41838; Etain Tannam, 'Cross-Border Co-Operation between Northern Ireland and The Republic of Ireland: Neo-Functionalism Revisited', *The British Journal of Politics & International Relations* 8/2 (2006) pp. 256–76; Cathal McCall, 'European Union Cross-Border Cooperation and Conflict Amelioration', *Space and Polity* 17/2 (2013) pp. 197–216.

10. Scott (note 5) p. 49.

11. James Wesley Scott and Henk van Houtum, 'Reflections on EU Territoriality and the "Bordering" of Europe', *Political Geography* 28/5 (2009) pp. 271–73.

12. A prominent example of this logic is the yearly monitoring exercise documenting developments and gaps in implementing reforms required for EU access. The 2014 document reported Bosnia "at a standstill" in the process. The 2016 document flags some progress, yet it also continuously highlights key challenges in co-operation, coordination and policy harmonisation across entities and levels of governance. Arguably these challenges are enabled and exacerbated precisely by Dayton's govern-ance regime. See 2014 and 2016 Progress Reports, available at <http://ec.europa.eu/enlargement/pdf/key_documents/2014/20141008-bosnia-and-herzegovina-progress-report_en.pdf>, accessed 12 Oct. 2015, and <https://ec.europa.eu/neighbourhood-enlar gement/sites/near/files/pdf/key_documents/2016/20161109_report_bosnia_and_herze govina.pdf>, accessed 2 Aug. 2017.

13. Eric Gordy, 'Dayton's Annex 4 Constitution at 20: Political Stalemate, Public Dissatisfaction and the Rebirth of Self-Organisation', *Southeast European and Black Sea Studies* 15/4 (2015) pp. 611–22.

14. Ibid.; Andrew Gilbert and Jasmin Mujanović, 'Dayton at Twenty: Towards New Politics in Bosnia-Herzegovina', *Southeast European and Black Sea Studies* 15/4 (2015) pp. 605–610.

15. Personal interviews with EU officials, Sarajevo, 21 and 27 Aug. 2015.

16. Personal interviews with EU officials, Sarajevo, 21 and 27 Aug. 2015.

17. See <http://projects.europa.ba/About>, accessed 6 Nov. 2015.

18. See <http://ec.europa.eu/enlargement/instruments/funding-by-country/bosnia-herzego vina/index_en.htm>, accessed 17 Oct. 2016.

19. McCall (note 7); Emma Hutchison and Roland Bleiker, 'Grief and the Transformation of Emotions after War', in Linda Åhäll and Thomas Gregory (eds.), *Emotions, Politics and War* (New York: Routledge 2015).

20. On the relevance of the everyday in peace/conflict, see, for example: Roger Mac Ginty, 'Everyday Peace: Bottom-up and Local Agency in Conflict-Affected Societies', *Security Dialogue* 45/6 (2014) pp. 548–64; Helen Berents, 'An Embodied Everyday Peace in the Midst of Violence', *Peacebuilding* 3/2 (2015) pp. 1–14. Feminist scholars have long drawn attention to the everyday life in war, these texts are but a few examples: Swati Parashar, 'Anger, War and Feminist Storytelling', in Linda Åhäll and Thomas A. Gregory (eds.), *Emotions, War and Politics* (New York: Routledge 2015); Carol Cohn, *Women and Wars: Contested Histories, Uncertain Futures* (Hoboken: John Wiley & Sons, 2013); Cynthia Enloe, *Maneuvers: The International Politics of Militarizing Women's Lives* (Oakland: University of California Press 2000); On the relevance of bottom-up border-making see also Chris Rumford, 'Towards a Vernacularized Border Studies: The Case of Citizen Borderwork', *Journal of Borderlands Studies* 28/2 (2013) pp. 169–80; Nira Yuval-Davis, 'A Situated Intersectional Everyday Approach to the Study of Bordering', *Euborder-Scapes Working Paper* 2 (2013), available at <http://www.euborderscapes.eu/fileadmin/user_upload/Working_Papers/EUBORDERSCAPES_Working_Paper_2_Yuval-Davis.pdf>.

21. One of the responses to citizens' protests saw EU representatives entered lengthy negotiations with the local elite which eventually led to the acceptance of BiH

candidacy in September 2016. It remains unclear whether this will enable any meaningful political and social change given that many of Bosnia's alleged inherent "deficiencies" remain unresolved. Rather than supporting citizens' demands for political transformation it has been suggested that this *new* approach will merely see a shift from a state of permanent crisis to that of perpetual candidacy. For an analysis of the protests and international responses see Daniela Lai, 'Transitional Justice and Its Discontents: Socioeconomic Justice in Bosnia and Herzegovina and the Limits of International Intervention', *Journal of Intervention and Statebuilding* 10/3 (2016) pp. 361–81; Cera Murtagh, 'Civic Mobilization in Divided Societies and the Perils of Political Engagement: Bosnia and Herzegovina's Protest and Plenum Movement', *Nationalism and Ethnic Politics* 22/2 (2016) pp. 149–71.

22. Aida Hozic, "The Origins of Postconflict", in Chip Gagnon and Keith Brown (eds.), *Post-Conflict Studies: An Interdisciplinary Approach* (New York: Routledge 2014).

23. For analysis of Europeanisation and cross-border co-operation that draw on the borderscape concept, see McCall, *The European Union and Peacebuilding*; Cathal McCall and Xabier Itçaina, 'Secondary Foreign Policy Activities in Third Sector Cross-Border Cooperation as Conflict Transformation in the European Union: The Cases of the Basque and Irish Borderscapes', *Regional & Federal Studies* 27/3 (2017) pp. 261–81.

24. See, for example: Nick Vaughan-Williams, *Border Politics: The Limits of Sovereign Power* (Edinburgh: Edinburgh University Press 2009); Rumford (note 20); Anke Strüver, *Stories of the 'Boring Border': The Dutch-German Borderscape in People's Minds* (Münster: LIT Verlag 2005); Anne-Laure Amilhat Szary et al., 'The Evolving Concept of Borders State of the Debate Report I', 2012, available at <http://www.euborderscapes.eu/fileadmin/user_upload/EUBORDERSCAPES_State_of_Debate_Report_1.pdf>; Thomas M. Wilson, *A Companion to Border Studies* (Hoboken: John Wiley & Sons 2015); Corey Johnson et al., 'Interventions on Rethinking "the Border" in Border Studies', *Political Geography* 30/2 (2011) pp. 61–9; Noel Parker and Nick Vaughan-Williams, 'Critical Border Studies: Broadening and Deepening the 'Lines in the Sand' Agenda', *Geopolitics* 17/4 (2012) pp. 727–33.

25. Prem Kumar Rajaram and Carl Grundy-Warr, *Borderscapes: Hidden Geographies and Politics at Territory's Edge* (Minneapolis: University of Minnesota Press 2007) pp. ix–xl.

26. Ibid.; Brambilla (note 3); Chiara Brambilla et al., *Borderscaping: Imaginations and Practices of Border Making* (Farnham: Ashgate 2015).

27. Brambilla (note 3) p. 25.

28. For a discussion of international intervention in BiH, see David Campbell, *National Deconstruction: Violence, Identity, and Justice in Bosnia* (Minneapolis: University of Minnesota Press 1998); For an analysis of Dayton's ethnopoltics see Dejan Guzina, 'Dilemmas of Nation-Building and Citizenship in Dayton Bosnia', *National Identities* 9/3 (2007) pp. 217–34; Maria-Adriana Deiana, 'Citizenship as (Not) Belonging? Contesting the Replication of Gendered and Ethnicised Exclusions in Post-Dayton Bosnia-Herzegovina', in *Beyond Citizenship?* (New York: Springer 2013) pp. 184–210.

29. See Dayton Peace Agreement full text, available at <http://www.nato.int/ifor/gfa/gfa-home.htm>, accessed 10 May 2016.

30. 'The Serbian Referendum in Bosnia and Herzegovina', *EurActiv.com*, 30 Sep. 2016, available at <https://www.euractiv.com/section/enlargement/opinion/the-serbian-referendum-in-bosnia-and-herzegovina/>.

31. Danijela Majstorović, Zoran Vučkovac, and Anđela Pepić, 'From Dayton to Brussels via Tuzla: Post-2014 Economic Restructuring as Europeanization Discourse/Practice in

Bosnia and Herzegovina', *Southeast European and Black Sea Studies* 15/4 (2015) pp. 661–82; Gordy, 'Dayton's Annex 4 Constitution at 20'.

32. Damir Arsenijević, *Unbribable Bosnia and Herzegovina: The Fight for the Commons* (Baden-Baden: Nomos Verlagsgesellschaft 2015); Radmila Gorup, *After Yugoslavia: The Cultural Spaces of a Vanished Land* (Redwood City: Stanford University Press 2013).

33. Selma Tobudić, 'Plenums and Protests: A Remembering', in Damir Arsenijević, *Unbribable Bosnia and Herzegovina: The Fight for the Commons* (Baden-Baden: Nomos Verlagsgesellschaft 2015) pp. 156–57.

34. Luiza Bialasiewicz, ed., *Europe in the World: EU Geopolitics and the Making of European Space*, Critical Geopolitics (Farnham: Ashgate 2011).

35. Useful here is the work that interrogates European integration as a multifarious process of governmentality. In this sense, "Peace through EU governance" can be read as one of the complex often incoherent and contingent techniques of governmentalization. These undergird a specific geopolitical, social, cultural and economic vision for and material demarcation of Europe as framed by the EU. Operating at different levels (e.g. state-building, civil society, cultural co-operation, cross-border-co-operation), through different actors (e.g. EU delegation in BiH and EU commission) and with different registers/themes, these assemblages ultimately work to legitimise the idea of Europe as a political project and international peace actor, make (potential) European citizens and ultimately uphold it as a model and space of democracy, progress and normality. See Jens Henrik Haahr and William Walters, *Governing Europe: Discourse, Governmentality and European Integration* (New York: Routledge 2004).

36. Stef Jansen, *Yearnings in the Meantime: 'Normal Lives' and the State in a Sarajevo Apartment Complex* (New York: Berghahn Books 2015).

37. My research in BiH suggests ways in which various local/international institutions and local/international actors normalise, reproduce, but also experience and constantly negotiate the 'road into the EU'. For many I have encountered during my fieldwork, European integration represents the possibility to conduct a normal life versus being 'stuck' in the post-Dayton impasse. In one occasion, I asked a local EU official if they could express a personal view on what, if any, could be the value of investing in the project of EU integration. The response poignantly stated: 'European integration is the way of living normal'. During my ethnographic fieldwork in Sarajevo in 2010 and 2015, friends, activists and other research participants I interviewed often expressed similar aspirations to a transition to normality and out of the never-ending post-conflict trajectory.

38. Johan Schimanski and Stephen Wolfe, 'Cultural Production and Negotiation of Borders: Introduction to the Dossier', *Journal of Borderlands Studies* 25/1 (2010) pp. 38–49; Chiara Brambilla, 'Navigating the Euro/African Border and Migration Nexus Through the Borderscapes Lens: Insights from the LampedusaInFestival', in *Borderscaping: Imaginations and Practices of Border Making* (Farnham: Ashgate 2015) p. 111; Michael J. Shapiro, 'HBO's Two Frontiers: *Deadwood* and *The Wire*', *Geopolitics* 20/1 (2015) pp. 193–213; Elena Dell'Agnese and Anne-Laure Amilhat Szary, 'Borderscapes: From Border Landscapes to Border Aesthetics', *Geopolitics* 20/1 (2015) pp. 4–13.

39. Johan Schimanski, 'Border Aesthetics and Cultural Distancing in the Norwegian-Russian Borderscape', *Geopolitics* 20/1 (2015) pp. 35–55.

40. Schimanski and Wolfe (note 38); Brambilla (note 38); Shapiro (note 38); Dell'Agnese and Amilhat Szary (note 38).

41. Brambilla (note 3); Brambilla (note 38).

CROSS-BORDER COOPERATION   161

42. Dell'Agnese and Amilhat Szary (note 38); Alan Ingram, 'Art, Geopolitics and Metapolitics at Tate Galleries London', *Geopolitics* 22/3 (2017) pp. 719–39.
43. Brambilla (note 38); Roland Bleiker, 'In Search of Thinking Space: Reflections on the Aesthetic Turn in International Political Theory', *Millennium* 20 (2017) p. 0305829816684262.
44. Michael J. Shapiro, *Cinematic Geopolitics*, 1st edition (New York: Routledge 2008); Maria Rovisco, 'Towards a Cosmopolitan Cinema: Understanding the Connection Between Borders, Mobility and Cosmopolitanism in the Fiction Film', *Mobilities* 8/1 (2013) pp. 148–65; Ana Cristina Mendes and John Sundholm, 'Walls and Fortresses: Borderscapes and the Cinematic Imaginary', *Transnational Cinemas* 6/2 (2015) pp. 117–22.
45. Rumford (note 20).
46. Dina Iordanova, *The Cinema of the Balkans* (New York: Wallflower Press 2006) p. 9.
47. Aida A. Hozic, 'Between "National" and "Transnational": Film Diffusion as World Politics', *International Studies Review* 16/2 (2014) pp. 229–39.
48. Mirza Redzič, 'Made in War (Boomed in Peace): The Sarajevo Film Festival', available at <http://www.narratives.eu/s/Made-in-war-boomed-in-peace-SFF-pxtz.pdf>, accessed 13 May 2016.
49. Kotecki (note 1).
50. Hozic (note 47); Sandra Ponzanesi and Verena Berger, 'Introduction: Genres and Tropes in Postcolonial Cinema(s) in Europe', *Transnational Cinemas* 7/2 (2016) pp. 111–17; Dina Iordanova, *Cinema at the Periphery* (Detroit: Wayne State University Press 2010); Lydia Papadimitriou and Jeffrey Ruoff, 'Film Festivals: Origins and Trajectories', *New Review of Film and Television Studies* 14/1 (2016) pp. 1–4.
51. After all the focus on national cinema has been a central element of the festival since organisers began to show documentaries in the midst of the siege. Personal interview with SFF Elma Tataragić, Sarajevo 18 Aug. 2015.
52. Kotecki (note 1); I. SFF Elma Tataragić points out that local government's funding is rather limited, accounting for around 15% of the Festival's overall budget. Personal interview with SFF Elma Tataragić, Sarajevo 18 Aug. 2015.
53. See <http://www.sff.ba/en/page/about-the-festival>.
54. Interview with Elma Tataragić, Sarajevo, 18 Aug. 2015.
55. Iordanova (note 46).
56. Interview with Rada Sesic and Martichka Bozhilova, Heads of Docu Rough Cut Boutique programme, reproduced in CityLink Industry Days -Where art meets Business, 19–22 Aug. 2015. The brochure was included in the welcome pack for accredited guests.
57. Kotecki (note 1).
58. Iordanova (note 46).
59. Rumford (note 38).
60. It is often through *conflict films* that the respective post-Yugoslav industries can enter international cinematic production networks, even though this might contribute to reify troubling stereotypes that satisfy the Western gaze, see also Kotecki (note 1); Iordanova (note 46).
61. Shine Choi and Maria-Adriana Deiana, 'Questioning the International: (Un)making Bosnian and Korean Conflicts, Cinematically', *Trans-Humanities Journal* 10/1 (2017) pp. 5–30.
62. There is a rich repertoire of independent local films that provide critical/artistic reflections on the war. See, for example, cinematic productions from and about Bosnia-Herzegovina such as Ademir Kenović's The Perfe Circle, Jasmila Zbanic's

Grbavica, Pjer Zajlic's Gori Vatra and Aida Begic's Snijeg. Full listings and film synopsis for the various editions of the Festival are available at http://www.sff.ba/en/page/about-the-festival, accessed 13 May 2016.

63. Personal interview with Timohir Popovic, YIfHRBiH, Sarajevo, 25 Aug. 2015.
64. Mac Ginty (note 20).
65. Author's participant observation, Sarajevo, 16–22 Aug. 2015.
66. Author's participant observation and personal communications with Docu Corner attendees, Sarajevo, 16–22 Aug. 2015.
67. Hutchison and Bleiker (note 19) p. 210.
68. Jansen (note 36).
69. I am grateful to Giulia Carabelli for suggesting this term as an interesting and fluid category of identity at the festival.

ORCID

Maria-Adriana Deiana ⓘ http://orcid.org/0000-0003-4310-1728

Index

Note: Figures are indicated by italics. Tables are indicated by bold. Endnotes are indicated by the page number followed by 'n' and the endnote number e.g., 20n1 refers to endnote 1 on page 20.

The Accession 126
acquis communautaire 24
acquis envisions 21
adjacent remoteness 87
Adriatic Sea 133
Aghtamar 118n9
Akdamar Church 118n9
Akuryan 104
Anderson, A. 49
Anderson, Benedict 132
Anderson, James 5
Anglo-centric nationalism 14
Ankara Agreements 84, 85, 99–100, 111
the Annan Plan 83–4
Ardahan 105
Arkzin 130, 135
Armenia 6, 98–100, 104, 106–8, 110, 112, 116, 118n16
Armenian Kingdom of Vaspurakan 118n9
Armenian-Turkish border 115
Arsenijević, Vladimir 134–5
articulation of 'national' in 1990s 125–6
Assemblies of Croatian European Movement (CEM) 126
Atatürk, Mustafa Kemal 74
Azerbaijan 99–100, 107–10, 113

Babić, Nemanja 155
Bakić-Hayden, Milica 138n10
Bakuła, Bogusław 41, 47
Baku-Tbilisi-Erzurum natural gas pipeline (BTE) 109
Balkanism 131
Balkans 122, 125, 128–9, 134, 136
Ballet Theatre 44
Barbero, I. 19
Barikade 130
The Barricades 130
Beauvois, D. 41, 42
The Belfast Agreement, 1998 25; *see also* Good Friday (Belfast) Agreement (GFA)
Belgrade 136
Berezin, M. 44

Berg, E. 14, 17–18, 20–1
big players 50
BIHCGHRSR-space 134, 139n15
bleeding island theme, Greek Cypriot 81–2, *82*
Bleiker, Roland 156
bloody cartopolitical imagination *83*
Bogišić, Vlaho 129
Bollens, S. A. 39
border guards 28
borderlands of Europeanisation 143
borderless world 98
border regimes 8, 14; EU external 20–2; Features of 17–19; Island of Ireland 25–30; multiperspectival analyses 16–18; UK–Ireland border 22–5
borderscape 5–6
borderwork 5
Bosnia-Herzegovina (BiH) 6, 142–7, 149, 154, 156, 160n37
Bosnian films 152
Bosnian-Serb entity 2
Brambilla, Chiara 6, 17
Brexit 2, 16
Britain 31
British Commonwealth 23
British Empire 87
Buckley, P. H. 49
Bulgarian literatures 129, 130
Bulgarian question of Croatian culture 126
Bulgarica 130
bureaucracy 107
Butazzoni, M. 24
Byzantium 68

cartocolonialism 63, 68
cartopolitical heterotopias 70
cartopolitical *idée fixe* 88
cartopolitics 6, 62, 88n5
Ceci n'est pas la Ligne Verte 59
Central Asia 110
Central Europe 131–3
Chasing a Dream 154
Christian Orthodox 66, 70

chronotopes 62, 70
Civilitas Foundation (CF) 118n16
civilized Cypriots 65
civil societal organisation 111–13
Coast Guard Agency 20
collective consciousness and memory 105
Collective Security Treaty Organisation (CSTO) 108
Common Travel Area (CTA) 22, 23–4, 28–30, 31n7
Communist-run Yugoslavia 39
communist threat 104
conceptualization 105
conflict transformation 5–10
Congress 125
consciousness 42, 66, 105, 109, 126–8
constructivist turn 117n1
contemporary societies 5
contradiction 126
The Conversations with Miroslav Krleža 133
convivencia 60, 88n1
Copenhagen 155
cordon sanitaire 68
Corner, Docu 155
Council of European Municipalities and Regions 39
The Crisis Novels 129
crisis of sovereignty 15
Croatia 122, 126, 127
Croatian European Movement (CEM) 126, 127
Croatian literary 123–4
Croatian silence 139n16
Croatia Today 127
cross-border contacts 55
cross-border initiatives 116–17
cross-cultural space 131, 132
Crown Dependencies 23, 31n6
Cypriot Orthodox Church 76
Cypriots 58–61, 64, *65*, 66, 87–8
Cyprus 6, 9, 59, 63, 89n10
Czech–German 55

dance at the Élysée Palace 127
Dayton Peace Agreement 145, 146
debordering 2–3
Declaration on the Name and Position of Standard
  Croatian 138n7
(in)definite topography 124, 137n1
*Deklaracija o nazivu i položaju hrvatskog književnog
  jezika* 138n7
Delacroix, Eugène 72
de-territorialisation 132
dispersed nature 126
dispute on literary left 137n3
distant closeness 87
Doğangün, Gökten 9
Doğu Kapı 104
dominant ethnonational fault lines 147
Dubrovnik Summer Festival 139n17

Eastern Turkey 105
Economic Policy Research Foundation of Turkey
  (TEPAV) 118n16
Ehin, P. 14, 17, 18, 20, 21

The Electoral Commission, 2016 26
Élysée Palace 126–7
Enej 55
Erdoğan, Recep Tayyip 83, 86
ethnarcs 66
ethno-nationalist 2, 9, 60, 80, 81, 118n12, 143, 145,
  147, 149, 151–3
ethno-national prejudices 98
EU Border Politics 2–5
EUBORDERSCAPES researchProject 6
EU external border regime 20–2
EU foreign policy 2
EU Framework Programme 6
EU-funded projects 113
EU-led cross-border cooperation 9
EU27 Member States 32n14
Eurasian Economic Union (EEU) 108
Eurasia Partnership Foundation (EPF) 118n16
European anti-Semitism 88n2
European 'book' 129–30
European Border 20
European Commission 85
European Community (EC) 81, 126–7
European Days of Good Neighbourhood 38, 52, 54
European Economic Community 85
European integration 1, 98, 115, 122
Europeanisation 2–5, 122, 129, 144–6, 153
Europeanise the Balkans 153
European Neighbourhood Policy (ENP) 98, 100
Europeannes 153
European politics 108
European space 144
European Travel Information and Authorisation
  System 30
European Union (EU) 1, 13, 32n14, 37, 39,
  40, 53, 54
Europe Today 127
EU's cross-border cooperation: border conflict,
  Turkey and Armenia 103–4; and conflict
  transformation 100–3
Euskirchen, M. 21
Evropa danas 127

The Flags 127–9
The Flags as Krleža's philosophy of history 125–6
Flotel Europa 155
The Fog of Srebrenica 155
France 114, 117n7
freedom of knowledge 31n4
freedoms of movement 13
Frontex 21

Garry, J. 26
genocide 6, 105, 108
geographical-biological organism 69
geopolitical totality of Mitteleuropa 132
Germany 114
the Global South 62
Glocal Green Line *see* Green Line
Good Friday (Belfast) Agreement (GFA) 14, 25, 30
Gorgolewski, Zygmunt 44

INDEX

The Government of Ireland Act, 1920 22–3
graffiti 48, **49**
grassroots 48
Great Britain 25
Greater Greece, map of *69*
Great Idea 69
Greece 117n7
Greece on the Ruins of Missolonghi 72
Greek and Turkish ethnic lines 66
Greek Cypriots 60, 61, 63, 66, 68, 70, 71, 76, 77, 80, 81–2, *82*, 83–7; EOKA members 89n9
Greekness 60
Green Line 2, 9; adjacent remoteness 87; after 1974 80–1; Brutish British sophistication 63–8; competing imperial cartopolitics 72–6; Cypriots 87–8; Cypriot segregation 58–61; decolonisation and further glocalisation 76–8; distant closeness 87; EU's imperial conflict resolution 81–6; Hellenic and Ottoman antagonism 68–70; imperial cartopolitics 61–3; imperial logic of the US 78–80; religious antagonism 71–2; textbook nationalism 71
Grivas, Georgios 76
Grundy-Warr, Carl 159n25
guilt perception *43*
Gymri 108

Happy Peace Operation 81
hard border 26–8
Hayward, K. 8, 24
Hellenism 72
Hellenist irredentism 85
Hellenization of Cyprus 71–2
Helsinki Citizens' Assembly (hCa) 118n16
Herbert Kitchener's map of Cyprus *67*
Herzegovinian 152
heterotopias 62
High Sun 154
Hobsbawm 88n3
Hozic, Aida 146
Hrant Dink Foundation 104, 106–7, 118n16
Hrvatska danas 127
hrvatska šutnja 139n16
Hud, B. 41
Hutchinson, Emma 156

illegal migration 115
imagined community 132
Immigration Act, 1971 28
Immigration Order, 1972 28
impenetrability 16
imperial nationalism 68, 88n6
Iran 110
Ireland 2
Irish border regimes 3, 14
Iron Curtain 39
Island race 14
Istanbul 99, 111, 112

Jergović, Miljenko 135, 137
Justice and Development Party (JDP) 83

Kafkaesque scenario 145
kaleidoscopic view 146, 156
Kaptolski kolodvor Predraga Matvejevića 124, 132
Kaptol station 124
Karadağ, Yelda 9
Kars-Tbilisi-Baku railway (KTB) 109
Kars Treaty 118n11
Kolossov, V. 15
Komarova, M. 8, 24
Kostanjevac 124
Kraków 43, 50
Krleža, Miroslav 123, 124, 130, 132, 135
Krležianity 125, 131, 136
Krležologija ili povijest kriticke misli o Miroslavu Krleži 125
Krležologists 123, 126, 129, 133, 134, 136
Krležology or The History of Critical Thinking about Miroslav Krleža 125
Kryłów 53

La Francophonie 88n6
La Hispanidad 88n6
Latham, R. 18
Lebuhn, H. 21
Lederach, J. P. 4
Liberation Committee 76
Libya 1
liminality 133
The Ljubljana's Report 125
Ljubljanski referat 125
LódŸ 43
Lódz 50
London–Zürich agreements 78, 84
Lublin 43, 50, 51
Luketić, Katarina 135
Lvis and its Polish partner cities **49**

MacGinty, Roger 4
Magris, Claudio 132, 133
mainstream media 15
Makarios 89n8
Malhowice–Niżankowice border 52, *52*
Mandić, Igor 129
Matvejević, Predrag 133
McCall, C. 4, 15, 38, 98
Mediteranski brevijar 133
Mediterranean 59, 63, 70, 79, 101, 123, 131–3
Mediterranean Breviary 133
Mediterranean Cuba 80
Megali Idea 69, *74*
Mehanović, Samir 155
mental borders 104–7
Michelangelo 139n17
micropolitics 8
migration crisis 15, 20
Minsk Agreement, 2014 1
Minsk group 114
mission civilisatrice 63
Mitrović, Mladen 154
Mitteleuropa 123, 132–4
Mitteleuropean space 132, 134, 136, 138n8

Montenegrin 134
Mudri predsjednikov savjetnik Miroslav Krleža 130
Muslim–Christian syncretism 66
Muslim Cypriots 66
The Muslim World 62

Nagorno-Karabakh conflict 99, 107–10, 114, 116, 117n4
National Academic Opera 44
national issue 105
nationalist rhetoric 106
National League of Cities 39
National Organisation of Cypriot Fighters (EOKA) 76–80
national self-identification process 123
national silence 135
nation-building process 122
NGOs 107, 113
non-European periods 129
Northern Ireland 6, 7, 13, 22, 25–7, 30, 31, 32n9
Norwegian-Russian border 150
Nowicka, Klaudia 8

O'Dowd, Liam 5
One Day in Sarajevo 142, 143, 154
'One Nation' approach 14
"ordinary" citizens 6, 7, 28, 149
the Orient 62
Orthodox Church 72
Ottoman Empire 72, 75–6, 117n8
Our Motherland Turkey 71
'Our' space 134–6

Peace Agreement, 1998 8
permissibility 18, 19
Petković, Nikola 131
phantoms 133
Ploughing of the Sea 132–4
Poland 6, 41–3, 51–2
poleis 39
Polish cities 46
Polish–German 55
Polish Home Army 53
Polish January Uprising of 1863 42
Polish November Uprising of 1830 42
Polish Scouting and Guiding Association 46
Polish–Ukrainian conflict 38
Polish–Ukrainian cross-border cooperation 41, 43–7, 55–6
post-conflict moment 146
post-Dayton borderscape 144, 145, *148*
post-Dayton Bosnia 9–10, 143, 146
post-Dayton Bosnia–Herzegovina 2
post-Dayton Peace Agreement 143
post-Westphalian 97
post-Yugoslav space 1–2, 134–6, 143, 145, 156
Povratak Filipa Latinovicza 124
Predrag Matvejević's Kaptol Station 132
The President's Wise Counsellor Miroslav Krleža 130
Princip, Gavrilo 142

prism of *cartopolitics* 9
Pristup 126
privileged partnership 84
problématique 8, 16, 30
pro-Brexit movement 15
Proclamation of the Verkhovna Rada of Ukraine 40
protracted conflict 61
Przemysl 43, 50
Public Journalism Club (PJC) 118n16

Queen's University Belfast 22

Ray, G. 21
Razgovori Miroslavom Krleža 133
real partners 50
rebordering 2
Referendum 22
regional rhetoric 134, 136
regional socio-political realities 136
Regional Studies Centre (RSC) 118n16
Republika Srpska 147, 152
The Return of Filip Latinovicz 124
Ristic, Marija 155
Romani krize 129
Romantic embodiment, Greek nation *73*
Rumford, Chris 5, 16, 19
Russia 1, 107, 108, 110, 114
Russian Revolution of 1905 42
Russo-Georgian war 117n5
Rzeszów 43, 50, 51

Sagan, Iwona 8
Sarajevo Film Festival (SFF) 10; borderlands of Europeanisation 143; Bosnia-Herzegovina 143; EU external frontier 144–6; post-conflict border-making 146–9; post-Dayton border landscape 144; post-Yugoslav space 156; re-thinking border politics 150–3; World War I 142; Zbanic's film 143
Sarkozy, Nicolas 85
Schengen Agreement, 1985 24, 29
Schengen Zone 24
Schimanski, Johan 150
Scotland 13, 25, 26
Scott, James 3, 15, 115
security 19
Serbia 126
Serczyk, A. W. 41
settled status 29
SFRY successor states 148
sine qua non 110
Sister Cities programme 39–40
small diplomacy: cross-border contacts 55; culture 47–51; partner cities 38–41; Poland and Ukraine 41–3; Polish–Ukrainian border 43–7; shadow of conflict 51–4
small players 50
small-scale cities' cooperation 41
Snatching Cyprus away from Anatolia *86*
SOCAR Turkey Energy 118n15
soft power 116–17
South Caucasus 107, 116

sovereignty 30
Soviet Armenia 118n13
Soviet Union 97–8, 104, 105, 116
spillover logic 145–6
Stanko Lasic 123, 125, 126, 128–30
status quo 110–11, 113
strategic partnership 108
striking sites 15
stronger borders 15
The Structure of Krleža's 'The Flags' 128
Struktura Krležinih 'Zastava' 128
Studzinska 8
Support to the Armenia-Turkey Normalisation
   Process 112
Svoboda 47
Switzerland 70

Takahashi, A. 49
Technocratic EU programmes 149
telecommunication industry 108
territoriality 98
The Three Essays about Europe 126
Tomic, Vladimir 155
Treaty of Maastricht, 1993 31n8
Tri eseja o Evropi 125, 126
TRNC 81–3
Tuđman, Franjo 130
Turkey 1, 6, 98–9, 104, 106, 107, 109, 112, 113–
   14, 116
Turkish-Armenian border 9, 98, 99, 105, 111,
   115, 116
Turkish-Armenian case 100, 104
Turkish-Armenian conflict 106, 116
Turkish Cypriots 60, 61, 63, 66, 68, 71, 76, 77, 79–
   80, 86, 87
Turkish invasion of 1974 66–7
Turkishness 60
Turkish Republic of Northern Cyprus (TRNC) 80
Turkish Resistance Organisation (TMT) 78
turkophobic historiography 70

UK–Ireland border 14–15, 22-5, 30
Ukraine 1, 6, 41–3, 51–2
Ukrainian Insurgent Army 42, 53
Ukrainian Lviv 43
Ukrainian–Polish cooperation 40, 41
Ukrainian Revolution of 1917–1921 42
UK Referendum, 2016 14–15
The Unidentified 155
unionists 26
United Kingdom (UK) 13, 28–30, 32n14
United States 104, 114
Ural Mountains 59

Van Houtum, H. 3, 115
Vijenac 129
Viskovic in Radakovic-Vinchierutti,
   1993 125

Wapiński, R. 41
Warschawski, M. 41
the West 62
Western Armenia 105
White Eagle Association 46
wider Europe 98, 117n3
WikiLeaks 80
World War I 39, 72, 75, 117n8, 128, 142
World War II 3, 6, 8, 39, 42, 47, 53, 76
Wrocław 43, 50

Yerevan 99, 105, 108, 111–14, 117n5
Youth Initiative for Human Rights 155
Yugoslav federation 122, 123, 125, 131
Yugoslav literature 129

Zastave kao Krležina filozofija povijesti 125–
   7, 138n6
Žbanić, Jasmila 142
Žbanić's film 143
Zbereże 53
Zurich Protocols 110

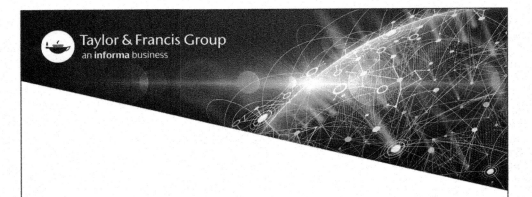